VIOLENT ACCOUNTS

QUALITATIVE STUDIES IN PSYCHOLOGY

GENERAL EDITORS: MICHELLE FINE AND JEANNE MARECEK

This series showcases the power and possibility of qualitative work in psychology. Books feature detailed and vivid accounts of qualitative psychology research using a variety of methods, including participant observation and field work, discursive and textual analyses, and critical cultural history. They probe vital issues of theory, implementation, interpretation, representation, and ethics that qualitative workers confront. The series mission is to enlarge and refine the repertoire of qualitative approaches to psychology.

Violent Accounts

Understanding the Psychology of Perpetrators through South Africa's Truth and Reconciliation Commission

Robert N. Kraft

NEW YORK UNIVERSITY PRESS

New York and London

NEW YORK UNIVERSITY PRESS
New York and London
www.nyupress.org

Excerpt from *The Cure at Troy: A Version of Sophocles'* Philoctetes by Seamus Heaney.
© 1990 by Seamus Heaney. Reprinted by permission of Farrar, Straus and Giroux, LLC. and
Faber and Faber, Ltd.

Excerpt from *Regarding the Pain of Others* by Susan Sontag. © 2003 by Susan Sontag.
Reprinted by permission of Farrar, Straus and Giroux, LLC. and Penguin Books, Ltd.

References to Internet websites (URLs) were accurate at the time of writing.
Neither the author nor New York University Press is responsible for URLs that
may have expired or changed since the manuscript was prepared.

Library of Congress Cataloging-in-Publication Data
Kraft, Robert Nathaniel.
Violent accounts : understanding the psychology of perpetrators through South Africa's
Truth and Reconciliation Commission / Robert N. Kraft.
pages cm. — (Qualitative studies in psychology)
Includes bibliographical references and index.
ISBN 978-1-4798-2160-0 (cloth : alk. paper)
1. South Africa. Truth and Reconciliation Commission. 2. Apartheid—South Africa—
Psychological aspects. 3. Violence—South Africa—Psychological aspects. 4. Restorative
justice—South Africa—Psychological aspects. I. Title.
DT1974.2.K73 2014
968.06—dc23 2013042412

New York University Press books are printed on acid-free paper, and their binding materials
are chosen for strength and durability. We strive to use environmentally responsible
suppliers and materials to the greatest extent possible in publishing our books.

Manufactured in the United States of America

10 9 8 7 6 5 4 3 2 1

Also available as an ebook

For Virginia Petersen

CONTENTS

ACKNOWLEDGMENTS

Few activities reveal the limitations of oneself and the generosity of others more convincingly than writing a book. Although my name is the only one to appear under the title, many people contributed to the actual writing of this book—including people I have never met. It is with profound gratitude that I now acknowledge these generous individuals and their considerable offscreen contributions.

I thank my friends and colleagues at Otterbein University who advised me, in particular, Pegi Lobb, Noam Shpancer, Alice Wiemers, Allan Cooper, Beth Daugherty, and Marsha Aman. I am especially grateful to Pegi Lobb for carefully reading each of my chapters—more than once—and providing knowledgeable, focused insights each time. I am also grateful for her genuine encouragement of my work and her enlightened belief in the potential of restorative justice. I thank Noam Shpancer for his wisdom and discerning friendship—and for inadvertently motivating me by starting and finishing three books while I was writing this one. I also thank the historian Alice Wiemers for her observant critique of chapter 2.

I am indebted to the sabbatical program at Otterbein University, to the NEH Faculty Development Fund for allowing me to study at the Bodleian Library, to my overworked department chair, Michele Acker, and to academic deans who patiently supported my research even when its pace seemed glacial. I thank my students, present and past, for challenging and reinterpreting my ideas, and while doing so, encouraging humility—especially Stan Darling, Danielle Gagliano, Tanya Brown, Phillip Cantor, and MaryBeth Bailar.

At NYU Press, I am grateful to Jennifer Hammer for her distinctive blend of firmness, subtlety, and tact as she skillfully edited my manuscript. Her quickness and grace in answering my questions were remarkable. I also want to acknowledge the thoughtful, persuasive suggestions of Jeanne Marecek at Swarthmore College and the encouragement of Michelle Fine at the CUNY Graduate Center. I should note that I acknowledged Jeanne Marecek more than a decade ago in my previous book, which means she has now demonstrated unrequited altruism twice. In addition, I express my appreciation for the thoroughness and acuity of Constance Grady and Alexia Traganas in bringing about the publication of this book. Finally, I thank the unseen and unidentified reviewers who took the time to read my manuscript carefully and to offer well-defined, incisive suggestions that clarified and elaborated earlier drafts of this book.

I am grateful to Fathali Moghaddam for the perceptiveness and utility of his staircase model of terrorism. I thank the talented Matthew Kelley of Lake Forest College for supporting my work and giving it an audience as I was just beginning to develop my ideas. And I thank Heleen le Roux and Riki Botha at the South African Broadcasting Corporation for helping me assemble a research archive of videotaped testimony.

I am most indebted to my family. I thank my parents, Allen and Lillian Kraft, for their wholehearted, unwavering support of my work, and I thank my sister, Amy Kolen, for continuing to show me the power of the personal essay. I dedicate this book to my late wife, Virginia Petersen, who encouraged me and my research as I watched many hours of videotaped testimony in my home office. Though she lost her struggle with multiple sclerosis in 2010, her elegance and dignified resolve taught everyone around her to live life fully and honestly—and to have fun. I give thanks to my daughter, Jessica Carew, for insightfully revising my early chapters and for thinking of inventive ways to attract more people to read my book—critiquing, provoking, enlivening, questioning, and always motivating. I am grateful to my son, Samuel Dane, for inspiring me with his dedicated work in Teach for America and his accomplishments in architecture and sustainable design, creatively advancing theory and practice. I am also thankful for the talent, precision, and moral centeredness of my son-in-law, Jordan Elias, the poise and compassion of Erin Lau, the mischievous humor of my first granddaughter, Simone Odiya, and the quiet courage of my newest granddaughter, Lazarre Opal.

Finally, I thank the Amnesty Committee of South Africa's Truth and Reconciliation Commission for not only getting to the bottom of illegal violence during apartheid but—unlike so many other commissions— getting to the top as well. Ultimately, this book would not exist without the transcendent wisdom of Nelson Mandela and the hard work and daily heroism of all the members of the Amnesty Committee as they conducted the amnesty hearings and guided South Africa's search for truth and reconciliation.

Introduction

Crimes of Allegiance

Someone who is perennially surprised that depravity exists, who continues to feel disillusioned (even incredulous) when confronted with evidence of what humans are capable of inflicting in the way of gruesome, hands-on cruelties upon other humans, has not reached moral or psychological adulthood.

Susan Sontag, *Regarding the Pain of Others*[1]

In July 1997, Captain Jeffrey Benzien sat before the Amnesty Committee of South Africa's Truth and Reconciliation Commission and gave testimony about his illegal activities during apartheid. In the course of this testimony, Benzien provided extended accounts of his activities with the "terrorist tracking unit" of the South African Police, finding and detaining antiapartheid activists and locating their ammunition and weapons. He described his general duties and he recalled the specifics of his most notorious expertise: the "wet bag" method of torture interrogation. He would force a wet canvas bag over the head of a bound prisoner and then alternately tighten and release the bag, repeatedly bringing the prisoner to the brink of asphyxiation while conducting his interrogation. He disclosed this procedure in his testimony:

> It was a cloth bag that would be submerged in water to get it completely wet. And then the way I applied it, was I get the person to lie down on the ground on his stomach . . . with that person's hands handcuffed behind his back. Then I would take up a position in the small of the person's back, put my feet through between his arms to maintain my balance and then pull the bag over the person's head and twist it closed around the neck in that way, cutting off the air supply to the person.

He detailed the torture interrogations of several activists, describing the various cruelties he inflicted on these men, including torture through the application of electric shocks, and he gave extensive testimony regarding the killing of an antiapartheid activist during a covert operation. During the hearings, Benzien's former victims listened to his sworn testimony, and one at a time, they confronted Benzien with questions, disputing some of the testimony and offering alternative accounts.

Over two full days of testimony, Jeffrey Benzien exhaustively described what he called his "heinous" acts and endeavored at length to explain his thought processes and motivations at the time he committed these acts. He said that he was genuinely sorry for the mistreatment of the individuals he interrogated but not for his efforts to maintain security and to fight the efforts of antiapartheid activists. His perspective was that of a diligent professional who tried to accomplish all that was asked of him, but whose very diligence had led him astray. Although inconsistent and incomplete, Benzien's testimony offered a sincere and revealing account of how one human being became a killer and serial torturer for the apartheid state and began answering the general question of how ordinary people develop into violence workers (Benzien, July 14–15, 1997).

After the amnesty hearings, discrepancies between Benzien's testimony and the testimony of his former victims remained unresolved, and the limitations of an individual perpetrator to recall years of illegal violence work became a matter of record. Even with these limitations, however, the case of Jeffrey Benzien ultimately showed how unconstrained testimony can disclose the phenomenology of the perpetrator, the existence of multiple truths, and the possibilities for reconciliation.

* * *

A remarkable set of events occurred in South Africa in the final half decade of the twentieth century—events that are now mostly forgotten. Many people outside South Africa still remember the stormy transition from apartheid to democracy and Nelson Mandela's triumphant victory in May 1994 as South Africa's first democratically elected president, but few recall the truth commission that followed. In 1995, guided by President Mandela and mandated by an act of Parliament, South Africa created the Truth and Reconciliation Commission (TRC), a massive, temporary institution whose mission was to reveal the specifics of widespread human rights abuses and to begin repairing the damage from nearly half a century of violent oppression known as apartheid.

Officially introduced in 1948 as a policy of forced segregation, apartheid was designed to control the nonwhite majority of South Africa and to preserve a privileged way of life for the white minority. Over a period of decades, the ruling National Party then enacted apartheid through a succession of increasingly oppressive laws restricting every major aspect of the lives of nonwhite South Africans, beginning with the forcible removal of millions of people from their homes and communities and deportation into segregated homeland areas and overcrowded, underserved townships (Adam 1997; Mamdani 2000; Thompson 2000). Those who resisted faced imprisonment, torture, and death at the hands of the government security forces. As the oppression of apartheid grew and the brutal enforcement of the apartheid government became more widespread, so did the violent conflicts between the government forces and the various organizations fighting to end apartheid and establish a democracy. As these conflicts escalated throughout the 1970s and 1980s, and into the early 1990s, deadly clashes eventually enveloped much of the country, with horrific violence committed by all sides.

It was during the hearings of the TRC that the brutal violence of apartheid was publicly investigated and openly discussed. Many of the government's atrocities that had been covered up for decades within South Africa and only briefly glimpsed in the world media were uncovered and documented. Names not heard of outside South Africa and no longer talked about today, even within South Africa—Jeffrey Benzien, Dirk Coetzee, Eugene de Kock, Robert McBride, Adriaan Vlok—commanded the attention of millions of South Africans with their testimony about the violent political crimes they committed during apartheid.

Analyses and critiques of the South African TRC have now resulted in the largest literature ever produced about a truth commission, with dozens of scholarly books and scores of research articles, representing a distinctive biblio-monument to the TRC—its goals, its accomplishments, its compromises, and its legacy. In the process, the TRC created a comprehensive archive of the proceedings, housed in the National Archives, with its final report serving as a road map for the TRC archive.

Today, however, as new challenges have overwhelmed the second decade of democratic South Africa—the AIDS epidemic, widespread poverty, debilitating unemployment, and violent crime—political leaders in South Africa have devoted their efforts to addressing these challenges, placing apartheid and the TRC behind them. In the West, the TRC is largely absent from contemporary discussions of national and geopolitical conflicts, pushed aside by the demands of current economic, environmental, and military urgencies. More broadly, the TRC has faded from view because it occurred during a period of time that is obscure for us now: in the words of noted publisher and correspondent Rupert Hart-Davis, "too old to be news and too young to be history—the day before yesterday" (Hart-Davis 1978, 116).

Yet it was the TRC that transformed an emerging set of principles for finding truth and resolving long-term national conflicts into an established tradition, a tradition that continues today in a handful of countries working to adapt its principles to their own national traditions (Amnesty International 2009; Bronkhorst 2006; Hayner 2011; Lobb 2010; U.S. Institute of Peace 2009). For those countries traumatized by sustained violence, the findings of the TRC represent news in the making, but for the rest of the world, the TRC remains the day before yesterday.

Over the next generation, however, all this will change. Inevitably, growing economic and social forces will demand creative methods for resolving long-standing confrontations that do not involve the expense and destructiveness of prolonged lethal force. At the local level, community leaders and participants in the justice system are recognizing the effectiveness of restorative justice in resolving protracted civil conflicts and reconciling victims and perpetrators in criminal cases (Johnstone 2003; Sherman and Strang 2007; Strang and Braithwaite 2002; Zernova 2007). As these methods continue to be studied and implemented, awareness of the TRC will grow and propagate. More generally, now that the foundational concepts of restorative justice and truth commissions have entered our cultural lexicon, it is only a matter of time before they enter our political discussions and our national public policy. Within a generation, the TRC is likely to become both news and history. The extensive analyses of the TRC will be rediscovered and the TRC itself—along with its struggles and limitations—will achieve lasting historical significance as the foundational national institution for uncovering truth and for helping to promote the reconciliation of long-standing conflicts.

Beginning a Study of Perpetrators

The research for this book took root at a provocative 1998 conference at Yale University entitled "Searching for Memory and Justice: The Holocaust and Apartheid." Cosponsored by the Fortunoff Video Archive for Holocaust Testimonies and the Orville H. Schell Jr. Center for International Human Rights, the conference brought Holocaust scholars together with researchers and officials from South Africa at the time the TRC was conducting its hearings. It was at this conference that I first encountered what seemed to me a radically new concept: restorative justice. Until that time, for me, justice was retributive: people who committed crimes were apprehended by the police, tried by the state, and punished by the criminal justice system. At the conference, I learned that restorative justice is rooted in the concept of Ubuntu, which translates generally as "humaneness," and is conveyed in the expression "A person is a person through other people" (Simpson 2002, 248; TRC 1999a; Tutu 1999b, 31). Ubuntu seeks to redefine crime away from offenses against the state and toward an understanding of crime as violations against other human beings and their communities. In the context of Ubuntu, restorative justice seeks full accountability, with perpetrators facing the people they victimized and working to repair the damage they inflicted. Based on reparation, it endeavors to heal all sides of a conflict, encouraging victims and perpetrators to be directly involved in resolving the conflict (TRC 1999a).

I was invited to participate at the Yale conference as a Holocaust scholar. I had been studying oral testimonies of Holocaust survivors in the Fortunoff Video Archive as a way of learning about deeply traumatic memory and its enduring aftermath. At the time of the conference, I had analyzed nearly seventy videotaped testimonies from victims of Nazi ghettos and concentration camps and had begun characterizing the distinctive patterns of Holocaust memory. In these testimonies, Holocaust survivors detailed the brutal acts of the SS officers, the Wehrmacht, the camp guards, the ghetto officials, and local police, but they remained understandably uncomprehending about how their

tormenters could have behaved with such relentless cruelty and brutality. Martin S., for example, described this incredulity as a child in the
slave labor camp of Skarzysko:

> I just kept asking, Why? And I couldn't get the answer. I remember, I
> walked by a spot, and a guard hit me very hard over the head. After I
> recovered—because he did put me into a sort of semiconscious state
> for a few minutes—I turned around and I said, he doesn't know me. I
> wasn't even thinking of the fact that I was a child. He doesn't know me. I
> don't know him. Why does he have such a hatred for me? . . . I could not
> understand the brutality. (Tape HVT-641, testimony of Martin S. 1986)[2]

As I continued to study the testimonies, the unanswered questions of
Martin S. grew more and more insistent, and I became increasingly
aware of my ignorance of the people who were offscreen: the perpetrators of the Nazi monstrosity. I also recalled the words of Primo Levi
from *The Drowned and the Saved* (1988), after he acknowledged the
importance of recording the perpetrators' accounts of their atrocities:
"Much more important are the motivations and justifications: Why did
you do this? Were you aware that you were committing a crime?" (26).

In 2002, after seven years of studying Holocaust testimonies, I completed my work in the form of the book *Memory Perceived: Recalling the
Holocaust* and then directed my research toward the study of perpetrators. But the Nazis were not talking. The problem then was to find an
archive with extensive testimony from perpetrators. At the time, however, no such archive existed, and it was this lack of perpetrator testimony that led me back to the Yale conference four years earlier and to
the monumental work of the South African TRC.

In terms of testimony, the TRC consisted of two great halves: the collection of victim testimonies by the Committee on Human Rights Violations (HRV) and the documentation of perpetrator testimonies by the
Amnesty Committee. Victims gave testimony to the HRV to document
the crimes committed against them and their families and to apply for
reparations. Perpetrators gave testimony to the Amnesty Committee to
inform the nation of the specific crimes they carried out during apartheid and to obtain amnesty for these violent crimes. The newly constituted South African Broadcasting Corporation then recorded every

public hearing of the HRV and every public hearing of the Amnesty Committee, making a permanent record of the victims' testimonies and the perpetrators' testimonies, with the TRC posting the transcripts of these hearings on its website (www.doj.gov.za/trc).

Thus it was that the difficult work of the Amnesty Committee resulted in the most extensive collection of perpetrator testimony ever recorded. All that remained to begin my research on perpetrators was to select a representative sample of videotaped perpetrator testimonies from the hearings of the TRC Amnesty Committee and to proceed with a detailed analysis of this testimony.

I should note that my juxtaposition of the Holocaust and apartheid in this introduction does not imply that the two historical events are somehow comparable. Each historical event should be studied in depth and not *in relation to* the other. In fact, framing one historical event in the categories of another distorts our understanding of both and diminishes the distinctive consequences of each. Regarding the Yale conference on the Holocaust and apartheid, the archivist of the Fortunoff Video Archive made it clear that "there was no intent or effort to make comparisons" and that the conference "offered a unique opportunity for examining and discussing the impact and memory of two different traumatic histories." She also addressed *commonalities,* saying that much could be learned by studying "oppressive governments that legally inflict such suffering upon their own citizens" (Rudof 2000, 9). It is with this perspective that I analyzed the perpetrators in apartheid South Africa: as one distinctive example of widespread oppression that also revealed the universal themes of systemic cruelty, sustained repression, and ideology unmotivated by compassion. After studying more than 120 hours of perpetrator testimony, it is clear to me that the testimony given to the Amnesty Committee of the TRC provides the comprehensiveness, the immediacy, and the unsummarized specificity for a thorough and generalizable analysis of violent perpetrators.

A Qualitative View

The unlived analysis is not worth doing. Studying the testimony of perpetrators in apartheid South Africa demanded an initial examination of my own attitudes toward the events at the time and my limitations in understanding these events. Raised and educated in the American Midwest during the second half of the twentieth century, I grew up mostly unaware of the history and struggles of South Africa. In the 1960s and 1970s, the evening news occasionally depicted the tragic events in the townships—the massacre in Sharpeville, the mass killing in Soweto—and I interpreted the antiapartheid movement in South Africa in terms of the civil rights movement in the United States. Later, in the 1980s, as the apartheid government came under more intense media scrutiny, my awareness of its injustices and cruelties increased appreciably. The international media stepped up their coverage of apartheid South Africa during the politically volatile years of the early 1990s, which then came to a celebratory end in May 1994 with the election of Nelson Mandela as president of the new South Africa.

It was only after the fall of apartheid that I began a social scientific study of South Africa's struggle with the painful memories of apartheid and with its devoted efforts to reconcile. As a foreign observer without experiential knowledge of life under apartheid, my perspective will always be that of an outsider, with the outsider's advantage of distance and the corresponding disadvantage of missing the shared knowledge and obvious subtleties of daily life.

As a qualitative researcher, it is necessary not only to reflect on my own experience with the subjects of my study but also to reflect on the analytical process itself. My original motivating goal for this book was to understand violent perpetrators in violent organizations by studying testimony from the amnesty hearings of the TRC. My analysis then began by identifying generalizable patterns of thought, motivation, and social influence that cause ordinary people to perpetrate extraordinary brutalities for a political cause. An extensive analysis of testimony from these violent perpetrators is presented in chapter 3.

As my analysis of perpetrators proceeded, however, related goals emerged. The confrontations between perpetrators and victims during the amnesty hearings revealed enduring insights about collective violence, but they also disclosed honest and profound discrepancies between the memories of the perpetrators and the memories of the victims for the violent crimes being investigated. These discrepancies and the interactions between the testimony and the goals of the Amnesty Committee could only be accommodated by the existence of multiple—and sometimes contradictory—truths. The study of perpetrator testimony therefore required an analysis of these discrepancies and of different kinds of truth. This analysis is presented in chapter 4.

As perpetrators and victims offered new facts and narratives about the crimes of apartheid, and as the confrontations between victims and perpetrators defined the contours of acceptable discrepancies, the interactions that occurred between victims and perpetrators directly influenced the opportunities for reconciliation. These confrontational interactions then demanded an analysis of the complexities of reconciliation, identifying those interactions that promoted reconciliation and those that foreclosed it. This analysis of testimony and reconciliation is presented in chapter 5.

Finally, as these analyses came to completion, it became apparent that my findings about perpetrators, about multiple truths, and about face-to-face confrontations between victims and perpetrators needed to be integrated and *applied* to the challenge of implementing future truth commissions as well as other programs of restorative justice. This integration and application is presented in chapter 6.

Each chapter, then, presents a different topic in the study of perpetrator testimony, moving from methodology (chapter 1) to the history of apartheid and the TRC (chapter 2) to an analysis of violent perpetrators (chapter 3) to the kinds of truth that emerged during the amnesty hearings (chapter 4) to the complexities of reconciliation between perpetrators and victims (chapter 5), and finally to the applications of the findings (chapter 6). Throughout the book, all the analyses were motivated by the same underlying goal: to understand the etiology, maintenance, and aftermath of collective violence through a comprehensive analysis of testimony from the amnesty hearings of the TRC.

As social-cognitive research on collective violence, the book asks two overarching questions: How do mostly ordinary people transmogrify into individuals who repeatedly perpetrate illegal acts of violence against others and how do perpetrators and victims manage in the aftermath? To answer these questions, the book presents a qualitative study of testimony from violent perpetrators who operated within governmental and political organizations in apartheid South Africa, focusing on the thoughts and motivations of the individual perpetrators, as well as the social-political context for their destructive actions. Based on the analysis of this testimony, the book offers several interrelated findings. It reveals the stepwise interactions between decisions and consequences that move individuals to cruelty and violence, the cognitive basis for maintaining brutality against others, the unexpected insights that arise when victims confront their tormentors, the reality of multiple truths, the complexities of reconciliation, and the lessons that transcend the particulars of the South African TRC.

* * *

My method involved close analysis of individual testimonies, with a focus on the remembered experiences of the perpetrators and the observations about these remembered experiences by the perpetrators and the confronting victims. My general strategy was to study each testimony repeatedly and to identify patterns of thought and motivation across the different testimonies. By studying many testimonies, the analysis revealed commonalities in the individual experiences of the perpetrators, with the particulars of the testimonies coalescing into generalizable themes. My method was consistent with other phenomenological approaches by analyzing each testimony as a valid source of information about the perpetrator's own thoughts and beliefs and by identifying descriptive commonalities across individuals. My method differed from established phenomenological analysis by generalizing beyond the particular sample of participants in the study, moving from individual experiential descriptions to categories of specific experience to an organization of these categories that constituted an explanatory framework, with existing theoretical concepts informing the final stage of the inductive analysis. In general, this method integrated the personal and experiential immediacy of phenomenological analysis with the goal of identifying broader theoretical principles.

A necessary reference throughout the writing of this book was the final report of the TRC, a set of seven volumes, with the first five volumes published in 1999 and the final two in 2003, two years after completion of the TRC. This final report is not a work of literature. Rather, it is a patchwork of historical scholarship, reportage, descriptive statistics, psychological interpretation, tables, graphs, lists, maps, cartoons, photographs, financial records, and policy recommendations.

Although flawed and inconsistent, it is also a remarkably comprehensive document, reflecting the ambitious scope of the TRC hearings, the demanding research of the TRC staff, and the improvisations of the TRC commissioners during six years of hearings, challenges, political interventions, and internal decisions.

In fact, in this final report, one of the commissioners suggested, "A qualitative analysis of the data that has been collected . . . would have made a very valuable contribution to a better understanding of our society and the underlying endemic risks of the conflicts of the past repeating themselves in different forms" (Malan 1999, 455). In that sense, this book begins a new volume of the TRC report.

1

Regarding Perpetrators

Studying Collective Violence

A fundamental question confronts any research psychologist interested in studying the problem of collective violence: How does one conduct meaningful behavioral research on violence? Historically, one approach has been to *simulate* collective violence within the confines of an experiment, with the two most prominent examples being the Milgram experiments on obedience in the early 1960s (Milgram 1963, 1965, 1974) and the surprisingly destructive and illuminating six days of the Stanford Prison Experiment (Zimbardo 1973; Zimbardo, Maslach, and Haney 1999). These and other, similar experiments have provided distinctive insights from the laboratory about violence to others, demonstrating the pervasive influence of the situation on the behavior of individual perpetrators. Yet the realism and the complexity of such laboratory simulations are obviously limited by ethical and legal constraints. As researchers, we are not permitted to terrorize our participants. Moreover, since these early laboratory studies of more than thirty years ago, institutional review boards have mostly not allowed psychologists to simulate collective violence in such forceful ways. How, then, do we study collective violence?

One effective solution is to *interview* those individuals who have actually carried out collective violence in the past and to analyze their responses, characterizing the powerful influences and destructive actions of the perpetrators from their remembered experiences. Robert Lifton's seminal and provocative work, *The Nazi Doctors* (1986), introduced this approach by analyzing interviews with twenty-eight physicians involved in Nazi medicine, five of whom had worked in concentration camps as SS physicians or in medical experiments. In the past decade, three major studies have continued and extended Lifton's approach. In *Violence Workers* (2002), Martha Huggins, Mika Haritos-Fatouros, and Philip Zimbardo analyzed interviews with twenty-three Brazilian policemen, fourteen of whom were torturers and killers for the Brazilian military regime that ruled the country from the mid-1960s through the mid-1980s. *The Psychological Origins of Institutionalized Torture* (2003), authored by Mika Haritos-Fatouros, studied primarily sixteen former Military Policemen who had served under the Greek military junta of 1967–1974, five of whom were confessed torturers. For *Machete Season* (2005), Jean Hatzfeld collected statements from ten Hutu men who had killed Tutsis in the Rwandan genocide in the spring of 1994.

Christopher Browning's (1998) groundbreaking investigative work, *Ordinary Men,* should also be introduced here. Although Browning did not conduct interviews, he did analyze the legal interrogations of 210 men from Reserve Police Battalion 101, a squad of approximately 500 men who shot to death tens of thousands of Jewish people in the villages of Poland during the summer and fall of 1942. His analysis of these legal interrogations yielded valuable historical information about the killing squads during World War II. But, as Browning described, several important factors limited the interrogations as a source of *psychological* disclosure: the "conscious mendacity" of the men, the legal focus on collecting evidence only for specific crimes, the amount of time that had lapsed between the events and the interrogations (twenty to twenty-five years), and the German law defining homicide as involving a base motive, such as anti-Semitism, effectively eliminating the expression of personal animosity in the legal proceedings (Browning 1998, xviii).

Each of these interview studies was informative and heroic, revealing strong influences and individual decisions responsible for horrifying violence work. The studies were also understandably clandestine, with small samples of perpetrators and no videotaping of the interviews. Moreover, the perpetrators in the studies were those at the bottom of the violence hierarchy (often referred to as "foot soldiers") or, in the case of Lifton's study, physicians who were not in leadership or managerial positions where they could initiate policy.

One strategy for overcoming the limitations of secretive data gathering, small samples, and the lack of access to different levels of the violence hierarchy is to study perpetrator testimony gathered by truth commissions. Unlike clandestine interview studies, hearings for perpetrators who testify in front of truth commissions can be public and open-ended, with hundreds of testimonies available for analysis from various levels of the violence hierarchy. Each testimony documents a distinctive set of particulars about perpetrating violence and divulges personal reactions and details that can then be compared to the accounts of other violent perpetrators. Analyzing many such testimonies can reveal general patterns of social and political influence, as well as the cognitive-emotional states of each perpetrator when participating in crimes against humanity. Analysis of testimony from a truth commission presents a way of retrospectively knowing the thoughts and motivations of a diverse set of violent perpetrators, disclosing the phenomenology of the perpetrator: one's state of mind while planning and carrying out violence.

Perpetrator Testimony from the South African TRC

Testimony given to the Amnesty Committee of the TRC distinguished itself in several important respects. To begin, perpetrators testified in public, in open hearings held before audiences at different locations around the country. The public hearings were then filmed by the South African Broadcasting Corporation (SABC), with full transcripts posted on the TRC website (www.doj.gov.za/trc/).[1] To promote inclusiveness, all eleven official languages of South Africa were spoken at the amnesty hearings, requiring more than 1,500 interpreters during the course of the hearings.[2] Second, amnesty was granted to the perpetrators in exchange for *full disclosure,* thereby motivating the perpetrators to provide detailed and comprehensive testimony about their crimes. Full disclosure also required the testimony to extend and corroborate forensic evidence whenever possible, revealing previously unknown historical events. Third, the testimony was subject to examination by legal representatives and open to questions and dispute from witnesses and victims, encouraging perpetrators to analyze their actions and their thought processes—then and now. Fourth, more than 1,600 perpetrators qualified for the amnesty process, with 255 public amnesty cases and 1,632 days of amnesty hearings (TRC 2003a, 736). Finally, the perpetrators who gave testimony to the TRC represented *multiple levels* within the apartheid system: foot soldiers, managers, executives, members of the cabinet, and even the former president, F. W. de Klerk. The requirements of openness, full disclosure, safe confrontations between perpetrators and victims, and participation from different levels on all sides of the conflict combined to create distinctively revealing testimony. From a researcher's perspective, the amnesty hearings of the TRC constitute the most comprehensive set of data ever collected on violent perpetrators.

Before giving testimony, perpetrators were sworn in under oath, with attorneys for all sides present. The perpetrators were then subject to cross-examination about their testimony by the evidence leader of the Amnesty Committee, by attorneys representing the victims and their families, and by the former victims themselves. The perpetrators gave their testimony and confessed their misdeeds in order to persuade the Amnesty Committee to grant them amnesty—a requirement that generated strong extrinsic motivation for comprehensiveness and honesty.

The *confrontations* between perpetrators and victims were especially informative about the perpetrators' motivations and actions, encouraging unexpected revelations as well as surprising interactions. Consider one such confrontation in the case that opened this book, the hearings for Captain Jeffrey Benzien of the South African Police. One of Benzien's former victims, Tony Yengeni, repeatedly questioned Benzien's testimony and presented conflicting accounts of what transpired during and after the interrogation sessions. At one point in the confrontation, Yengeni made a direct request of Benzien about his wet bag method of torture interrogation: "I have never seen this bag being used myself or on any other person. Even when it was used on *me*, I never saw it. And I think it would be in the interest of the public and the Commission for you to *demonstrate* the use of this bag" (Yengeni, July 14, 1997).

More concerned about his diminished agility than the immorality of the act, Benzien agreed to demonstrate the wet bag technique of torture using a volunteer from the audience, with a donated pillowcase serving as the wet bag. Although the transcript of this interaction conveys a flat dialogue of cryptic comments about the particulars of the demonstration, the videotaped testimony presents a powerful piece of impromptu theater, with the volunteer from the audience lying facedown on the

floor with a pillowcase over his head and Benzien straddling him, placing his considerable weight on the small of his back. Benzien sat on
the volunteer prisoner, alternately pulling up on the pillowcase and
pushing down his head, forcing the volunteer's face into the floor, as he
helplessly succumbed to the demonstration. As Jeffrey Benzien demonstrated the wet bag technique of torture, pantomiming his actions
with the volunteer from the audience, the camera alternately showed
Benzien sitting astride the volunteer prisoner and Tony Yengeni watching intently, involuntarily squeezing his own neck in sympathy with his
remembered self being tortured (Benzien, July 14, 1997).

Analyzing the Testimony

This research involved close analysis of individual testimonies given
to the Amnesty Committee of the TRC, with a focus on the remembered experiences of the perpetrators and the observations about these
remembered experiences by the perpetrators and the confronting victims. The primary source material for this analysis was testimony from
seventy-four perpetrators who testified in front of the Amnesty Committee of the TRC, consisting of a complete set of transcripts and 126
hours of videotaped testimony. The testimony was taken from ninety-
six days of amnesty hearings that spanned a period from November
1996 through November 2000, including twelve major amnesty cases
that involved confrontations between victims and perpetrators. (Refer
to the appendix for a detailed listing of the testimonies.) In this sample,
the testimony originated from several levels in the hierarchy of collective violence: the executives and commanders who translated political
doctrine into general strategies, the managers who turned these general
strategies into specific plans, and the staff working under these managers—the hundreds of "foot soldiers" in a particular region who carried
out the instructions of these managers. Although my emphasis is on
the large middle of this hierarchy (the managers of collective violence),
testimonies from the commanders and the foot soldiers are integrated
throughout, and differentiated.[3]

   In terms of political categories, the testimony originated from three
groups of perpetrators: (1) the defenders and enforcers of apartheid,
mostly the security forces of the South African Police (SAP); (2) those

who fought within the liberation movements, primarily the military wings of the African National Congress (ANC) and the Pan African Congress (PAC); and (3) those involved in township conflicts, primarily members of groups affiliated with the Inkatha Freedom Party (IFP) who were in conflict with members of groups linked to the ANC. Initially, my plan was to maintain this tripartite political distinction while analyzing the testimony, clearly separating the pro-apartheid forces from the liberation movements. As the analysis proceeded, however, it became apparent that the testimony, especially from the first two groups, provided the same discernible themes about perpetrating violence, about the reactions to this violence, and about its justification, with explicit commonalities in the experiences of the perpetrators and in the influences of their organizations. In fact, these common themes were shaped by the similar relationships between the individuals and the structures of their organizations. The first two groups of perpetrators—the enforcers of apartheid and the members of the liberation movements—operated within hierarchical organizations, employed unorthodox methods to fight a clearly defined enemy, and were influenced by the same national events. The third group was more loosely organized and more spontaneous in its actions.

Although this study found precise commonalities in the testimony from different kinds of perpetrators, these commonalities do not imply moral equivalence between those fighting for liberation and those defending deadly oppression. The analysis was of individuals within organizations committing violent crimes because of their allegiance to these organizations. In fact, the Amnesty Committee itself, while well aware of the profound questions of power, historical injustice, and economic and educational disparity, was mandated to treat the testimony from all sides of the struggle equally.[4] Later in this chapter, I juxtapose the testimony from a commander in the ANC with testimony from a commander in a notorious security unit fighting against the ANC. Again, this juxtaposition is not meant to suggest moral equivalence in the causes of these two organizations but to convey the similarities in the motives and justifications of the individuals who perpetrated illegal violence in service to these organizations.

Historically, my method of analysis is rooted in the inductive methodologies developed and elaborated over the past decade and a half for the qualitative study of complex psychological phenomena in natural settings (e.g., Camic, Rhodes, and Yardley 2003; Smith 2003; Tolman and Brydon-Miller 2001; Wertz et al. 2011; Willig and Stainton-Rogers 2008). More specifically, my method adapted and extrapolated phenomenological analysis (Giorgi 2009; Smith 1996; Wertz 2011) to reveal commonalities in the individual experiences of the perpetrators, as well as the social-political influences responsible for widespread violations of human rights: the phenomenology of violence and the topography of the crimes. Through this analysis, the particulars of the individual testimonies coalesced into broader themes, with a subset of cases cited as exemplars for each theme. The following section presents the specific steps involved in this analysis.

Progressive Phenomenological Analysis

My method for analyzing testimony began with the phenomenological approaches of Jonathan Smith (Smith and Osborn 2003) and Amadeo Giorgi (Giorgi and Giorgi 2003) and extended these approaches by structuring the analysis of reported experience into generalizable frameworks and by integrating existing theories. As with these other phenomenological approaches, my method assumed that people's descriptions of their remembered experiences are valid sources of information about their own thoughts and beliefs and focused on how people understand these experiences. As Smith and Osborn (2003) noted, the researcher's goal is to make sense out of the participants making sense of the world.[5]

My emphasis differed from established phenomenological approaches by using the detailed analysis of each person's experience to identify commonalities across individuals and by generalizing beyond the particular sample of participants in the study (Chapman and Smith 2002).[6] Reflecting this difference, my method required a considerably larger sample size than most phenomenological analyses (Smith and Osborn 2003).

For my study, I adapted Giorgi's four-step method for analyzing lived experience (Giorgi 1975, 1985, 2009; Wertz 2011) to the analysis of testimony, employing the following general steps: (1) taking an overview of each testimony, (2) identifying and listing individual ideas within each testimony, (3) organizing the individual ideas into meaningful psychological categories, and (4) structuring the ideas and categories into generalizable themes, with the goal of building a theoretical framework.

Each step overlapped with the others. With the videotaped testimony, I studied each testimony once in its entirety, taking an overview (step 1). I then studied the testimony in its entirety again, identifying idea units and creating a list of the different ideas expressed in each testimony (step 2).[7] Each identified idea consisted of a summary label, an excerpt of testimony, and the location of the excerpt in the overall testimony. I then re-studied selected portions of the testimony, verifying and transcribing extended examples for each identified idea and referencing the official transcripts of the TRC. With amnesty hearings that were unavailable on videotaped recordings or with tapes that were untranslated, I analyzed the full transcripts with the same four-step procedure.

Step 3 consisted of comparing the exemplified ideas in the particular testimony being analyzed to the exemplified ideas from *other* testimonies and developing *categories* for the different ideas. As I continued to analyze the testimonies in this step, I found new exemplified ideas for existing categories, while also identifying ideas that constituted new categories.[8] As the analysis proceeded, some categories became increasingly reinforced with subsequent testimony, while others divided, becoming more differentiated and detailed.

At its least compelling, the perpetrator testimony could be general and repetitive. At times, in fact, I needed to verify that I had not unknowingly listened to a particular perpetrator earlier in my research. The same themes could be expressed repeatedly, almost verbatim, with different events and at different times. But this independent repetition became a valuable source of thematic emphasis. "Following orders," for example, instead of an evasion, became an explanatory theme, especially when elaborated. "I had no choice" became a commentary on the phenomenology of the perpetrator just before committing a violent act.

After half the testimonies were analyzed, I began step 4 by organizing the categorized testimony into *superordinate and subordinate themes:* (1) finding larger themes that were supported by several categories and numerous examples and (2) subdividing some of the categories into subthemes. In this step, I looked to create a partially hierarchical structure to organize the themes and subthemes and to characterize these themes in terms of general principles. With each new testimony, I repeated this procedure. In addition, I re-studied testimonies analyzed earlier in the process and repeated steps 3 and 4.

This fourth step also involved integrating *existing theory* with the inductively derived categories. In the analysis for chapter 3, for example, I applied Moghaddam's (2005) staircase model of terrorism to the categories of influence that led people to commit violence against others. For chapter 4, I integrated the TRC's (1999a) four categories of truth, Tilly's (2006) four types of explanation, and Baumeister's (1997) concept of the magnitude gap to help explain the disagreements between the recall of perpetrators and victims and the discrepancies between forensic evidence and remembered events. For chapter 5, I applied theoretical distinctions among different kinds of forgiveness to account for the process of reconciliation between victims and perpetrators (Andrews 2000; Hamber 2007; Kriesberg 2000). For chapter 6, I synthesized the findings in the previous chapters to codify general lessons for future truth commissions.

The process of analyzing the testimony moved back and forth between the individual testimonies and the categories, with each influencing the other. I termed this approach *progressive phenomenological analysis:* (1) studying each individual testimony in its entirety, (2) identifying and listing exemplified ideas expressed in each testimony, (3) comparing the analyses of *different* testimonies and developing categories of exemplified ideas across these different testimonies, and (4) grouping the categories into superordinate and subordinate themes and building a theoretical framework to generalize beyond the set of analyzed testimonies (Kraft 2002, 2007, 2011).

Although each theme about perpetrators was revealed explicitly in the testimony, the resulting theoretical framework moved to a level of analysis that was not directly experienced and was not part of the phenomenology of the perpetrators. Thus, the analysis moved from the experiential descriptions of the perpetrators and other participants to categories of specific experience and then to an organization of these categories that constituted an explanatory framework. This method of analysis does not begin with theory to bracket the observations but rather *builds* theory by applying the initial categories from earlier inductive analysis to later analysis of the testimony. It then integrates existing theoretical concepts into this inductive analysis, further defining, refining, and organizing the categories in later observations.[9]

Analyzing the Testimony: An Example

Consider testimony from Aboobaker Ismail, the commander of special operations of the military wing of the ANC. An overview of the selected portion of Ismail's testimony (step 1) showed that he was explaining the context for the ANC initiating violent actions against members of the South African military, as exemplified in the following statement: "We are talking here of a country at war with itself. We are talking of a nation that was broken up on the basis of apartheid, on the basis of a racist ideology." The main ideas in this contextualizing explanation (step 2) were that South Africa was in a civil war and that the cause of this war was the divisive, immoral ideology of apartheid. Ismail then elaborated on the necessity of killing civilians:

> When people enter the Defense Force, when they are typists and others that work for the Defense Force, they become part of that military machine. During World War II, more civilians died than military people. During World War II, in order to get at the Nazi beast, the Allies went in and went on blanket bombings. In those days they couldn't target specific targets. They bombed cities. All of those are considered legitimate. Were they tried? No. They were considered victors. They were considered as liberators from the Nazi beast. In our case, we considered we had to destroy, by whatever means we had at our disposal, those security forces which defended apartheid, and that's what we struck at. (Ismail, May 6, 1998)

In this statement, Ismail's main rationale for targeting civilians in South Africa is that they, too, contributed to the war against the ANC and were therefore legitimate targets for the ANC. To support this rationale, Ismail proposed a direct analogy between the struggle against apartheid and the fight against the Nazis, which meant that the methods used against Nazism could justifiably be used against apartheid. For step 2 of my analysis, I listed Ismail's main ideas that the ANC was at war with the Defense Forces, that everyone who worked for the Defense Forces was a target, and that modern warfare necessitates the killing of civilians. I also listed the type of explanation, which in this case was an analogy to an agreed-upon extreme example.

To illustrate step 3 of the analysis, this example compares Ismail's testimony to the following testimony from Captain Dirk Coetzee, commander of a secret unit in the security forces at Vlakplaas, as he justified ordering and leading illegal violence *against* members of the ANC:

> Never before I joined Vlakplaas did I commit any murders, stole cars, or anything to that extent, and never thereafter. It was a war situation as I saw it, and it was a question of using the same methods that the enemy used—illegal methods—to achieve our goals, namely to try and prevent the total onslaught from succeeding, the revolutionary onslaught. (Coetzee, November 6, 1996)

The overview of this testimony (step 1) was Coetzee presenting a general rationale for engaging in illegal violence. The analysis in step 2 revealed five related ideas: (1) Coetzee's exemplary conduct outside the influence of Vlakplaas, (2) the unique role of Vlakplaas in encouraging illegal, violent activities, (3) being *at war*, (4) reciprocity—matching the methods of Vlakplaas with the illegal methods of the enemy (the ANC) to achieve victory, and (5) the larger idea of protecting the entire country.

The similarity in reasoning of the two commanders on opposing sides of the struggle is noteworthy, with both Ismail of the ANC and Coetzee of the state security forces categorizing the enemy as a profound threat to the nation and to humanity in general and citing war as the justification for illegal violence. From these brief excerpts of testimony, the analysis in step 3 identified two categories of influences that support sustained violence in crimes of allegiance: (1) an abbreviated ideology that idealizes oneself and vilifies one's adversary and (2) the use of war to justify any act of illegality.

Further analysis of these testimonies and others in step 4 evinced three higher-level themes (italicized here), supported by categories identified in step 3 (in parentheses): (1) influences for *joining* violent organizations (political ideologies, specific memories, national events, the narrowing of choices, and the rewards for joining); (2) influences for *continuing* to perpetrate violence within these organizations (ongoing battles between government forces and the liberation forces, the incremental process of carrying out violent acts, teamwork, directives from others); and (3) *immediate causes* for violent behavior (unanalyzed orders and a sharp focus on the logistics and mechanics of the violence). In step 4, categories could also subdivide. It became clear, for example, that the category of political ideologies was composed of three distinct subcategories: concepts of self, concepts of the enemy, and concepts of the worsening situation. Eventually, the four steps of analysis in this example were applied to all the testimonies in the study.

Defining Concepts

This chapter closes with a discussion of two concepts that are fundamental in communicating the analysis of testimony presented in this book: *evil* and *perpetrator*. This section examines these two concepts and their limitations.

Evil

In referring to gross violations of human rights, I avoid the term *evil*, primarily because it shuts down the possibility of explanation. As a concept, evil stands alone and absolute, and open to abuse. People cannot be partially evil or understandably evil, and labeling people or political groups as "evil" sets them aside and condemns them as the impenetrable other, unable to be understood—outside the world of evil. In fact, a more distant view of such stigmatized people may even hold them blameless, possessed by a devil, leaving no recourse except quarantine or exorcism. My decision to eschew the concept of evil does not dismiss it from serious discussions of ethics or theology. Rather, as a social scientist seeking to understand the cognitive and social influences that lead to sustained, violent oppression, I find the invocation of evil distracting and unnecessary, with other terms more useful in describing criminal violations of human rights.

There is also the problem of definition, which will necessarily be incomplete. Zimbardo (2004) defined evil as "intentionally behaving, or causing others to act, in ways that demean, dehumanize, harm, destroy, or kill innocent people" (22). Impressively concise and comprehensive, this definition fits into the lexicon of social science, but it does so only by transferring evil to other concepts (demean and dehumanize) and to other observable actions (harming, destroying, or killing). A more direct approach is to use these more specific concepts and actions when describing and explaining violent perpetrators. Waller (2002) defined evil even more succinctly as "the deliberate harming of humans by other humans" (12), but this elegant brevity blurs distinctions among very different instances of violence and ends up including nearly all adult human beings.

These and other definitions also bring with them the controversy of requiring explicit intentionality. In an armed political struggle, for example, it is difficult and often self-serving to maintain a moral distinction between *planning* to kill fifty innocent people and fully *expecting* to kill fifty innocent civilians—but not trying to. Moreover, as with most psychological definitions of evil, these definitions exclude cruelty to animals and willful despoliation of the natural environment.

When addressing the behavior of perpetrators in general terms, my approach is to use secular and more circumscribed concepts, such as cruelty or brutality. When discussing the specific abuses perpetrated in apartheid South Africa, I refer to particular examples of the four defined categories of human rights violations introduced in South Africa's Promotion of National Unity and Reconciliation Act: killing, torture, severe ill-treatment, and abduction.[10]

BANALITY AND EVIL

Many essays analyzing the motives and actions of perpetrators in apartheid South Africa invoke Hannah Arendt's (1994) ubiquitous phrase "the banality of evil," but often without adequate skepticism. With Arendt, *banality* resonated because of the stark contrast between Eichmann's monstrous deeds and his bland demeanor and quotidian reasons. Yet the pervasiveness of the phrase is unhelpful. The destructive accomplishments of executives in charge of state-sponsored brutality are certainly not banal, and *evil* conveniently blurs the distinction among different crimes and cruelties, conveying a bumper-sticker simplicity when complexity is called for. Arendt also stated that "Eichmann was not Iago and not MacBeth, and nothing would have been farther from his mind than to determine with Richard III 'to prove a villain'"

(287). Again, this kind of phrasing creates a normalizing opacity that hides the complexity of real perpetrators. Although an apt characterization of Eichmann's self concept, Arendt's theatrical analogy is problematic because it conflates reality and literature. Eichmann was not a character from a Shakespearean tragedy but, in fact, a real person—one who was instrumental in committing industrial mass murder: not banal, not a fictive character, but an individual influenced by a willfully murderous system who carried out his destructiveness from a consuming self-interest to excel at his chosen goals.

Perpetrator

I use the word *perpetrator* primarily because those who applied for amnesty did perpetrate crimes against others, crimes considered by the TRC to be gross violations of human rights. This lexical choice, however, is not without controversy. To begin, the word *perpetrator* itself is conflicted. Its Indo-European root is *pəter,* referring to *father.* Yet the destructive actions of those applying for amnesty were anything but paternal and not the actions of fathers supporting their families and protecting them from harm. In contrast, however, the Indo-European root of *pəter* is fitting because nearly all of the identified perpetrators in apartheid South Africa were male, and many of them were fathers. In fact, when using the singular possessive or third-person pronoun in reference to the concept of perpetrator, I use *his* or *him*—not for linguistic convenience but because in apartheid South Africa, the perpetrator was male.

More broadly, any categorical label for human beings is necessarily reductive and limiting. Instead of *perpetrator,* a fuller description would be "a person who perpetrated," maintaining Korzybski's distinction between the complexity of each individual and a circumscribed set of behaviors. In fact, such a distinction is not merely academic. Nearly all of those who applied for amnesty did not think of themselves primarily as perpetrators but as complex human beings who had behaved badly for a time. For practical reasons, however, repeatedly using the full phrase "a person who perpetrated" was simply too cumbersome.

One could argue that *former perpetrator* would be more appropriate, especially given the motivation to reconcile. But the distancing effect of *former* would prematurely close off discussion of the very crimes that the TRC wanted to bring to light, which is why the Amnesty Committee officially referred to the applicants as perpetrators. These were the people responsible for wrongdoing during apartheid. These were the people who committed the crimes and who were seeking amnesty for those crimes. Notably, *perpetrate* means "to be responsible for; commit" and the Latin root *perpetrāre* means "to accomplish, to bring about," both of which suit the amnesty applicants (*American Heritage* 1996, 1349). For the victimized, the perpetrators were already being presented with an opportunity for amnesty, so as a minimal requirement, it was fitting to acknowledge their destructive actions—as perpetrators. Ultimately, the extensive testimony to the Amnesty Committee conveyed the requisite complexity to expand and redefine the initial label of perpetrator.

2

Apartheid and Amnesty

Managing a History of Sustained Oppression

Apartheid was a sustained program of segregation imposed by South Africa's ruling National Party to maintain control over the nonwhite population of South Africa and to preserve a privileged way of life for the white minority. Through a succession of laws from 1948 through the mid-1980s, the National Party strengthened and codified its subjugation of nonwhites, enforcing its laws of apartheid through a repressive system of internal security. In the process, the apartheid government uprooted millions of black South Africans, stole their land and their citizenship, restricted their employment, divided their families, impoverished their education, banned their unions and political organizations, and inflicted a myriad of daily humiliations, transforming them into foreigners in their own country (Adam 1997; Mamdani 2000; Thompson 2000).

Over several decades, the state Security Police diligently enforced apartheid through intimidation, arrest, detention, torture, and assassination—with tacit approval from those who benefited from the government's policies. In opposition to these punitive violations of human rights, antiapartheid liberation movements in South Africa carried out public protests and political resistance against the actions of the apartheid government. In response, the government implemented even harsher restrictions and more violent reprisals. Over time, with each new set of government restrictions, more people joined the liberation movements and more militancy arose within their ranks. As confrontations grew, the struggle in South Africa became increasingly violent, with each government restriction leading to new protests, more brutality by the state, violent attacks by the liberation movements, still harsher laws, deadlier operations against the apartheid government, and more destructive reprisals by the government security forces, with the violence on all sides escalating unabated.

It is the testimony from these perpetrators—on all sides of this violent struggle—that forms the basis of this study. Thus, to provide the necessary context and detail for presenting a comprehensive psychological analysis of this testimony, this chapter reviews the history of apartheid, outlines the goals of the TRC, elaborates the procedures and difficulties of the Amnesty Committee that gathered the perpetrator testimony, and highlights several prominent cases. The chapter also discusses apartheid South Africa as a paradigmatic example of an oppressive government fighting an organized resistance, with generalizable patterns of influence that exist in other systemically repressive countries, past and present. The chapter begins with an overview of how apartheid came into being and how it was maintained for nearly half a century.

A Brief History of Apartheid

As World War II was ending in Europe, the Afrikaner leadership in South Africa directed its efforts to organizing and consolidating its political power within the National Party. (The term *Afrikaner* refers to the South African descendants of Dutch, German, and Huguenot settlers who came to South Africa beginning in the mid-seventeenth century and who speak the language Afrikaans.) At this time, the National Party began designing a policy of rigorous segregation, including the abolition of political representation for all nonwhites, the establishment of separate educational systems for whites and nonwhites, and the forceful regulation of labor, including the separation of migrant African workers from their families. While developing this policy, the leaders of the National Party chose to label their policy of segregation *apartheid,* literally meaning *apartness*—a word introduced into the national discussion of race by Afrikaner intellectuals in the 1930s.

In the first postwar election in 1948, the National Party ran against the incumbent United Party on its newly developed policy of apartheid and managed to win a plurality of seats in the South African Parliament. As a result of the election, the National Party gained control of the South African government and maintained this control for nearly half a century—until the election of the ANC and Nelson Mandela in 1994 (Thompson 2000). Following its political victory in 1948, the National Party government built on the foundational principles of the prewar segregation era and began to enact a series of laws that implemented and then elaborated the segregational policy of apartheid, using its new institutional power to fulfill Afrikaner ethnic goals as well as broader white racial goals for controlling nonwhite communities—a minority of 10 percent effectively dictating all important aspects of public and private life for 90 percent of South Africa's population (Thompson 2000).

The legislative origins of apartheid can be traced back to the *Land Act* of 1913, which restricted the black population in South Africa to designated reserves, prohibiting black Africans from owning or renting land outside these reserves—about 7 percent of the land. Throughout the country, the Land Act set in motion the massive forced removal of African people from their own land, establishing both the geographic and the economic foundations for apartheid thirty-five years later. It did so by specifying the territorial separation of Whites and Africans and by destroying the thriving African agricultural community. After the election of 1948, the National Party adapted the Land Act as its foundation and set a course of ambitious legislative accomplishments, officially segregating every aspect of political, economic, educational, and social life (TRC 1999a).

Over a period of forty years, from 1948 through the end of the 1980s, the apartheid government of the National Party passed nearly a hundred laws that systematically restricted the lives of nonwhites: laws that specified basic segregation, laws that blocked social contact among racial groups, laws that defined security measures for containing and punishing political activism, laws that limited employment, laws that barred political representation, laws that regulated the ownership of land and property, and laws that restricted education.

The year 1950 saw two major planks of this legislative framework: the *Population Registration Act* and the *Group Areas Act*. The Population Registration Act required people to be identified and registered from birth as belonging to one of four designated racial groups: *White, Colored, Indian,* and *African*—also known as *Bantu*. A White person was "one who is in appearance obviously white," a Colored person was "a person who is not a white person or a Bantu," an Indian person was one whose family came from the Indian subcontinent, and an African or Bantu person was one who was "generally accepted as a member of any aboriginal race or tribe of Africa" (TRC 1999a, 30).

The Group Areas Act specified the areas of the country for exclusive use by each of these four racial groups, demarcating the entire country into zones for each designated racial group.[1] Effectively, the act enabled the apartheid government to evict nonwhites from their own property and to force them into undesirable areas that were less developed and more poorly serviced than the whites-only areas. Many nonwhite South Africans living in cities were deported from their neighborhoods to specific areas on the periphery of the cities known as *townships,* which soon swelled into overcrowded urban residential areas.[2] In many cases, residents of the townships worked in the affluent whites-only areas during the day and returned to the townships only at night, forced by legal restrictions and economic necessity to abandon their families. Some of these townships became the sites for violent clashes with the state police, resulting in killings of unarmed residents—later investigated by the TRC, including Alexandra, Boipatong, Guguletu, Katlehong, Mamelodi, Sebokeng, and Sharpeville. Soweto was actually a group of townships.[3]

The designation of four racial groups (White, Colored, Indian, and African) became part of everyday life in South Africa and part of the common parlance of the country, with only the white minority able to participate fully in the electoral process. This division of humanity in South Africa was motivated by four ideological principles of apartheid policy: (1) the physical reality of distinct racial groups in South Africa; (2) the destiny of white people to maintain absolute control over the state; (3) the primacy of white interests, with no obligation to provide comparable facilities for "subordinate races"; and (4) a single nation of South Africa for white people only, with Africans assigned to smaller areas outside the larger nation of South Africa (Thompson 2000, 190).

In tandem, the Population Registration Act and the Group Areas Act effectively segregated the entire country and forced nonwhites into crowded, underserved townships, as part of the larger system of separate and fragmented homelands. In keeping with the philosophy of apartheid, the National Party imposed the two acts with perverse creativity, despite legal wording that was especially vague and crude. As Nelson Mandela observed in his autobiography, "Where one was allowed to live and work could rest on such absurd distinctions as the curl of one's hair or the size of one's lips" (Mandela 1995, 122).

Other well-known laws were the *Prohibition of Mixed Marriages Act* (1949), the *Immorality Amendment Act* (1950), and the *Separate Amenities Act* (1953) that imposed codes of moral behavior for nonwhites; the *Bantu Education Act* (1953) that mandated separate and inferior education for African students; the *Extension of University Education Act* (1959) that prohibited black South Africans from attending the university of their choice; the *Unlawful Organizations Act* (1960) that allowed designated organizations to be declared unlawful, immediately banning the ANC and the PAC; and a set of infamous acts known collectively as the "pass laws" that required black South Africans in particular to carry passports to travel from one area to another within the country (TRC 1999a, 450–477).

Forceful resistance to these laws was organized and carried out by the liberation movements. The oldest and most influential of these movements was the African National Congress, which was founded in 1912 in an effort to achieve democracy and human rights for all South Africans, denied to Blacks since colonization. The second major liberation movement was the Pan African Congress, a rival organization that formed in 1959 as a result of ideological and strategic differences with the ANC and that concentrated more on regaining the land and resources of Africa taken away by what the PAC referred to as "settlers." For decades the ANC engaged in peaceful protest—until the Sharpeville massacre on March 21, 1960, when sixty-nine unarmed black people were shot and killed by the state police after marching to oppose the pass laws. After the massacre, both the ANC and the PAC called for armed struggle. Also noteworthy in the history of the resistance movements is the June 1976 massacre in Soweto of more than 500 students engaged in a peaceful demonstration against the Bantu education laws.

With the increasing oppression and brutality of the apartheid state came corresponding societal losses: loss of social conscience, loss of creativity in commerce and the arts, loss of international goodwill, loss of security, and eventual economic hardship in the form of boycotts of goods and athletics. By the mid-1980s, hostilities had increased markedly on all sides, with an accelerated ratcheting up of oppression and protest, forceful subjugation, and forceful response. In the ANC, 1985 was the "Year of the Cadre," and 1986 was the "Year of Umkhonto we Sizwe—the People's Army"—the military wing of the ANC. The apartheid government was in crisis, facing its strongest challenges both at home and abroad. One telling statistic is the number of detentions without trial of the apartheid government's political opponents, especially during emergency legislation. It is estimated, for example, that during the state of emergency from June 1986 to June 1988, more than 30,000 people were detained without trial by the Security Police (Coleman 1998). By this time, the intermittent battles between the security forces of the apartheid state and the military wings of the liberation movements had grown into a civil war.

It was only in the late 1980s that the National Party began passing laws and issuing decrees that began to withdraw the restrictions imposed by the laws of apartheid, including the portentous unbanning of the ANC and other liberation movements in 1990. But the bloodshed was not yet over. In the period from July 1990 to April 1994, as negotiations between the ANC and the apartheid government were taking place, violence became even more widespread, with the majority of this violence occurring in the provinces of KwaZulu-Natal and Gauteng. During this period, nearly 14,000 people died as a result of politically motivated violence, a rate of more than 300 deaths a month. (Transposed to the present United States, that would be more than 110,000 deaths due to political violence in a four-year period, and a rate of *more than 2,300 deaths every month.*) During that same period in South Africa, there were more than 22,000 serious injuries from politically motivated violence, nearly 30,000 arrests, and ninety-one documented major massacres (Coleman 1998).[4]

Although the particulars of this struggle are unique to apartheid South Africa, the pattern of increasing repression and increasing resistance can be seen in other countries with established governments and entrenched bureaucracies that sustain the oppression of designated groups of people. After the oppressive government falls from power, the new government must then manage the aftermath of the widespread destruction and violence. In the case of South Africa, the new ANC government designed a truth commission to help heal the many victims of apartheid, to hold the perpetrators accountable, and to promote reconciliation between the victims and the perpetrators and their communities. The next section describes the methods of restorative justice that South Africa planned and implemented to begin recovering from nearly a half century of apartheid.

The Truth and Reconciliation Commission

For nearly three decades, truth commissions have been implemented to resolve long-standing national conflicts, primarily in Latin America, Africa, and Asia. Since the development of the modern truth commission in the early 1980s, thirty countries have conducted some form of truth commission, with others calling for commissions in the next several years (Amnesty International 2009; Bronkhorst 2006; Hayner 1994, 2002; Posel and Simpson 2002a; U.S. Institute of Peace, 2009). Ideally, truth commissions function to disclose past abuses of human rights and to encourage reconciliation among former enemies. They perform their truth-gathering function by collecting material evidence and by recording the testimony of those who were directly involved in the human rights abuses.

To date, the most extensive and well documented of the truth commissions has been South Africa's TRC, mandated by an act of the South African Parliament in 1995 and conducted over a period of six years, from 1996 through 2001 (TRC 1999a, 2003a). The stated purpose of the TRC was to gather information about human rights violations during apartheid and to promote reconciliation in a country devastated by decades of violent struggle. To help accomplish its eponymous goals of truth and reconciliation, the TRC obtained testimony from the victims and from the perpetrators of apartheid. The victims gave testimony to document the crimes committed against them and their families and to apply for reparations. The perpetrators gave testimony to inform the nation of the specific crimes they carried out during apartheid and to obtain amnesty for these crimes. If the perpetrators' crimes against humanity were judged to be politically motivated, and if they made *full disclosure,* they were granted amnesty. If the perpetrators were in prison—and more than 70 percent of them were—the granting of amnesty meant immediate release from prison and permanent immunity from any legal or civil action (Boraine 2000; Pigou 2002a; TRC 2003a). In the words of the TRC chairperson, Archbishop Desmond Tutu, "Freedom was granted in exchange for truth" (1999a, 7). The very lives of the perpetrators depended on the perceived accuracy and comprehensiveness of their testimony.

The TRC comprised three committees: the Human Rights Violations (HRV) Committee, the Reparation and Rehabilitation (R&R) Committee, and the Amnesty Committee. Designed to work in concert, these three committees were mandated to document the gross violations of human rights during apartheid, to restore human and civil dignity to the victims through public testimony and through reparations, and to grant amnesty in exchange for full disclosure of crimes committed with a political objective (TRC 1999a). The HRV Committee investigated human rights abuses and collected statements and public testimony from victims, placing in the public record their identities, the nature and extent of the harm they suffered, and the individuals and organizations responsible for their mistreatment. The R&R Committee allocated support to the victims identified by the HRV and formulated policy recommendations on the rehabilitation of the survivors, their families, and the larger communities.

The Amnesty Committee evaluated applications for amnesty from perpetrators who had committed gross violations of human rights during apartheid. For amnesty hearings to be considered, the human rights violations were required to be politically motivated and committed within the time frame between the Sharpeville massacre (March 1, 1960)[5] and the inauguration of Nelson Mandela (May 10, 1994), with the final deadline for submitting an application on the last day of September 1997. If the applications met the initial requirements for further consideration, the applicants were then required to testify in public, making full disclosure of their human rights violations and demonstrating to the satisfaction of the Amnesty Committee that these violations were politically motivated and proportionate to their political goals. Based on the testimony from the perpetrators and the exchanges between the perpetrators and the former victims and their families, the Amnesty Committee deliberated and then decided to grant or refuse amnesty for each crime specified in the perpetrators' applications.

In practice, the TRC hearings served two general functions: to gather and acknowledge the accounts of the victimized and to document the testimony of the perpetrators. As the TRC conducted its hearings, the initial focus was on the testimony of victims in the hearings of the HRV Committee, but by the end of the first year, it was the Amnesty Committee that drew the most public attention, becoming by far the most widely discussed and thoroughly analyzed of the committees (TRC 2003a; Valdez 2000).

The Amnesty Committee

The Amnesty Committee of the TRC was established by the Promotion of National Unity and Reconciliation Act, No. 34 of 1995, known as "The Act." In particular, the Act authorized the Amnesty Committee to consider amnesty for crimes committed with a political objective while the applicant was a member or supporter of a publicly known political organization or an employee of the state. That is, applicants for amnesty were limited to those whose crimes were committed to advance the goals of a political organization or the apartheid state. In determining the political objective of a crime, the Amnesty Committee weighed motive, political context, the individual's authority, and the proportionality of the act in relation to the objective. During the hearings, the applicant was then required to make full disclosure of the relevant facts concerning the crimes. The Act defined gross human rights violations in terms of four categories: *killing, abduction, torture,* or *severe ill-treatment* of any person—or any attempt, conspiracy, or command to commit these violations. These four categories were further operationally defined with examples to include eighteen types of killing, thirteen types of torture, sixteen types of severe ill-treatment, and two types of abduction (TRC 1999a, 1999c).

To fulfill its mandate of investigating gross violations of human rights, the Amnesty Committee was set up with three structural requirements: (1) amnesty would be granted only to individual perpetrators, (2) the Amnesty Committee would have the power to subpoena, and (3) the amnesty hearings were to be held in public. As a statutory institution, the Amnesty Committee had the ability to make legally enforceable decisions, releasing people from prison or not releasing them; as a quasi-judicial body, however, it did not have the power to impose fines or sentences (Jeffrey 1999; Posel and Simpson 2002b).

The Amnesty Committee consisted of experienced members of the legal community who adapted their legal training to the quasi-judicial environment of the amnesty hearings (TRC 2003a, 17–35). Although there was a set order for presenting testimony and for cross-examination, unlike the HRV Committee, the Amnesty Committee did not have a defined protocol for gathering testimony (TRC 1999a, 2003a; Verdoolaege 2008). Perpetrators could plan their opening statements, but after these statements, the interactive process of gathering testimony took over, drawing out testimony that informed and that could be compared to the available forensic evidence and the testimony of witnesses and victims. Most amnesty applicants were not trained in the art of courtroom rhetoric. Their focus was on telling their side of the story and on answering the questions put to them. As a result, there was considerable spontaneity and revelation in the disclosures, and by the end of each hearing, the specific outcomes could not have been predicted from the structure of the proceedings or the initial amnesty applications.[6]

With regional offices in several cities and headquarters in Cape Town, the Amnesty Committee acted as an itinerant *axis mundi,* moving from Durban to Pretoria to Johannesburg to East London to Pietermaritzburg and to Cape Town to hold its hearings. In the process, the Committee ultimately amassed the largest collection of testimony from perpetrators ever assembled, with 255 public amnesty cases and 1,632 days of amnesty hearings, open to public participation and scrutiny. The amnesty hearings were conducted from May 1996 through December 2000, and the amnesty decisions were handed down through 2001, with some remaining decisions in 2002 (TRC 2003a, 736).

Videotaping of the hearings focused on the amnesty applicant, but also on the individuals who questioned the applicant, the reactions of the audience, the victims, and the family members, providing personal and spatial context for the millions of observers who watched the hearings on television. When members of the Amnesty Committee remarked on the testimony and questioned the applicants, they were on camera, in effect making them the faces of the amnesty process and well known to the viewing public.[7]

When the amnesty hearings began, five members served at all hearings of the Amnesty Committee: three judges (appointed directly by President Nelson Mandela), including the chair and the vice-chair of the Committee, and two commissioners, as mandated. With many more people applying for amnesty than anticipated and with increasingly complex cases, however, more judges were appointed. As the hearings proceeded and became more numerous, the TRC sometimes deployed a smaller subset of three members to constitute the Amnesty Committee. Other participants supporting the legal process during the actual hearings were the evidence leaders from the TRC and the attorneys representing the amnesty applicants and the victims and their families (TRC 1999a, 48–57).

Full disclosure meant that the perpetrators provided details about previously unknown crimes, supplying answers to unsolved bombings, murders, beatings, and disappearances and giving information about secret organizations and activities. As the hearings proceeded, the TRC demonstrated notable success in uncovering these unknown truths, unearthing much of the workings of the apartheid state that was either unknown or merely suspected (Sarkin 2004; TRC 1999c). As the chair of the TRC documented, the amnesty hearings uncovered the particulars about many hidden crimes, which could only have been solved through the testimony of the perpetrators (Tutu 1999b).

Understandably, as the hearings took place, many people who had been victimized sincerely questioned the application of restorative justice with perpetrators—restoring the perpetrators' dignity and integrating them back into civil society through testimony and amnesty. Heinous crimes had been committed. Tens of thousands of people had suffered lasting physical harm from these specific crimes, and hundreds of thousands had endured considerable hardship, both personally and economically. One reasonable approach, then, would be to *punish* those who had committed the wrongdoing. After all, Franz Kafka wrote *The Penal Colony*—not *The Reconciliation Colony,* and Dostoyevsky did not write *Crime and Amnesty.*

Much has been written about the relative merits of restorative and retributive justice, but the overriding argument in favor of restorative justice in South Africa was its relative effectiveness in the two fundamental goals of the TRC: uncovering truth and promoting reconciliation. Moreover, from a practical perspective, there were simply too many crimes and not enough evidence. As Graeme Simpson noted, the few famous cases (e.g., the murders of Stephen Biko and Griffiths Mxenge) would have stood an excellent chance in the criminal and civil courts, but according to Simpson (2002), "the harsh reality is that the vast majority of apartheid's victims probably stood to gain more from the opportunity to tell their stories (coupled with the meager reparations promised by the TRC) than from the criminal justice system" (233). Responding to critics who had forgotten the raison d'être for amnesty, the TRC chair, Archbishop Desmond Tutu, penned his famously simple statement, "Amnesty is not meant for nice people. It is intended for perpetrators" (Tutu 1999a, 12).

The Amnesty Hearings

The amnesty hearings were held throughout South Africa in public halls that could accommodate a small audience from the local community as well as victims and their families. Each of the hearings involved introductions, testimony, examination, and cross-examination, with the amnesty applicants providing testimony in three phases.[8] First, guided by their counsel, the applicants described the details of their crimes, usually in episodic narratives supported by specific facts. Second, the applicants gave testimony during cross-examination by the victim's counsel and by the evidence leader for the Amnesty Committee, leading to an extended series of specific questions and focused answers, with the applicants typically responding directly and without undue elaboration. Third, victims or their family members could choose to confront the amnesty applicants, encouraging more in-depth answers from the applicants and an accompanying opportunity to begin reconciliation.[9]

Before giving testimony, applicants were sworn in with the following canonical oath: "Do you swear that the evidence you are about to give to this commission will be the truth, the whole truth, and nothing but the truth? If so, raise your right hand and say, 'So help me God.'" Small variations occurred in the phrasing of the oath, but the gist remained the same throughout. Applicants also had the option to affirm the truth of their testimony without swearing to God. Witnesses were also sworn in. Victims, however, could decide whether or not to provide testimony under oath. Balancing the constitutional need for amnesty with the goal of promoting a safe environment for victims to confront the amnesty applicants meant relaxing the strict legal requirements of sworn testimony from victims and the cross-examination of victims.

Throughout the testimony and cross-examination, the chair and other members of the Amnesty Committee could intervene with questions, observations, and brief rulings on the proceedings. Typically, during the initial leading of testimony by the applicant's counsel, the applicant provided descriptions of his crimes and the rationale for committing these crimes. Cross-examination by opposing counsel, the evidence leader, and members of the Amnesty Committee often led to blunt exchanges of direct questions and revealing answers.[10] Later questioning by the victims involved more open-ended questions from the victims and lengthier responses from the applicants. In general, the amnesty hearings demonstrated a blend of structure and improvisation, with principled decisions and necessary inconsistencies, repeated themes and unexpected revelations, and a persistent tension between truth gathering and healing.

Disclosing in Public

Giving testimony in front of an audience that could include victims and their families, the amnesty applicants clearly entered into a stressful situation, and many applicants arrived anxious about the uncertainties and confrontations of the hearings. Once the introductions were concluded and the testimony began, however, applicants focused their attention on describing their actions and motivations and answering questions from counsel and members of the Amnesty Committee. To encourage applicants to speak freely, the Committee provided sufficient opportunity before cross-examination for an opening statement and for the applicants to tell their version of events while being guided by their own counsel. The stated requirements for amnesty, the constraints of the amnesty proceedings, and the expectations of the amnesty applicants could influence the initial testimony, but once the hearings were under way and the perpetrators began giving testimony and answering questions, the effort to remember took over as the guiding force shaping the testimony.

As applicants recalled violent incidents and past thoughts at length, the presence of an audience became less influential than the act of recalling itself. As testimony proceeded and as questioning continued, nearly all the applicants in this study answered the questions put to them and disclosed their remembered experiences sincerely and determinedly, recalling their crimes and the reasons for committing them. Later, if confronted by the people they had victimized, the applicants made efforts to explain themselves, even if those efforts fell short of the victims' expectations. In fact, when the applicants' accounts did not match the remembered experiences of the victims or the witnesses, most of these discrepancies could be explained by their differing perspectives and by the magnitude gap in memory (discussed in chapter 4).

For many applicants, the *intrinsic* motivation for giving testimony and disclosing their crimes was to reconcile with the victims and their families—to "put the record straight"—and to explain why they had carried out violence (Abrahamsen and van der Merwe 2005, 7). In contrast, the emphasis of the Amnesty Committee was on gathering information about the crimes. These two goals, nonetheless, led to the same outcome: the disclosure of the crimes and the revelation of the influences and reasons for committing the violence. Being confronted by the victims and their families was an intimidating challenge for the amnesty applicants but also an opportunity to explain themselves and to reconcile.[11] In fact, this two-edged sword ended up encouraging testimony more than inhibiting it. In its supervisory role, the Amnesty Committee was less motivated to maintain the traditional adversarial procedures of the courtroom and more motivated to draw out testimony that provided new information or could be compared to available forensic evidence.[12]

Allowing the victims and their counsel to confront the perpetrators and ask questions provided impetus for unprecedented revelations. Without such confrontations, for example, Captain Jeffrey Benzien would not have acted out the wet bag method of torture interrogation with a volunteer from the audience. Captain Dirk Coetzee would not have described in involute detail his remembered thoughts during the killing an ANC activist or his deep regrets afterward, offering sincere statements of self-loathing and condemnation for his actions. Zahrah Narkedien would not have disclosed Robert McBride's state of mind after his car bombing of Magoo's Bar that killed three young people and seriously injured scores more. Bheki Mbuyazi would not have confessed his personal reasons for murdering three women affiliated with the IFP. Paul van Vuuren would not have detailed his methods of torturing ANC activists or his private initiative in learning these methods. More generally, in restorative justice programs for criminal cases, when victims confront perpetrators in a safe environment supervised by law enforcement officials, the results are invariably more revealing about the motivations of the perpetrator than in the traditional courtroom (Lobb 2010; Sherman and Strang 2007; Zernova 2007).

Defining Apartheid by Extremes

The mandate for the Amnesty Committee of the TRC was to address specific violations of human rights that were *illegal* under apartheid, and not the large-scale destructiveness of lawful apartheid in general. The amnesty hearings focused on murder, torture, abduction, rape, and theft—all outside the law in apartheid South Africa—and not on the widespread repression of apartheid itself. In this regard, Mamdani (2000) criticized the TRC for producing a narrow truth that did not convey the overall destructiveness of apartheid, and he compared the TRC to a truth commission in the old Soviet Union that said nothing about the Gulag. Referring to Hannah Arendt, Mamdani (2000) asked, "What happens when crime is legal, when criminals can enthusiastically enforce the law?" (60).

One answer to this criticism is that any maintenance system that normalizes cruelty will necessarily move to extremes and break its own laws. When people enthusiastically enforce unjust laws, they inevitably transgress into criminality. Moreover, by examining the excesses of the perpetrators who *did* break the law, we see the contours of apartheid itself: the secrecy, the shadow groups within larger, established organizations, the abuse of power, and the perversion of morality. During the hearings of the TRC, apartheid was given national scrutiny through the violations of its own laws—by the abuses in its own abusive system (TRC 1999c). Revealing these crimes during the TRC hearings ultimately revealed the nature of the system that gave rise to them, exposing apartheid more broadly (Tutu 1999b).

Another answer to the criticism that the TRC was too narrowly focused is that the larger oppressions of apartheid were part of public policy and already known, whereas the individual cases of human rights violations were not. The devastating effects of apartheid legislation on black communities were a matter of record, but the specific criminal activities were clandestine, covered up, and reframed. Moreover, these individual violations were crimes, and as such they needed to be investigated (Sachs 2000). Still another answer to this criticism is that outside the work of the Amnesty Committee, the TRC investigated institutional violence, holding special hearings on the practices of the apartheid government in business and labor, the legal community, the health sector, the national media, and prisons, with special hearings on compulsory military service, children and youth, and the treatment of women (TRC 1999a).

Amnesty Numbers

By the closing date of September 30, 1997, the Amnesty Committee had received 7,116 applications for amnesty, although a large majority of these were denied before they went through the full review process because they failed to meet the basic requirements of the Act. The primary reasons for disqualification were that the violent incidents named in the applications had no political objective, that the violence was for personal gain, or that the incidents did not involve gross violations of human rights. In total, 5,442 applications were denied for these reasons, initially leaving 1,674 applications that met all requirements. Another 28 cases were either withdrawn or judged insufficient later, so that number eventually became 1,646—still considerably larger than anticipated. Nearly all of the qualifying applications came from the African National Congress and its allied organizations (998), the South African government's security forces (293), the Pan African Congress (138), and the Inkatha Freedom Party (109) (Foster, Haupt, and de Beer 2005, 13–14; TRC 2003a).[13] On the last day of March 2001, the Amnesty Committee eventually completed its daunting mission of hearing and deciding more than 1,600 separate cases. Two years later, the TRC presented the last two volumes of its final report to President Thabo Mbeki.

Regarding Veracity

As stated in the final report of the TRC (2003a), "Amnesty applicants were legally required to give a full and truthful account of the incidents" in accordance with Section 20(1)(c) of the act of Parliament that mandated conditional amnesty. The report also stated that "where an applicant's version was untruthful on a material aspect, the application was refused." To be granted amnesty, applicants were required to disclose fully about the incidents for which they were seeking amnesty, which meant they had to provide "a full and truthful account of their own role, as well as that of any other person, in the planning and execution of the actions in question" and "any other relevant conduct or steps taken subsequent to the commission of the particular acts" (TRC 2003a, 10).

Although these statements seem straightforward in prospect, in actual practice the testimonies could be limited by the applicants' need to maintain dignity and forestall emotional testimony, by the shortcomings of memory, and by each applicant's particular perspective of the events. In addition, the emphasis on disclosure of the incidents in question meant that other, more general information about illegal activities was not required. Thus, the applicant's own limitations and the Amnesty Committee's focus on particular incidents could lead to testimony that appeared selective and constrained, especially to victims and their families, and also to researchers evaluating the overall comprehensiveness of the revelations during the amnesty hearings (James and van de Vijver 2000; Mamdani 2000; Posel and Simpson 2002a; Sarkin 2004; Villa-Vicencio and du Toit 2006). The following two sections discuss the aspects of perpetrator testimony that led to concerns about full disclosure and truthfulness– and the responses to these concerns.

Absence of Emotion

For victims as well as researchers, one major shortcoming of perpetrator testimony was the lack of emotion. Many perpetrators seemed unable to express appropriate affect as they described their crimes, even as the descriptions of their motivations and violent actions were informative (Gobodo-Madikizela 2003; Payne 2004, 2008; Ramsey 2006). In fact, it was this juxtaposition of flat affect and detailed expressions of brutality that was most unsettling to victims and researchers (Foster 2000; Payne 2004). Unable to find the appropriate vocabulary to express emotion, perpetrators often resorted to cliché as they described their own reactions to the cruelty they inflicted.

Importantly, Foster (2000) maintained that it was not the content of the perpetrators' testimony that created difficulties but rather the attitude of emotional hardness. Foster proposed that the apparent insensitivity was a protective covering to maintain dignity in the emotionally challenging environment of the amnesty hearings, citing what Baumeister (1997) referred to as the perpetrator's preference for a "detached minimalist style" (19). According to Ramsey (2006), many perpetrators believed that openly showing sympathy for the victims would reveal weakness and shame in front of the Amnesty Committee, and it was this fear and avoidance of shaming that prevented the appropriate expression of emotion, even though it did not prevent the disclosure of one's actions or motivations or even one's state of mind. In fact, the emotional flatness in the disclosures could be accompanied by considerable self-analysis.

After describing his role in the brutal murder of an ANC activist, for example, Captain Dirk Coetzee disclosed profound self-criticism, but he did so in a flat, measured style, without displaying the emotions that would ordinarily accompany those words (Coetzee, November 6, 1996). When David Tshikalanga testified about his role in the murder of ANC activist Griffiths Mxenge, he seemed hesitant about his knowledge of the murder and the cover up afterward. Tshikalanga explained, "It's so dreadful that sometimes I used to get worried considerably, in such a way that I couldn't just say what happened because it was difficult" (Tshikalanga, November 6, 1996). Ramsey (2006) reported that in her interview with one of the young men who killed Amy Biehl, he described his actions in detail but only in the third person, saying, "It is the only way I can talk about Amy's death without experiencing overwhelming feelings of shame and self-loathing" (130). In her study of six violent perpetrators from South Africa, Ramsey found that as the hearings proceeded and the perpetrators confronted the victims or their surviving relatives, all six men took fuller responsibility for their actions and expressed sincere remorse.

Unsatisfying Explanations

Related to the problem of emotional flatness was the difficulty some perpetrators had recalling the details of their illegal actions and the particular rationale for engaging in these actions. In this regard, perpetrators were demonstrating limitations and distortions of memory well documented in the literature on personal event memory: omitting details, combining different episodes into one event, allowing self-concepts to shape specific memory descriptions, and considerable forgetting (e.g., Alba and Hasher 1983; Kraft 2000; Neisser 1988; Pillemer 1998; Reyna 1998; Schacter 1999). These basic memory processes were especially frustrating when perpetrators could not remember information that others—particularly counsel for the victims and their families—judged to be important.

In general, dissatisfaction with the perpetrator's testimony stemmed from a combination of the limitations of memory and disagreements over what should have been remembered. An example of this dissatisfaction occurred in the testimony of Jeffrey Benzien, as he gave his account of killing ANC activist Ashley Kriel. According to Benzien, when he went to arrest Kriel for his illegal support of the ANC, Kriel physically resisted. During the struggle, Benzien disarmed Kriel and then used Kriel's own gun to shoot him. Benzien's explanation was that the gun went off accidentally and that during the struggle, events happened too quickly to remember. In contrast, the victim's family maintained that Benzien had planned to shoot Kriel even before he went to arrest him. The following excerpts of testimony focus on why Benzien kept Kriel's gun during the struggle and why he failed to subdue Kriel in a nonlethal way. In answering questions from the counsel for the victim's family, Benzien made the following statements (Benzien, July 14, 1997):

1. I don't know how many people have been involved in a struggle or a fight, especially of this nature. It is a continuing act of rolling around and there is a lot of motion, and it is very difficult to describe the events in the exact order in which they happened.
2. I was the policeman on the scene, making the arrest. I have just disarmed a person with a firearm. With *hindsight* and knowing how this tragic experience developed, I could say yes, it would have been the best thing to throw the firearm away, but I don't think anybody throws a weapon away to equal the playing field. At that stage it was not a case of a boxing or wrestling match.

3. At this stage I was grappling with a terrorist. The only weapon which was available in this split second action was the weapon which I had in my hand. I don't think that anybody in similar circumstances should consider actually throwing the weapon away—what purpose would that serve?

4. To handcuff a person who does not want to be handcuffed is no easy job.

5. This whole turmoil was not taking minutes, it was *seconds.*

6. The weapon went off in my hand. I suppose I could have hit him on the head if I wanted to, but it is hard to say what possibilities flash through your mind.

After this testimony, the following exchange took place with Benzien and two members of the Amnesty Committee:

JUDGE NGOEPE: Did you not keep the firearm with the view that you should shoot him?

JEFFREY BENZIEN: I didn't think at that stage at all, Your Honor.

JUDGE MALL: At that time, did it occur to you that you could have hit him and decided that you were not going to hit him on the head?

JEFFREY BENZIEN: Mr. Chairman, with all respect, I don't know what I was thinking at that stage.

Jeffrey Benzien was consistent in his own perspective on the killing and forthcoming in his answering of the questions put to him, but he was unable to recall the details of the killing and he did not admit to a planned murder. Even after repeated questioning, it was clear that Benzien could not go beyond his version of the events. Explaining a killing by saying that it happened too abruptly to control and too quickly to think about can be profoundly unsatisfying for family members and for those looking for deep insight into the details of the killing, but it was a frequently cited explanation, repeated over different events and different perpetrators.

Perpetrator testimony could also be judged unsatisfactory when it was at odds with the remembered experiences of victims. Often, victims remembered more details of the critical incidents, more events leading up to the incidents in question, and more vivid experiences afterward. Victims also attributed more responsibility to the individual perpetrators, whereas perpetrators remembered having little or no choice in the matter. As discussed in chapter 4, many of these differences can be accounted for by accepting the sincerity of *both* versions and by applying the findings on the magnitude gap to explain the differences. Moreover, as Baumeister (1997) has reported, although there is understandable sympathy for the victim's perspective, there is no general empirical reason for privileging victim testimony over testimony from perpetrators.

Perpetrator testimony was also challenged as unsatisfactory when it was inconsistent with forensic evidence, although this observation does not necessarily mean that the testimony was dishonest or insincere. Inconsistency with forensic evidence occurs with traditional courtroom testimony as well, as shown by the large literature on well-meaning eyewitnesses who provide partially accurate descriptions of events that omit important details and include vivid inaccuracies about such information as the people who were present, what the people looked like, the sequence and duration of events, and pertinent details involving the people and their actions (e.g., Kassin et al. 2001; Lindsay 2007; Schacter 1999; Wells and Olson 2003; Wells and Quinlivan 2009).

Clearly, some perpetrators tried to get away with lies or purposeful obfuscation during the amnesty hearings. In fact, one general goal of chapter 4 is to address this complex issue of veracity, distinguishing testimonies that are sincere and understandably flawed from those that are insincere and withholding in the recall of critical events. To this end, chapter 4 examines the TRC's (1999a) categories of truth and the established findings on the magnitude gap, identifying those characteristics of perpetrator testimony that distinguish truthfulness and evasiveness. In short, many accounts by the perpetrators in this study contained narrative truth, but some did not.

Even with suppressed emotions, the forgetting of critical details, meaningful gaps in the testimony of perpetrators and victims, and discrepancies between perpetrator accounts and forensic evidence, sincere testimony from perpetrators provided valuable information about the crimes they committed, the influences and choices that led to these crimes, and the experience of being a violent perpetrator. Although highly critical of the perpetrators' unwillingness to take full responsibility during their public confessions, Payne (2004) nonetheless acknowledged the value of the perpetrators' testimony, saying that "audiences can take advantage of highly imperfect confessions to advance the search for truth, accountability, and acknowledgment." She then concluded that these audiences can "pull truths about past events out of even these imperfect confessions: what happened, when, and who was involved" (9).[14]

Crimes of Allegiance in Apartheid South Africa

South Africa under apartheid presents a paradigmatic case of a complex government bureaucracy designed to repress a large segment of the population through systematic violations of human rights. As a perversion of decolonialization, apartheid was historically distinctive, but the structure and the methods of the apartheid government exist in many diligently repressive regimes dedicated to the suppression of fundamental rights. As in many repressive countries, the South African government considered itself under serious threat from within and without and set up secret, independent policing units to combat this perceived threat (Haritos-Fatouros 2003; Huggins, Haritos-Fatouros, and Zimbardo 2002; Malinowski 2008). As in many repressive countries, South Africa's Security Police operated within a bureaucratic hierarchy that removed direct responsibility from their leaders, separating those who created policy from those who actually carried out the illegal, violent acts. As in many repressive countries, to justify the expansion of bureaucratized violence, the National Party increasingly supported the need for violations of human rights, such as prolonged detainment without trial, specific forms of torture, and selective killing of their designated enemies.[15] As in many repressive countries, resistance groups formed to bring down the existing state government by force—using whatever means possible—and to implement a new government.

Studying the extensive testimony from members of the security forces who violently defended apartheid and members of the liberation movements who violently resisted reveals a generalizable set of influences explaining the etiology and maintenance of widespread collective violence in systemically repressive countries. The following chapter focuses on the psychology of the perpetrator, presenting a comprehensive analysis of testimony from individuals who worked within the violent political organizations of apartheid South Africa. In their testimony, the perpetrators disclosed their specific actions, their motives, their thoughts, and their observations about the social and political influences acting on them as they advanced the mission of their political organizations. Based on this analysis, the chapter identifies the situational influences and individual decisions that coerced ordinary people to carry out brutal and deadly violence against others.

Highlighted Cases

Although the analysis in the following chapter is based on the testimony of more than seventy individual perpetrators, a subset of these perpetrators is highlighted for the purpose of exemplifying the general themes. In addition to Captain Jeffrey Benzien, introduced in chapter 1, another manager of collective violence highlighted in this analysis is Paul van Vuuren, a police officer during the 1980s who worked in a torture and killing squad in the Northern Transvaal Security Branch of the ironically named Civil Cooperation Bureau. Van Vuuren was referred to as "apartheid's electrician" for his favorite method of torture interrogation, which involved using a small electric generator to repeatedly shock sensitive parts of a prisoner's body (Pauw 1998). Two upper-level managers in the Security Police are also highlighted in this analysis: Captain Dirk Coetzee, a commander in the Security Police headquarters at the notorious compound in Vlakplaas who supervised and carried out sabotage and murder against the antiapartheid opposition, and Colonel Eugene de Kock, the man who replaced Dirk Coetzee and who greatly expanded the killing operations. De Kock himself was responsible for more than eighty murders, many of them especially cruel. He was dubbed "Prime Evil" during the TRC hearings and was repeatedly compared to Adolph Eichmann (Gobodo-Madikizela 2003). De Kock's closely reported trial in 1996 (before the amnesty hearings) provided the public with lengthy disclosures from one of the main killers in the security forces, and in October of that year, he was sentenced on eighty-nine separate charges (Foster, Haupt, and de Beer 2005).

This analysis also emphasizes two separate operations that involved the full hierarchy of the apartheid state's domestic security forces, resulting in the bombing of ANC-affiliated buildings in downtown

Johannesburg. The first, in May 1987, targeted COSATU House, the building that housed the national offices of the Congress of South African Trade Unions. The second, sixteen months later, targeted Khotso House, a community center that housed the head office of the South African Council of Churches (SACC) and the national headquarters of the United Democratic Front (UDF)—a loose federation of different social, civic, and political organizations, united in opposition to the apartheid government and increasingly supportive of the ANC. According to the testimony, the COSATU operation served as a model for the destruction of Khotso House.

Three cases are highlighted to illustrate the operations of the liberation forces against the apartheid government. Robert McBride was the leader of an individual cell in Umkhonto we Sizwe (MK), the military wing of the ANC. He organized numerous acts of violent sabotage, which culminated in his most notorious mission: a car bombing outside a crowded Durban nightclub that killed three young women and seriously injured sixty others, known as the *Magoos Bar bombing.* Referred to in the national media as the "Durban bomber," McBride was caught and sentenced to death for this operation. Another case is the *St. James Church massacre,* which involved the armed wing of the PAC known as the Azanian People's Liberation Army (APLA). Three members of APLA attacked the congregation of a church during a service, killing eleven people and seriously wounding another fifty-eight. One of the APLA operatives, Gcinikhaya Makoma, testified, "As the hand grenades exploded, we took cover behind the doors, re-entered, and while the people inside were screaming, we started to shoot. We shot indiscriminately, and I finished my full R4 magazine, some 31 rounds of ammunition" (Makoma, July 10, 1997). A third case is the *Heidelberg Tavern massacre,* which involved three members of APLA who shot the customers at a popular tavern, killing three young women and critically injuring many others.

The Magoos Bar bombing, the St. James Church massacre, and the Heidelberg Tavern massacre are examples of what many people would consider acts of *terrorism:* setting off a car bomb outside a bar crowded with young people, shooting into a church with automatic weapons and throwing nail-studded hand grenades at the worshippers, and firing automatic weapons and grenade launchers into a tavern frequented by university students. Studying the perpetrator testimony from these cases is one way of learning directly from the perpetrators themselves about the motivations for planning such murderous acts and the cognitive processes while carrying them out.

Testimony from the state perpetrators revealed the choices and influences that shaped them to commit illegal, violent acts against citizens designated as enemies of the state. Testimony from those in the liberation movements revealed the choices and influences that led to violent operations against government institutions and against individuals associated with these institutions.

3

Understanding Crimes of Allegiance

Patterns of Violent Influence

Any study of violent perpetrators confronts a fundamental paradox: the abundance of cruelty throughout human history and the absence of people who think of themselves as cruel. To help resolve this paradox and to account for systematic, widespread brutality, this chapter analyzes the testimony of violent perpetrators, identifying the influences and choices that shaped ordinary people to behave with extraordinary brutality and the thought processes that motivated and rationalized these behaviors. The focus of the chapter is on the remembered experiences of violent perpetrators when planning and carrying out attacks on others—the phenomenology of collective violence, as disclosed in testimony to the Amnesty Committee of the TRC.

The main goal of this analysis is to reveal the structural and conceptual foundations of systemic violence: the necessary organizational and cognitive influences for motivating and maintaining collective violence.[1] Testimony to the Amnesty Committee of the TRC revealed that the motivations and actions of perpetrators were neither so simple that they could be summarized in a few maxims nor so complicated that they could not be identified and categorized. Studying many individual cases revealed patterns of systemic influence, as well as commonalities in the thought processes of perpetrators: the underlying beliefs, the thoughts at the time of planning and committing the acts of violence, and the reactions afterward.

A Structural Framework for Collective Violence

To account for the actions of violent perpetrators, this chapter begins with a case analysis of mob violence and then applies this analysis to more sustained collective violence, adding necessary influences that maintain the violence and allow it to be carried out repeatedly.

The Violent Mob

The shocking murder of Amy Biehl in August 1993 illustrates the dynamics of mob violence. Amy Biehl was a twenty-six-year-old Fulbright scholar from California who went to South Africa to help in the transition from apartheid to democracy. As she was riding through Guguletu with some friends, a mob of young people forced her out of the car, chased her through the streets, and killed her.

Four young men were convicted of the mob murder of Amy Biehl and sent to prison: Ntombeku Peni, Easy Nofemela, Mongesi Manqina, and Vusumzi Samuel Ntamo. Four years later, in July 1997, these men gave testimony to the TRC as applicants for amnesty. Back in 1993, the first three applicants were members of the Pan African Students Organization (PASO), an organization affiliated with the Azanian People's Liberation Army (APLA), the armed wing of the PAC. All four men had just attended a PASO rally that exhorted them to kill white people—in order to make the country ungovernable. All four of the applicants threw stones at Amy Biehl from very close range, Mongesi Manqina tripped her, and then Manqina and Easy Nofemela stabbed her to death after she collapsed on the ground, dazed and bleeding from the head. Viewed from the United States, the brutal murder of Amy Biehl appeared obscene and inexplicable. Four years later, during the TRC hearings, the public learned about the killers: their personal histories, their motives, and their thoughts—then and now. Their testimony revealed that nothing but a direct physical barrier would have prevented them from killing Amy Biehl that day. The violence was primed through speeches and slogans before it was committed, and the decision to kill was made before the actual act.

To explain how people end up committing mob violence, I adapt the structure of Moghaddam's (2005) staircase model of terrorism, separating the events into three levels of influence: (1) a *platform* of personal history, consisting of collective knowledge and specific memories; (2) active *priming* from immediate events, such as rallies, inflammatory speeches, or mass distribution of pamphlets; and (3) a specific *triggering* event.[2]

In testimony, Easy Nofemela directly invoked the first two levels of influence: a platform of personal history and priming: "On the day in question and during that period, I was highly politically motivated, not only by *the political climate in the township*, but also by the *militant political speeches* made at the PASO meeting which I attended." Ntombeku Peni focused on the second level, priming: "On the day in question when Amy Biehl was killed, the PASO leadership implored and instructed us to assist APLA in its struggle in making the country ungovernable and by preparing the groundwork for APLA operators." Later Peni said, "If we were not sent out to act, I would not have done it." In fact, Peni and Mongesi Manqina interpreted these priming speeches by the PASO leadership as orders. Peni said, "At the time we were told to act and help APLA to fight and burn down government vehicles so that South Africa would be ungovernable. We obeyed the orders." Manqina added, "When the PASO executive members ordered us . . . to make the township ungovernable, I regarded this as an instruction to also harm, injure, and kill white people."

Manqina spoke directly of the trigger: "When I saw that the driver of the vehicle which we had stoned, and which had come to a standstill, was a *white* person, I immediately asked one of the comrades in the crowd for a knife." Nofemela also described the triggering event: "That day we were very much emotional *and we find Amy in our location.*" Nofemela then elaborated on the final moments: "I saw Amy Biehl stumble across the road. I jumped off the bakkie and ran toward her also throwing stones at her. As we pursued her, Manqina tripped her. I had a knife and . . . I stabbed at her about three or four times."

Three of the applicants strongly emphasized emotion as guiding their actions, describing themselves as "excited," "inspired," "highly motivated," and full of "high spirits." Easy Nofemela said, "Our emotions led us to throw stones at this white person because our land was taken from us by the white people." He then blamed a force that was both part of himself and separate: "During that time, my spirit just said I must kill the White." There was also joy in the mob, more exaltation than debasement, and a sense of accomplishment afterward. Emotion then served to vivify the instructions to take violent action against white people. Ntombeku Peni said, "At the time we were in very high spirits and the white people were oppressive, we had no mercy on the white people. A white person was a white person to our eyes."

When the chairperson of the Amnesty Committee, Judge Hasan Mall, asked, "Why on this day?" Nofemela focused on the trigger: "It's because she came to Guguletu during a very wrong moment." Judge Mall then followed up, asking what was wrong with that moment, and Nofemela answered, "It's because students who were in PASO really wanted the land to go back to the Africans and we were in very high emotions." Judge Andrew Wilson of the Amnesty Committee then probed Nofemela further: "And yet you see this unfortunate girl running across the road, you jump out, chase her, throw stones at her and stab her—tell me why?" Nofemela explained the inevitability of the violence as a mix of uncontrollable emotion and the idea of taking back what was rightfully theirs: "There was nothing that could cause us to cool down. We were still in very high emotions. . . . They said that the African land has to return back to the Africans. Our emotions led us to throw stones at this white person because our land was taken from us by the white people."

A mob that forms is not planned, but it can be set in motion by the leaders of violent organizations. In the murder of Amy Biehl, the political climate and personal memories constituted the platform, the inflammatory speeches by the PASO leaders primed the mob violence, and the sight of a white woman in a vehicle in Guguletu triggered the killing. (The preceding testimony, questions, and comments about the killing of Amy Biehl were given to the TRC Amnesty Committee on July 8, 1997, by Ntombeku Peni, Easy Nofemela, Mongesi Manqina, Judge Hasan Mall, and Judge Andrew Wilson.)

A Planned Operation with Unintended Violence

The next case involves an operation with minimal planning that resulted in unintended violence, an operation less spontaneous than mob violence but less planned than the sustained operations that are the main focus of this chapter. This case is typical of the violence that broke out in South Africa in the late 1980s and early 1990s between the IFP and the ANC and between rival liberation movements.

The analysis focuses on a double killing in 1986 on a farm in the township of Mbekweni, just north of Paarl in the Western Cape. In the late 1980s, violent confrontations had broken out sporadically in Mbekweni between members of the Azanian People's Organization (AZAPO) and individuals affiliated with the ANC, as a result of a feud between the two liberation groups. As in most instances with organized attacks against the ANC and its affiliates, the police supported the groups opposed to the ANC, regardless of political ideology. The case in question involved three young men from Mbekweni who were affiliated with the ANC-supported United Democratic Front (UDF) and the Paarl Youth Congress (PAYCO): Philemon Maxam, Madoda Tisana, and Crosby Ndinisa. In April 1986, Maxam, Tisana, and Ndinisa broke into a nearby farmhouse with the intent of stealing firearms for the UDF, but in the confusion of the poorly conceived operation, Maxam shot to death two people who worked on the farm: a domestic worker, Anne Foster, and a gardener, John Geyser. All three perpetrators were eventually arrested, convicted, and sentenced in the murder of Foster and Geyser, with Maxam receiving the death sentence. Ten years later, all three men went before the TRC to present their case for amnesty with respect to those convictions.

The organizer of the operation, Philemon Maxam, began his testimony with background information: "Between 1985 and 1987 there was a group of people, the AZAPO, at Mbekweni. I was a member of UDF. Within the AZAPO there would also be police. Therefore, there was no order at Mbekweni because we would fight a lot with the police." He explained his rationale: "Sometimes the police would come to our township. Our township would be at peace and they would just throw tear gas canisters at us. In fighting such things, if we were approached in a violent manner, we would retaliate in a violent manner."

In their testimony, the applicants revealed that the motivation for the break-in came directly from the ANC in the form of instructions from ANC president Oliver Tambo. The "Tambo text" as presented to the Amnesty Committee by Advocate John Lourens read as follows:

> We must now respond to the reactionary violence of the enemy with our own revolutionary violence. The weapons are there in white houses. Each white house has a gun or two hidden inside to use against us. . . . We

must deliberately go out to look for these weapons in these houses. *It is a matter of life and death* to find these weapons to use against the enemy. (Lourens, July 8, 1997)

The applicants viewed this text as direct instructions from the president of the ANC to steal weapons from homes of white landowners. Thus it was that Maxam, Tisana, and Ndinisa planned their operation.

According to the testimony of Maxam and Tisana, they waited until the owner of the farm had driven away before they approached the main house. They spoke first to Anne Foster, a domestic worker, asking her for a glass of water. As she was handing them the glass, Tisana grabbed her arm and explained that they were looking for guns and that they did not intend to harm her. She refused to let them in and began screaming. Maxam described what happened next: "I took out my gun as she was screaming, and I shot inside. As I was shooting, I was pointing toward her, even though I did not realize that." After the first shot, the third assailant, Crosby Ndinisa, ran to the gardener, John Geyser, who begged not to be shot. Ndinisa then tied him up with wire and told Maxam not to shoot him. All three men then broke open the door, entered the house, and ransacked the rooms. Finding no firearms, Maxam stole a box of bullets and Tisana some jewelry and money. Shortly after that, an alarm went off, and the three men fled in different directions. As he was running out of the house, Maxam shot Anne Foster again as she was lying on the kitchen floor, and once outside, he shot the gardener, John Geyser, as he lay tied up on the ground.

At the amnesty hearings, Maxam described his experience ten years earlier: "Everything happened very quickly. This is why I get confused as to what happened at the end, because we all ended up running away." Then he elaborated his rationale for shooting the two people:

> As I was running, I shot the lady again, and I shot the gardener as I was running, so that they were not able to identify us to the police or which direction which we had run to or what we were wearing. I did it so that we could have enough time to run away because there was an open field. . . . It is self-defense, it is protection. You are protecting yourself when you are shooting somebody so that they are not able to identify you.

Maxam concluded with retrospective rationale: "It was not our aim to shoot people, but we were forced by circumstances" (Maxam, July 7, 1997).

In his testimony, Madoda Tisana described grabbing Anne Foster and then explained that his proximity to the unexpected shooting caused him to go into shock: "At the time of the shooting on this day, I became unconscious—because I did not expect that people would be shot. It was not our aim and we did not want anybody to be killed." He continued: "We just wanted to get weapons so that we can defend ourselves and protect ourselves from what was happening in the township, but it happened that people were shot. I cannot remember everything that happened that day because I was dizzy, as I did not expect it to happen." Tisana concluded, "When we went to the farm we did not intend on killing people. We just wanted weapons. It just happened— the shooting just happened. . . . I did not think at that time, because it happened automatically" (Tisana, July 7, 1997).

The tense political environment, the sporadic outbreaks of violence with AZAPO, and the inaction of the police were the immediate influences on the applicants to join PAYCO and the UDF to defend themselves and their families. These two organizations, in conjunction with the ANC, then provided the political and ideological *platform* for violent action. The meetings of PAYCO in general and the Tambo text in particular *primed* the applicants to break into houses owned by whites and to steal weapons for the ANC. During the break-in at the farmhouse, when Anne Foster screamed and refused to let Maxam and the others inside, Maxam shot her, without premeditation, triggered by her screaming and her refusal to allow them to enter. Only after ransacking the house and only after the alarm went off did Maxam come up with his reasons for shooting John Geyser, and shooting Anne Foster a second time. He feared being identified and turned in to the police. All three applicants said that the events happened too quickly to think, which is a recurring theme in many testimonies describing unplanned assaults and killings. The theft was primed by ANC doctrine—and planned, but the triggering of the murders was unforeseen and spontaneous.

Although this analysis diminishes the agency of the perpetrators, it does not do away with it altogether. During any of the steps in the planning process and during the initial phase of the operation, right up until the break-in, the perpetrators could have broken off the operation.

Moreover, if interventions had been made in the community or in the political communiqués, the violence could have been prevented. Had there not been a feud between the ANC and AZAPO, had the community been effectively policed, and had Oliver Tambo not exhorted his followers to steal weapons from the houses of white landowners as a matter of life and death, these killings would not have occurred. Similar to mob violence, however, once a hastily planned operation is under way, if a triggering event occurs, it is very difficult to prevent violence. After being sufficiently primed and then triggered, the perpetrator reacts. In retrospect, from the perpetrator's perspective, the events seem to have happened too quickly to control.

Sustained Violence

The three-level model of platform, priming, and trigger can be applied to sustained forms of collective violence by elaborating each of the three levels. In particular, with sustained violence, the level of priming becomes considerably more complex, due to the elaborate organizational and conceptual influences required to maintain systemic brutality over time and to shape it into acceptable, everyday actions.

Initially, two categories of sustained violence were distinguished in terms of the amount of bureaucratic structure: (1) operations that involved extensive planning within a bureaucratic hierarchy, as with many operations of the SAP, and (2) actions that involved organizational guidelines and constraints but also considerable independence, as in the operations of individual cells of the ANC and the PAC. Based on the analysis of perpetrator testimony, however, these two organizational categories showed very similar patterns of influence and action and were therefore analyzed together in the general category of sustained collective violence, with identifiable differences noted when appropriate. This combined analysis does not imply historic or moral equivalence between those who perpetrated crimes in defense of the apartheid state and those who perpetrated crimes to overthrow apartheid; rather, with some noteworthy exceptions, the analysis revealed the same structural and conceptual patterns in both groups: identifiable and generalizable characteristics of individuals and organizations engaged in sustained, criminal violence in service of a political cause.

Platforms

During an ongoing and escalating armed struggle within a country, a society radically alters its norms of acceptable behavior for participating in the struggle (Haslam and Reicher 2007). As described in the previous chapter, apartheid was a stepwise process of instituting new restrictions on nonwhites, followed by protests and stepped-up violence to fight these restrictions, followed by more brutal and widespread repression by the apartheid government. All sides in the struggle ratcheted up their destructiveness, justifying it with specific strategies that came out of an increasingly rigid set of ideological beliefs. The transformation of societal norms then encouraged more people to join in the fight against apartheid and more intransigence in those fighting to defend the apartheid system.

Consider the effect on societal norms of a single catastrophic event in the United States. Before the attack on the World Trade Center on September 11, 2001, most Americans conceived of themselves at peace, welcoming the inevitability of surplus, prosperity, and security. After the attack, most Americans accepted deficits, recession, insecurity, and war. In turn, against the backdrop of this acceptance, the norms about particular kinds of brutality shifted. From the end of World War II to the end of the twentieth century, torture was condemned and execrated, with no place in the United States. After the events of September 11, 2001, the norms shifted abruptly, with strident defenses of particular kinds of torture, such as stress positions and water torture, continuing to this day.

In an *ongoing* violent struggle, each outbreak of violence normalizes destructive actions in substantial subsets of the population, encouraging more people to step onto platforms of destructiveness. With each nationally publicized violent confrontation, the norms for violence shift throughout the society, and the likelihood that people will join a violent organization increases correspondingly. For an individual, the path to sustained and systemic violence begins when that individual steps onto the platform of a violent organization and then commits to its cause.

Testimony from perpetrators on all sides of the conflict in apartheid South Africa revealed four general patterns of influence that encouraged people to commit to a violent organization: (1) a foundational ideology, (2) memories of specific events that support the ideology, (3) the belief that there is no other acceptable choice, and (4) the honor, excitement, and personal satisfaction of participating in the organization.

An Ideological Foundation

Perpetrators did not articulate comprehensive ideologies in the larger sense of the concept *ideology*—as a body of ideas forming the basis of a political or economic system. Yet in the most concise sense of ideology, as a small set of doctrines or beliefs that supports one's motivations and actions, many perpetrators did describe an ideology that formed the conceptual basis for their actions. For state perpetrators, ideology began in the family and the church and then expanded to school activities, civic groups, and professional organizations. For those in the liberation movements, family and church were typically not as supportive of forceful antigovernment action, and ideology came directly from the words and actions of the ANC and PAC leaders, from affiliated student organizations, and from local political groups. In testimony, ideology was expressed most expansively as a few deeply held beliefs or as cryptically as a slogan.

Captain Dirk Coetzee said, "We were God's own people . . . threatened with a communist revolutionary onslaught from the north, which—if it was ever to succeed—would plunge the southern tip of Africa into chaos" (November 5, 1996). Paul Erasmus said, "It was our duty to fight Communism, which was at the root of this evil that was going to rip our country to pieces" (November 27, 2000). In defending his orders to blow up two ANC-affiliated buildings in downtown Johannesburg, Adriaan Vlok, the former minister of law and order, equated himself to Theodore Roosevelt and compared his actions to those of Abraham Lincoln and Winston Churchill (July 21, 1998). The motivating concept could go from a noble idea to violence in one sentence. In testimony, Robert McBride spoke directly to the victims' families about his personal salvation, "It was in a quest for my own freedom and a quest to unshackle myself from the apartheid system that I brought about the deaths of your loved ones" (October 5, 1999).

With perpetrators on both sides of the conflict, circumscribed ideologies addressed three sets of concepts: *self-concepts,* concepts of the *other,* and concepts of the *situation.* In summary terms, state perpetrators conceptualized themselves as defenders and upholders of the law, whereas they conceptualized members of the liberation movements as violent, godless communists. ANC and PAC perpetrators conceptualized themselves as soldiers for liberation and freedom, whereas they conceptualized the state perpetrators as repressive, murderous racists. Both groups thought of themselves as engaged in *war:* state perpetrators fought for the preservation of Afrikaner culture and against those who would destroy their way of life; ANC and PAC perpetrators fought for democracy and the return of their land and against violent, authoritarian oppression.

Early Experience and Specific Memories

When perpetrators testified about personal experiences, they referenced immediate influences and discrete events and rarely brought up more distant and general interactions in childhood and adolescence.[3] When early experiences were alluded to in testimony, it was the state perpetrators who did so, and not the members of the liberation movements. Although this testimony was limited, several members of the security forces independently identified a pattern of similar influences: nationalistic traditions, families with strict discipline, membership in the Afrikaans church (the Dutch Reformed Church), participation in patriotic civic organizations, indoctrination in the public schools, and specific political events (e.g., Coetzee, November 5, 1996; de Kock, July 29, 1998; Erasmus, November 27, 2000; Vlok, July 21, 1998). These earlier and larger influences had so strongly shaped the self-concepts of the individuals that by the time they decided to join and participate in violent organizations, they were conceived of as internalized predispositions. In these cases, Adorno's concept of the authoritarian disposition is pertinent—not as a defined trait of personality but as a strong belief in loyalty to a particular group, arising from early life experiences.

The state perpetrators who excelled at their destructive jobs were not pathological, but neither were they healthy and well balanced. The exceptional personal characteristic that many of the accomplished tormenters had in common was neither cruelty nor hatefulness but a highly developed aptitude for insulating themselves from the broader consequences of their destructive actions—a dogged unwillingness to conceive of another person's humanity, either over extended periods or during the circumscribed time frame in which the cruelty was perpetrated.[4] That an inclination toward insularity is present in most of us to some degree may make it seem ordinary, but the dominance of this characteristic to the exclusion of others requires persistent shaping, initiated by an upbringing focused on the supremacy of one's cultural group, encouraged by shifts in societal norms, and subsequently reinforced by violent organizations.

General Johannes van der Merwe, former police commissioner and chief of the Security Police in the late 1980s, was one of the few amnesty applicants who described his upbringing in some detail. He spoke of his mother and father as "conservative and fiery supporters of the National Party." He talked of the Afrikaner community of Ermelo in the Eastern Transvaal where he was born, and how he was insulated from views other than those of his family's social group. He recalled that beginning very early in his life, he supported the goals of the National Party, especially concerning "the policy of separate development which was subscribed and protected by the church, the school, the national media and the majority of the white community." As with many members of the security forces and all the presidents of apartheid South Africa (except F. W. de Klerk), van der Merwe belonged to the Dutch Reformed Church. He admitted, "There was very little influence on me which made me think that this policy was wrong. Most of the people I came into contact with believed in this policy and also supported it" (van der Merwe, July 22, 1998).

When members of the liberation movements spoke of influences earlier in their lives, they did not speak of their childhood or their religious and civic traditions. Rather, they focused almost exclusively on *adolescence* as a time of political awakening and the beginnings of activism. The main influences were typically untraditional: not church or family or public institutions, but rather their initial encounters with the political ideologies of the ANC and the PAC, promulgated by national leaders as well as local organizers.

Although general influences in early life were infrequently disclosed in testimony, many perpetrators did attribute their decision to join a violent organization to *specific events* in the past. Memories of these events provided touchstones for their ideology, with both sides citing personal memories to justify their actions, even many years later. Ideology was supported by these specific, documented events, with personal memories of these events increasing the potency and endurance of the ideology. In South Africa, one such event was the Soweto Uprising in 1976, which began as a protest against the mandatory use of the language Afrikaans in public schools and ultimately led to 500 black South Africans being shot to death, many of them students, many of them shot in the back (Thompson 2000). The mass killings in Soweto then became part of the collective knowledge of all South Africans in the struggle against apartheid, reiterated for many years in the pamphlets, posters, and manifestos distributed by the liberation movements.[5] Members of the liberation movements who gave testimony to the Amnesty Committee cited the uprising and massacre in Soweto as the specific event that led them to join the armed wings of their movements to fight against the apartheid government.

Similarly, members of the SAP also cited the Soweto Uprising as the reason for joining the Security Branch to fight against the liberation movements. Paul Erasmus said, "I was a very young policeman who'd never seen dead people or shot people. I went through the '76 riots in Soweto for five days, and I witnessed unspeakable horrors which changed my life." He continued, "Instead of leaving the police force as I could have at the end of 1976, I applied to join the Security Branch" (Erasmus, November 27, 2000). Captain Brian Mitchell, the police commander who later sought amnesty for the murder of eleven black people in the *Trust Feed killings,* also recounted the influence of the Soweto Uprising in his testimony.[6] Back in 1976, he directly witnessed the Soweto Uprising and based his primary career decision on that experience:

> As a young white South African I was for the first time confronted with an uprising that left me shivering in my boots. During this uprising, I experienced the solidarity of the black masses like never before, and the brutality of the law enforcers to put down the uprising. The hostility of the Blacks toward us was real and constant.

As a result, he committed to training "in counterinsurgency tactics and counterrevolutionary measures to stop the eventual onslaught" (Mitchell, 16 October 1996).

In the terminology of memory researcher David Pillemer (1998), specific memory for the uprising in Soweto was an *originating event:* a remembered personal event perceived as creating a new life course. For example, just after his conviction for terrorism, ANC activist Ashley Forbes told the South African Supreme Court that the violent breakup by police in 1985 of the march to Pollsmoor Prison was the "watershed event" in his decision to join the African National Congress and its armed wing, the MK (Forbes, September 21, 1988). Many perpetrators cited such events as originating events for joining violent organizations.

No Choice

Those who joined the liberation movements said that at the time they had "no choice" and that they were "forced by the situation." After his remarks to the Supreme Court, for example, Ashley Forbes made a statement to the national media about the charges against him, concluding, "To me there was no choice, I decided to fight" (Forbes, September 21, 1988).[7] Gcinikhaya Makoma, one of the perpetrators in the St. James Church massacre, said, "The situation in South Africa led us to do those things. We saw our fellow Africans being shot and killed by the Whites, and we were forced by the situation" (Makoma, July 10, 1997). Near the end of Vuyisile Madasi's hearing on the Heidelberg Tavern massacre, when confronted by the mother of one of the young women killed at the tavern, Madasi said, "It was the conditions in the country that led to such actions" (Madasi, October 28, 1997).

The perception of no choice was not only due to economic circumstances. Mohammed Shaik, a commander in the armed wing of the ANC, said, "I come from a middle-class family. I was quite comfortable and being politically involved was only to my detriment. However, I joined because of the violence of the apartheid system. . . . The apartheid state left us no choice but to take up arms" (Shaik, May 6, 1998). While in Pollsmoor Prison, when Nelson Mandela was offered amnesty by Prime Minister P. W. Botha in exchange for renouncing violence, Mandela refused, saying, "It was only when all other forms of resistance were no longer open to us that we turned to armed struggle" (Mandela 1985, 1).

Honor, Excitement, and Personal Satisfaction

Joining organizations of collective violence was reinforced by special status and privileges. Eventual perpetrators on all sides of the struggle in apartheid South Africa spoke of honor and excitement in joining their violent organizations. Colonel Eugene de Kock said, "With Vlakplaas and the security forces, it clearly was regarded as an honor if one was allowed to participate in an action. . . . We didn't have a gang-pressing system to get people to Vlakplaas, we had to keep them away" (de Kock, July 29, 1998). Captain Dirk Coetzee, the commander of Vlakplaas before de Kock, said, "It is each policeman's aspirations and wish to one day become one of this elite corps" (Coetzee, November 5, 1996). Paul Erasmus of the security forces elaborated:

> I started on the Security Branch, believing as a very young man that this would be exciting. It was something to which I could commit myself, this crusade against godless, satanic communism, as we were taught, and then I would be something of a James Bond type of character and lead this exciting life dealing with very important issues. (Erasmus, November 27, 2000)

About the torture and murder of ANC activists, Paul van Vuuren said he *enjoyed* what he did and that he thought it was the right thing to do: "It was the enemy we were killing. I felt I was busy with big and important things" (Pauw 1998, 24).

Joining an organization also provided meaning in one's life. After joining the MK, the armed wing of the ANC, Robert McBride explained, "For the first time in my life, I was able to do something against the system. For the first time in my life, I was regarded as a South African, full status, without racial categorization. This elevation in my status was for me the most empowering moment of my life." McBride made it clear that when he joined the MK, he was not pressured to do so, that it was his own choice, and that it immediately affirmed personal meaning in his life: "My sense of anger, frustration and helplessness in the face of this injustice came to an end when I was formally recruited to the MK" (McBride, October 5, 1999).

The Commitment

Once people committed to their violent organization, it was then that they decided to kill (and to die). Robert McBride said, "I did all of those discussions about killing—with myself—before I entered Special Ops" (McBride, October 6, 1999). Luyanda Gqomfa, who led the killings at the Heidelberg Tavern, said, "I joined the PAC to work for them, to work against the oppressors." About killing innocent people in a tavern, he said, "I was willing to do it" (Gqomfa, October 27, 1997).

In their testimonies, the perpetrators admitted to agency—not at the time of their destructive actions but *before,* when they committed to the violent organization. After that, they simply maintained their commitment, with diminished agency and without analyzing their actions. Vuyisile Madasi stated clearly that he made his decision to kill at the time he joined APLA, and that once the decision was made, he no longer questioned it. When asked what would have happened if he had disobeyed the order to kill people at the Heidelberg Tavern, he replied, "If I was going to defy the order I would have defied it . . . in the first place." He elaborated, "I was not forced to do what I did. And I did not do it because I did not want to. I joined APLA as an army that fought for the freedom of Africans" (Madasi, October 28, 1997). Madasi's partner in the massacre, Luyanda Gqomfa, concurred: "For any APLA soldier, we take an oath, and one of the conditions is that we should follow the orders from our commanders" (Gqomfa, October 27, 1997). One of the decisions that people made in joining a violent organization was to give up choice, later.

Priming

After people step onto the platform of a violent organization and commit to that organization, priming for violence begins with an initial period of training and indoctrination. In one testimony after another, members of the security forces invoked the theme of "never before" as a reason for their illegal actions. Until they committed acts of violence against others in service of their jobs, their organizations, and their country, they had been obedient, law-abiding citizens. On the other side, members of the liberation movements repeatedly referred to the conditions in their communities and in the country as requiring illegal, violent action.

Indoctrination and Training

To prepare participants for sustained violence work, organizations in South Africa provided a limited period of ideological indoctrination and tactical training, a focused and specialized approach to shaping personal history. Indoctrination typically emphasized the rightful place of the organization in the struggle against the enemy forces and the impending threat of these forces. Colonel Eugene de Kock, for example, spoke specifically of being indoctrinated early in his career, "regarding communist takeover of South Africa, regarding the most terrible things which were going to happen to the Whites in the country if a black government took over" (de Kock, July 29, 1998). Tactical training focused on the initial operations; preparation for later operations occurred as the operations proceeded.

Consider the case of MK operative Robert McBride. To receive his initial training, McBride crossed the South Africa–Botswana border into Gaborone, where he met two members of the ANC who provided the training, which McBride described: "They showed me how to pack and hide things, as I was not going to be used on an operation immediately. They showed me how to make an arms cache, to put the soil down in the same way as before, how to mark it, what kind of spot to pick— safe, but accessible." He then summarized this initial training: "They gave me instructions, both theory and practice, on weapons. It was only half an hour but very intense" (Rostron 1991, 101–102). Two weeks later, McBride drove to Botswana again and was given three days of training on explosives and firearms.

Thus it was that after an introductory half hour of training followed by three days of more intensive work, McBride was sent back into South Africa, with instructions to establish arms caches for guerrillas entering the country, to recruit an MK cell, and to conduct sabotage operations against the government in Natal (Rostron 1991, 104). As with many organizations that employ clandestine violence against existing institutions, including the car bomb (Davis 2007),[8] the ANC provided only brief, sufficient training in explosives to Robert McBride and then released him on his own to organize a small insurgent cell and to choose his targets—under general and flexible guidelines.

For the SAP, training could be self-motivated or inadvertent. On his own, Paul van Vuuren studied methods of torture to decide which ones would be best for him, analyzing the different techniques of Nazi torture as well as the methods of violence workers for Pinochet's secret police in Chile. Captain Jeffrey Benzien learned the wet bag method of torture when he was in the South African Air Force. As part of the aircrew training for escape and evasion, a version of the wet bag method of interrogation was used on crew members to prepare them for its possible use against them in the event they were captured. Benzien then mastered the technique on his own.

Similarly, prior victimization can be considered a form of unintended training, especially in the case of the antiapartheid activists who had been victimized by the SAP. Robert McBride and his partner Matthew Lecordier, for example, were repeatedly victimized by the police and by the apartheid system. Lecordier, in his testimony about the Magoos Bar car bombing, summarized the abuses of the SAP that trained him in violent activism: "I was arrested by the Security Police, and I was repeatedly assaulted, humiliated, intimidated, threatened, and abused by the Security Police in diverse ways" (Lecordier, October 11, 1999).

Based on analysis of the testimony given to the Amnesty Committee, it is clear that the SAP and the armed wings of the liberation movements did not need the intensive, around-the-clock indoctrination and brutal training described by violence workers in the studies of dictatorships in Greece and Brazil (Huggins, Haritos-Fatouros, and Zimbardo 2002; Haritos-Fatouros 2003). Clearly, there was indoctrination and training, with some of the training self-motivated and inadvertent, but the perpetrators were prepared in advance by collective knowledge and personal memories of violent events in South Africa, which meant less need for focused transformation of the individual. Without intensive indoctrination or extended training, Jeffrey Benzien and Paul van Vuuren tortured for the state, Brian Mitchell ordered the killing of innocents in the community of Trust Feed, Christopher Makoma shot worshippers in the St. James Church, Vuyisile Madasi and Robert McBride killed young people in popular taverns, and four young men in a mob murdered Amy Biehl.

The next phase in the process of becoming a violence worker is *sustaining* one's commitment to illegal work. After joining violent organizations and after an initial introduction to training and indoctrination, why do members of violent organizations continue to commit extraordinarily brutal acts?

Specific Memories

After the ideological indoctrination, memories of specific events were interpreted in ways that supported the prevailing ideology, maintaining and strengthening one's commitment to the organization. In testimony, Adriaan Vlok referred to his specific memories of ANC attacks on civilians: "All these scenes were scenes from hell. At these scenes you would find injured people, as well as the maimed bodies of innocent people, all caused by bombs of terror planted by terrorists" (Vlok, July 21, 1998). His specific memories then fortified his decisions to take illegal actions against the ANC, including bombings of buildings where members of the ANC were suspected to gather and employing hit squads to assassinate ANC activists.

Specific events were extrapolated into general motivational principles. Chief of the Security Police, General Johannes van der Merwe, said, "Certain horrible experiences which I was unfortunate to experience touched me in such a way that I did everything in my power to fight the revolutionary struggle." Van der Merwe elaborated, "Killings of people, killings of members of the security forces, specifically South African Police—car bomb attacks, limpet mine attacks, landmine attacks and other explosive devices—with targets that were very often innocent defenseless people, being both black and white." He then summarized the goal of his illegal operations: "The protection and the interests of the government was always my first priority" (van der Merwe, July 22, 1998).

Similarly, in pamphlets and other publications, the liberation movements referred to specific acts of deadly violence by the SAP in order to incite forceful and often murderous action among their followers, imploring them to use deadly force against the police and to bring violence to the white suburbs. General van der Merwe, in fact, referred directly to the role of these antiapartheid pamphlets and magazines in his own decision to combat them, indicating that they were effective in priming *both* sides of the armed struggle: "In my official capacity I had access to publications of radical organizations, for example the ANC/SACP alliance and the PAC. The cold-blooded way in which the masses in South Africa were whipped up or incited by these publications to commit violence convinced me that the revolutionary onslaught had to be stopped with everything in our power" (van der Merwe, July 22, 1998).

On the other side, the National Party and the State Security Council used rhetoric that the TRC called "reckless, inflammatory and an incitement to unlawful acts" (TRC 1999c, 215). This rhetoric was then highlighted in the speeches and pamphlets of the liberation movements in calling for deadly action against the National Party. In both cases, the priming for one side translated into priming for the other.

Reasons for Unreasonable Acts

Supported by ideological rationale and encouraged by specific events, perpetrators called upon a diversity of reasons for maintaining their commitment and their violent actions. These reasons made direct contact with the ideological rationale of the perpetrators and established *short circuits* for action. In this way, the reasons bypassed moral inspection and helped prime the violent, illegal operations. Both the liberation movements and the pro-apartheid forces offered such reasons. Although the particulars differed, as did the general themes, the underlying belief in the moral justification of these reasons was the same.

Those in the liberation movements justified their violent actions as (1) demanding necessary attention ("So the government will now listen to our grievances"); (2) afflicting their own hardships on the privileged ("Make white people come out of their comfort zone"); (3) raising awareness ("Until the war moves to the white community, they will not understand what is happening in the African townships"); (4) hurting the morale in the privileged communities ("To bring down the spirit of the oppressors"); (5) meeting larger goals ("To get the land back from the Whites who had taken it away from the African people through violent means"); and (6) reflecting their lack of choice ("When all other forms of resistance were no longer open to us, we turned to armed struggle").

Mass murder could be supported by the simple reason of *calling attention* to the injustices of apartheid. To justify killing eleven people worshipping at the St. James Church in Kenilworth, Bassie Mkhumbuzi said, "When there is violence in white areas, they would try and go to the government to lay their grievances—so that the government can listen to *our* grievances" (Mkhumbuzi, July 9, 1997). To justify civilian casualties in general, Aboobaker Ismail said, "We cannot allow the [apartheid] system to persist for the sake of saving a few lives. It is not so harsh when one considers how many lives apartheid has destroyed" (Ismail, May 6, 1998). Members of the ANC also used their own constraints as reasons for killing innocents. For example, one of Robert McBride's reasons for bombing a popular bar was that no children would be present.

Those in the security forces justified their actions primarily in terms of national security, with attention to (1) maintenance of order and protection of values ("the last line of defense," "combating terrorism," "fighting Communism," "preventing total anarchy and chaos"); (2) general strategic goals ("Not an inch will be lost and inches lost will be regained"); and (3) the underlying destabilizing effects of the armed struggle ("shattered foundations," "national psychosis").

Torture and murder were also justified by these reasons. After apprehending three men from the ANC, Paul van Vuuren and two other officers took the men to an open veld north of Pretoria, bound their hands and feet, tortured them with electric shocks, and then killed them. In 1996, after testifying before the Amnesty Committee, van Vuuren said, "I did it for my country and my people. I was fighting communism." He added, "We had to stop the killing of innocent women and children" (Pauw 1998, 20). When Jeffrey Benzien was asked why he tortured his prisoners, he replied, "I had to prevent deeds of terrorism," saying that his "sole purpose" was to take weapons away from those who might use them against military targets and "the innocent people in Cape Town." Benzien said, "I believed *bona fide* that due to my expeditious and unorthodox conduct, we made a big difference in the combating of terror" (Benzien, July 14, 1997). By "expeditious and unorthodox conduct," Benzien meant spending thirty minutes effectively using the wet bag method of torture.

Reasons could also be mundane and very practical. Captain Brian Mitchell of the SAP defended his violent actions by saying, "The average white South African male was sitting at home on a Saturday afternoon drinking beer and watching rugby, while the townships were ablaze with violence and unrest. We were ordered to stop such unrest at all costs" (Mitchell, October 16, 1996).

All sides appealed to *reciprocity* as a powerful reason. Aboobaker Ismail of the ANC and MK said, "If they are going to do that with us, is it not perhaps also right that we can do it to them?" (Ismail, May 6,

1998). On the other side, Captain Dirk Coetzee of the security forces independently agreed: "It was a question of using the same methods that the enemy used—illegal methods—to achieve our goals" (Coetzee, November 6, 1996).

Many reasons took the form of if-then conditionals, as *algorithms for violence*. The young men who killed Amy Biehl, for example, gave conditional reasons about calling attention to the injustice of apartheid: *if* we kill an innocent white person and create chaos, *then* the government will listen to us; *if* we kill an innocent white person, *then* we will get our land back. Similarly, Jeffrey Benzien stated that *if* he tortured ANC activists and they revealed the locations of their weapons, *then* he prevented terrorism.

At War

To prime the members of a violent organization to participate in extensive violence, the most frequently invoked reason on all sides of the armed struggle was clear: *war*. In a special hearing of the TRC, General Andrew Masondo of the ANC referred to the human rights violations that took place in the ANC camps: "People who it was found that they were enemy agents, we executed them, and I wouldn't make an apology. We were at war" (TRC 1999c, 262). In the mass murder known as the Boipatong massacre, individuals affiliated with the IFP attacked the residents of Boipatong, a settlement south of Johannesburg, killing forty-six men, women, and children thought to be related to members of the ANC. At the amnesty hearings for this massacre, Victor Mthembu, one of the perpetrators, said, "If it had not been a war situation between the Inkatha Freedom Party and the ANC, I would not have participated" (Mthembu, July 6, 1998).

In explaining the rationale for targeting clerks and secretaries for bombing attacks, MK commander Aboobaker Ismail maintained that the victims chose their fate. According to Ismail, civilians who worked for the Defense Forces were guilty of supporting the "military machine" (Ismail, May 6, 1998). In fact, justification for killing civilians began with the leadership. In 1983, Oliver Tambo, president of the ANC, declared in writing, "No longer can the ANC's military wing, Umkhonto we Sizwe, safe-guard civilians in our armed struggle. Military action against the enemy will inevitably take the lives of innocent civilians. However, these sacrifices will not be in vain" (Tambo 1983, 21).

To support this rationale, perpetrators carefully enforced the lexicon of war in their testimony. In his testimony about the Heidelberg Tavern massacre, Luyanda Gqomfa said, "First of all, we are soldiers. That is our job. In every war there are casualties. It is to be expected." Later, he insisted, "I am not a terrorist. I am a freedom fighter" (Gqomfa, October 27, 1997). ANC militant Mohamed Shaik said, "We were MK soldiers, an MK Unit. We were not hit squads" (Shaik, May 7, 1998). The concept of *soldier* is essential, as it connects to the larger rationale of war.[9]

Some reasons invoking war were painfully direct. Luyanda Gqomfa said his goal at the Heidelberg Tavern was "to kill or injure as many people as possible" (Gqomfa, October 27, 1997). In explaining the rationale for car bombs, Robert McBride said, "The purpose of the attacks was to kill or injure enemy personnel or collaborators." McBride admitted that he fully anticipated that innocent civilians would be killed but that he only targeted members of the security forces, implying a moral distinction with no practical difference: attacking security forces with the expectation that civilians would be killed versus purposely targeting civilians (McBride, October 5, 1999).

State perpetrators blamed war for creating a widespread imbalance in people's lives, and this imbalance was then cited as a reason for a variety of violent acts. In the hearings for the Trust Feed killings, Brian Mitchell described the effects of armed struggle against the UDF: "The riots shattered the foundations of many families of the police. It shattered the foundations of the South African Police as a whole." He continued, "It ended up that many policemen lost their homes, lost their families, and it ended up that some of us ended up as arsonists and murderers" (Mitchell, October 16, 1996). General Johannes van der Merwe justified his order to bomb an ANC-affiliated community center by saying, "We were in a war situation, and this unfortunately was part of the psychosis which spread from that situation" (van der Merwe, July 22, 1998).

War itself was invoked simultaneously as an end and a means. Commander Sabelo Phama, defense secretary of the PAC, stated, "Until the war moves to the white community, they will not understand what is happening in the African townships. . . . There can be no peace in the white suburbs" (Phama 1987, 6).

Slogans as Reasons

Testimony to the Amnesty Committee disclosed in painful specificity the very real motivational power of slogans. Political movements need slogans and violent political movements need slogans of violence. In general, slogans function as necessary crypto-ideologies, encapsulating an organization's complex and sometimes contradictory strategies, while motivating extreme behavior on the part of the followers. They originate in ideology but distill the ideological complexities into cryptic calls for violent action, often assuming murderous dimensions. In apartheid South Africa, anticommunist slogans served to motivate the torturers and hit squads working for the apartheid state, and antiwhite slogans incited violence in the liberation movements against the white minority.

One of the most notorious slogans of the era was "One settler, one bullet," which connected to an extended argument offered by the PAC that the land stolen from Africans by deadly force could only be taken back through deadly force. This slogan inspired many members of the PAC to commit violence, including the young men who murdered Amy Biehl. At the amnesty hearings for this murder, Easy Nofemela said, "We were told to implement the slogan, 'One Settler, one bullet,' and that each and every white person, we must stone that person in order to bring back the African country to the Africans." Nofemela also said, "The slogan 'One settler, one bullet' inspired me to hurt, injure or kill white people" (Nofemela, July 8, 1997). When asked why he stabbed Amy Biehl, Mongesi Manqina reiterated, "For me this was an opportunity to put into practice the slogan 'One settler, one bullet'" (Manqina, July 8, 1997). At the hearings for the Boipatong massacre, Victor Mthembu cited a slogan to explain why he would not exclude even young children from being targeted for killing: "A snake gives birth to another snake" (Mthembu, July 13, 1998). The murder of eleven family members in the Trust Feed killings was motivated by a doctrine of the state police encapsulated in the simple slogan "Not an inch will be lost." Even acronyms could take on the status of a slogan. When referring to their apartheid enemy, the PAC secretary for foreign affairs, Commander Gora Ibrahim, spoke neither of the National Party nor of the government of South Africa, but of "RSA"—Racist South Africa (Ibrahim 1987, 4).

Doing What Is Right

Within the tightly coiled norms of elite groups of violent perpetrators, expectations shift so radically that torture and murder are assimilated into ideology and maintained through social conformity and habit. The resulting habitual brutality is then supported by a strong belief in the goodness of one's actions. With state perpetrators in apartheid South Africa, this belief was buttressed by the religious doctrine of the Dutch Reformed Church, which specifically spoke to the divinity of Afrikaans stewardship of southern Africa. The religious doctrine then allowed members of the security forces to conduct their illegal work, satisfied that they were acting in good faith.

Regarding illegal bombings, sabotage, and torture and murder of ANC activists, Colonel Eugene de Kock said, "The only reason to go over those steps is an absolute commitment and a belief in what you are doing and the *correctness* of what you are doing." He continued, "It couldn't be taught to you, you had to believe it" (de Kock, July 29, 1998). After demonstrating his torture technique, Captain Benzien stated, "At the time, given those circumstances, how heinous it may sound, I was convinced I was right." When one of Jeffrey Benzien's former victims questioned him about the legality of the wet bag method of torture, Benzien replied quixotically, "I was engaged in a lawful activity, using unlawful, unconstitutional methods" (Benzien, July 14, 1997). Managers of apartheid believed in the virtue of their destructive actions just as they believed in the rationale of apartheid.

Even afterward, many years later, after discarding the old rationale and honestly admitting that one's actions were immoral and cruel, a belief in the virtue of these actions can still persist. Speaking to Tony Yengeni, Jeffrey Benzien said, "With my absolutely unorthodox methods and by removing your weaponry from you, I am wholly convinced that I prevented you and any of your colleagues . . . from being branded a murderer nowadays" (Benzien, July 14, 1997). The victim was tortured, in other words, for his own good.

One Step at a Time

The cumulative momentum of incremental decisions carried perpetrators to commit acts of violence that would have been inconceivable earlier in their professional lives. In his testimony to the Amnesty Committee, Captain Willem Mentz outlined his stepwise professional path. When he joined the SAP in the late 1970s, he was stationed in Pretoria in the Detective Branch. He then transferred to Murder and Robbery in 1980 and occasionally worked in cooperation with the Security Branch of the Northern Transvaal, which was how he came in contact with the members of the security forces at Vlakplaas. In the late 1980s, he was invited to join the operations at Vlakplaas, and it was there, more than a decade later, that he began participating in illegal operations against the ANC under the command of Colonel Eugene de Kock. At the time of his testimony in early 1997, he was still a member of the SAP, although his Vlakplaas unit had disbanded in 1991. In a series of choices, each one understandable as an individual decision, Captain Mentz moved from diligent officer in the SAP to part-time collaborator with the security forces to lethal operative in the illegal operations at Vlakplaas (Mentz, February 24, 1997). After that, once at the elite level within a violent organization, the progression to methodical brutality continued. Several perpetrators, for example, spoke of their first kill as traumatic and dissociating but also as a necessary step in their on-the-job training (e.g., Erasmus, November 27, 2000; van Vuuren, February 25, 1997). A specific operation was both a cause and a consequence of continued violence.

Similarly, in the armed wings of the liberation movements, initial operations began with less risky and nonlethal operations and progressed to the killing of innocents. Each operation then primed the next operation. Luyanda Gqomfa, for example, who eventually led the Heidelberg Tavern massacre, started with smaller bombings where no one was killed and then moved up to a crowded tavern where the objective was "to kill as many people as possible" (Gqomfa, October 27, 1997). After being formally recruited into the ANC, Robert McBride began with the missions to sabotage transformers inside electricity substations in Natal. In discrete steps, McBride progressed from small-time saboteur to car bomber, with the momentum of the individual operations culminating in the killing of three young women at a popular bar and the maiming of sixty others.

Team Spirit

For many perpetrators, strong social bonding within a team prevailed. General van der Merwe stated that in the Security Branch, "There was a team spirit like no other unit of the South African Police. . . . One learned to really trust your fellow members in the Security Branch under any circumstances" (van der Merwe, July 22, 1998). A useful irony for this clandestine violence was that the greater the illegality, the stronger the support within an illegal cell. Encouragement from others within a group reinforced the actions of individuals and their continuation of destructive initiatives.

With some perpetrators, there was direct evidence of increasing stress, but with others, the social bonding during illegal operations was experienced as unpressured. Tikapela Mbelo testified about his experience of being a foot soldier in an antiterrorist unit of the Security Police at the notorious compound in Vlakplaas. He was attached to a small group and was not told his duties or the specifics of the operations he was assigned to. When asked why he stayed at Vlakplaas, Mbelo answered with cavalier honesty, "Vlakplaas was like a holiday resort . . . a place for making money and having fun and being drunk all the time." He then elaborated, "We remained at the farm just lazing around, but whenever there was work for us to do, we would go out to different places to complete or accomplish our missions." When the evidence leader for the Amnesty Committee asked him directly, "Despite the torture, the death, the cross-border raids, you regarded Vlakplaas as a holiday?" Mbelo unhesitatingly replied, "That is correct" (Mbelo, November 18, 1997).

The Illusion of the Follower

The managers of violence in apartheid South Africa were not thoughtless bureaucrats, passively shaped by their responsibilities to participate in atrocities. They willingly accepted the destructive ideologies of their bureaucratic organizations and creatively developed and refined their methods of destruction. Within these shifted norms, perpetrators acted with inventiveness and ingenuity, dispelling the illusion of the follower.

In the apartheid government, the complex bureaucracy of the Security Branch protected the managers and foot soldiers of violence with a lightning cage of secrecy about many of their illegal activities and with public commendations for fighting terrorism. A similar pattern existed within the militarized cells of the liberation movements, with secrecy maintained in training and planning, but with the violent acts against the people and installations of the apartheid government openly acknowledged and supported.

When planning operations, between the actual acts of violence, the managers of collective violence engaged in considerable thought and initiative. They were not automatons obeying orders but professionals interpreting instructions from their commanders. Paul Erasmus of the Security Police exemplified this approach: "We certainly worked very hard to outdo each other, we became very inventive. I certainly flourished in this environment. . . . I developed new techniques of harassment and more bizarre ways, which were more effective than some of my colleagues or commanding officers could ever have dreamed of" (Erasmus, November 27, 2000).

Based in Vlakplaas, Paul van Vuuren was a police officer during the 1980s in the Northern Transvaal Security Branch. In this capacity, he developed expertise in torture interrogation that involved using a small electric generator to shock sensitive parts of a prisoner's body (Pauw 1998). Using this method, he tortured dozens of ANC activists. But before using this method, van Vuuren took the initiative to study and practice several methods of torture to decide which technique to master as his signature method. Many perpetrators demonstrated innovation, ambition, and effectiveness—qualities in a workplace or a classroom that most people would encourage and even reward.

In strict military organizations, the influence of "following orders" is direct and plausible. Soldiers are trained to follow orders, to complete missions, and not to question their commanding officers or the operations they were ordered to carry out. For violent operations within non-military organizations, however, direct orders are not given. Instead, general goals and suggestive encouragement are passed down, allowing the members of these organizations more latitude in choosing specific actions, as long as they conform to the stated goals of the organization. Captain Benzien made this clear in his testimony: "There were no written instructions in police manuals that said this is what you can do. I *do* know, and as have tried to explain before, that the mandate of the foot soldier was to glean that information as soon and as fully as possible by—let's say the unwritten word—any method" (Benzien, July 14, 1997). In Captain Benzien's case, the chosen method was water torture.

Žižek (2006) rightly pointed out that within established bureaucracies, explanations for torture should not invoke a simple dichotomy: isolated acts of misbehavior on the part of individual soldiers versus direct orders from above. Rather, torture results from "unofficial pressure, hints and directives . . . delivered in private, the way one shares a dirty secret" (370).

Agency and Interactionism

One foundational principle in the study of perpetrators is the *fundamental attribution error:* when making judgments about personal causality, people place too much emphasis on an individual's traits and not enough on the influence of the situation (e.g., Ross 1977; Zimbardo 2007). This heuristic principle has been integrated into the larger framework of *situationism:* individual behaviors—especially misbehaviors—are primarily a function of situational influences and not attributable to inherent traits of personality. For more than three decades, this framework emphasizing the primacy of the situation has been widely applied to explain deeply destructive behavior in otherwise normal human beings in a variety of settings (e.g., Bandura, Underwood, and Fromson 1975; Haney, Banks, and Zimbardo 1973; Milgram 1974; Waller 2002; Zimbardo, Maslach, and Haney 1999; Zimbardo 2004, 2007). Recently, however, there has been growing recognition of more agency in the perpetrators, beginning with the voluntary selection process in joining violent organizations (Foster, Haupt, and de Beer 2005; Haslam and Reicher 2007). In fact, perpetrator testimony given to the Amnesty Committee suggests that there is a fundamental attribution error with the fundamental attribution error: explanations have placed too much emphasis on the situation and not enough on the perpetrators' decisions, motivations, and distinctive talents.

Perpetrators in apartheid South Africa chose to become part of an organization and then chose to join increasingly more specialized and more secret organizations that enforced their own sets of rules, separate from the society at large. Decision by decision, the perpetrators proceeded, committing acts of increasing destructiveness, reinforcing the organization and being reinforced in return to continue their destructiveness. Eventually, with some perpetrators in violent organizations, their choices and actions of the past led to the most extreme behaviors in support of the goals of the organization, such as torturing detainees, assassinating opponents, and detonating bombs on civilian targets.

Arguing for an *interactionist* understanding, Haslam and Reicher (2007) proposed that both the person and the situation influence each other and are reciprocally transformed through this interaction and that extreme people and extreme groups are "interdependent and mutually reinforcing" (621). To begin, there is common ground between the individual and a potentially destructive group. People join an organization to be with other people like them. The organization then transforms the individual members by allowing them to express their dispositions differently. In extreme cases, those who enjoy hurting others are allowed and even encouraged to express that behavior on those who are not members of the group. These individuals, in turn, transform the group, in some cases by pushing it to even more extreme policies and actions. This malevolent cooperation between extreme individuals and their violent organizations transforms the individuals and the group.

The state perpetrators in apartheid South Africa were shaped by the conditions at each level, which further shaped them to move to the *next* level: from straightforward police work, to police work that collaborated with the security forces, to joining the security forces, and eventually to special, clandestine units that performed illegal activities rationalized by the ideology of national security. Captain Dirk Coetzee, a commander at the security headquarters in Vlakplaas, effectively summarized this process in his testimony, stating that he and his men were selected from the general police force because of "attitude" and "skills" and then encouraged to maintain their attitude and use these skills for illegal operations (Coetzee, November 6, 1996). In his seminal work, *The Roots of Evil* (1989), Staub also noted the reciprocity between individuals and destructive groups, with considerable choice by the individual perpetrators. With each decision, the individual changes, but the system is also changed by these individual decisions. Eventually, as the individual adapts to an increasingly destructive system, many of the decisions, according the Staub, are made automatically, without awareness of their moral implications (147).

Obviously, a young person does not wake up one morning and say, "When I grow up, I want to be a violence worker and torture other people. I think I'd be good at it." But people do choose to participate actively in the culture of their violent organization, and through a series of experiences and decisions, some of them learn to become torturers and killers. In apartheid South Africa, those who tortured for the state chose to do so—by conscientiously beating their prisoners or by applying electric shocks to sensitive parts of their bodies or by repeatedly forcing them to the brink of asphyxiation. Those who planned sabotage bombings and killings for the liberation movements were aware of the destructiveness and illegality of their actions, even if other influences clouded and at times hid this awareness.

Triggers

Most of the bureaucratic efforts in violent organizations and most of the individual justifications for violence are focused on priming, on maintaining the strength of the organizational and social influences so that the triggers for violent actions can work as efficiently as possible, within habit and without analysis. In such a system, one that effectively maintains itself through ongoing, multilayered interactions between the demands of the organization and the capabilities of the individuals, the trigger is typically not a dramatic event but rather the instructions for a specific operation. For executives within a violent organization, the trigger is an agreement about a problem that needs to be resolved. For upper-level managers, the trigger is the presentation of the problem, along with the clear implication that the problem needs to be taken care of. For midlevel managers, the trigger is the specific directive to solve the problem by any means necessary, with the clear implication that secrecy and extralegal methods are required. For foot soldiers at the lowest level of the violence hierarchy, the trigger is in the form of orders for specific actions to solve the identified problem.

Unanalyzed Orders

Within violent organizations, triggers continue to initiate cruel and destructive acts primarily because perpetrators perceive no choice once a problem is presented and an operation set in motion. In the bureaucracy of violence, triggers work efficiently, and usually quietly, because perpetrators are primed to focus on the operation. On all sides of the struggle in apartheid South Africa, a clear pattern showed itself: the higher the level of the operative, the more vague the instructions; the lower the level, the more specific the instructions. At all levels, instructions and orders were heeded, unanalyzed.

Wilhelm Riaan Bellingan was under the command of Colonel Eugene de Kock when he received orders to help bomb COSATU House, a trade union building in the middle of Johannesburg. Even though the operation was to bomb a civilian building in downtown Johannesburg, Bellingan said, "I believed in the order. Colonel de Kock never came to me with any unreasonable orders" (Bellingan, July 30, 1998).

Brigadier Jan Cronje supervised an operation that used a UDF organizer, Joe Tsele, as bait to catch a group of "terrorists," which resulted in the killing of Tsele. About this operation, Captain Jacques Hechter said, "I accepted that Brigadier Cronje was convinced that that was the correct action. I would not have doubted his decision in any way" (Hechter, February 24, 1997). Even commanders in the Security Police did not question orders from above. Captain Dirk Coetzee, commander of the main antiterrorism unit of the Security Police headquarters at Vlakplaas, said, "Never did I question any orders" (Coetzee, November 5, 1996). Even at the highest level of government, orders went unanalyzed. The president of South Africa, P. W. Botha, advised cabinet minister Adriaan Vlok about the building that housed the headquarters of the South African Council of Churches (SACC), telling Vlok, "You must make that building unusable." Without questioning the president's instructions, Vlok then supervised the operation that ended in the firebombing of the building (Vlok, July 21, 1998).

Hearings for the murderous attacks on the St. James Church and the Heidelberg Tavern revealed the clear perspective of those who carried out the attacks. Thobela Mlambisa, an APLA operative, was asked, "What did you think when you realized that it was a church that you were going to attack?" Without hesitating, he replied, "There was nothing I could do. I was just following orders from my commander. I have to obey orders" (Mlambisa, July 9, 1997). Gcinikhaya Makoma, who commanded Mlambisa during the massacre and who himself received orders, said, "An order is an order. You don't think who is there and who is not there. If an order is being instructed, you just do that." When asked how he could shoot to death eleven worshippers in a church, Makoma replied, "I was deeply involved in this, but there was nothing I could do—to let this not happen—because this was an order from above and as a soldier I had to obey the instructions" (Makoma, July 10, 1997). Vuyisile Madasi is clear about his role in the Heidelberg Tavern massacre: "I was not told about the people inside the tavern, I was just ordered to get there and shoot because there would be people there. . . . Where people were, I shot" (Madasi, October 28, 1997).

States of Mind

In apartheid South Africa, perpetrators committed specific acts of cruelty, often in directly interactive situations: unarmed activists were stabbed to death, bound prisoners were pushed out of airplanes, detainees were hung for hours, dangling by their handcuffs, prisoners were tortured with electric shocks. What were the perpetrators thinking?

One answer is that during the actual operations, they were *not* thinking—outside the confines of the specific actions. The structural feature that supported the systematic brutality in apartheid South Africa was a bureaucratic division of labor that allowed the perpetrators to focus on technical considerations and defer moral responsibility. Specific acts of violence were maintained through an intense focus on doing the job, completing the task, and doing it effectively. Once the destructive actions were triggered, ideological beliefs and organizational goals transmogrified into tightly focused selective attention, which was then followed by pathological rationalization.

The ability to commit methodical acts of brutality can be explained in part by *action identification theory,* which posits that people encode and represent their own actions in terms of different levels of identification (Vallacher and Wegner 1987; Wegner and Vallacher 1986). Consider the ordinary act of calling a hospital to inquire about a friend who has just had minor surgery. The act could be represented as genuinely caring about another person or as the gathering of medical information or as the movements of one's fingers on a phone pad. Caring about the health of a friend entails the moral responsibilities of close relationships and empathy. Gathering medical information involves a cognitive understanding of surgery and outpatient procedures, with faithfulness to factual accuracy. Pushing numbers on a phone pad involves a low-level identity as physical technician, with no moral meaning. Depending upon the level of action identification, the encoding and representation of the actions will differ.

As indicated by their own testimony, those who participated in violent and deadly actions against other people maintained a low-level identity, focusing on the specific actions and techniques that accomplished their task. For those who tortured for the state, that meant extracting information, keeping prisoners alive, and not leaving identifiable marks. For those in the armed wings of the liberation movements, that meant maximizing the destructiveness and lethality of one's operations and then getting away.

As a former MK operative, Robert McBride applied for amnesty for a number of violent attacks, and he described his state of mind while placing explosives that would eventually kill innocent people: "When you do an operation, you are trained, go and lay your charge, initiate it, and retreat. That's your frame of mind. I had been doing that on more than ten occasions: going, gaining entry and laying charges, and retreating. That's what it is. That's what your mind is on" (McBride, October 6, 1999). McBride repeatedly emphasized his mission and the particulars of completing his task. By carefully detailing how he selected a location for his car bomb that would kill three young women and seriously injure scores of others, he revealed an unsettling juxtaposition of the practical and the profane: when setting a car bomb, it is very important to find a good parking spot.[10]

This same perspective was revealed in the testimony of Captain Dirk Coetzee, as he provided a flat, businesslike description of the murder of an ANC activist, Sizwe Khondile, and the disposal of his body afterward. Khondile was handcuffed, abducted, taken to a deserted area, and then shot in the head. Coetzee concluded his testimony with a matter-of-fact story of completing a job:

Each grabbed a hand and a foot, put it onto the pyre of tire and wood, poured petrol on it, and set it alight. . . . and whilst that happened, we were drinking and even having a *braai* [barbecue] next to the fire . . . and a body takes about seven hours to burn to ashes completely, and the chunks of meat, especially the buttocks and the upper part of the legs, had to be turned frequently during the night to make sure that everything burned to ashes. And the next morning, after raking through the rubble to make sure that there was no big pieces of meat or bone left at all, we departed and we all went our own way. (Coetzee, November 7, 1996)

Captain Jeffrey Benzien was similarly focused on his job: "When interrogating a terrorist, you got your information as soon as possible, by using any methods at your disposal. . . . When it came down to getting the job done, I was the person who did it." In evaluating his technique of wet bag torture, Benzien's showed his technical focus with a blinkered professionalism. "I applied it well," he said, "and with caution" (Benzien, July 14, 1997).

In testimony, Gcinikhaya Makoma revealed that while perpetrating the massacre at the St. James Church, his focus was solely on carrying out the operation, using his weapon effectively and making sure he finished his full magazine of ammunition. In testimony after testimony, violent perpetrators disclosed that their focus was on the level of specific actions—completing their job and doing it well—and not on a level where motive and morality could be considered.

The moral irony is that just prior to the violent act, just before beginning a torture session or setting a car bomb or firing an automatic weapon into a group of worshippers, when reflective thought is needed the most for a moral decision, the perpetrator acts without reflection and directs attention and thought only to the particulars of the act. The moment before going into the interrogation room to torture yet another detainee, the perpetrator could refuse and decide not to. Prior to that moment, however, the perpetrator tacitly decides to carry out the torture. Before going out to detonate a car bomb, the perpetrator could refuse and decide not to. The tacit decision to carry out the operation then acts as a hidden trigger for the destructive act, a trigger that then leads to a radical change in the selective focus of the perpetrator.

Aftershocks of Perpetrating Violence
Doubling

To account for the sustained hurtful actions by individuals within a system, Milgram (1974) introduced a dichotomy: the agentic state and the autonomous state. In the agentic state, people conceive of themselves as agents carrying out the plans of others; in the autonomous state, people conceive of themselves as the primary decision makers for their own actions. In a hospital, for example, a nurse may experience the agentic state when administering medication on the instructions of a physician, focusing on the administration of the medication, the proper dosage, the insertion of the hypodermic needle, and the comfort of the patient. In that same hospital, the nurse may experience the autonomous state when taking on the responsibility of scheduling tests for each patient as determined by the demands of the immediate situation. According to this distinction, in a violent organization, people commit hurtful actions when they are in Milgram's agentic state, under the influence of other people within an institutional setting.

Lifton introduced a similar dualism in *The Nazi Doctors* (1986) with the concept of doubling. In doubling, one set of self-concepts lies dormant, while the other remains active in order to carry out the acts of violence. Doubling, then, is a nuanced version of Milgram's distinction, involving a *simultaneity* of different selves rather than a dichotomy. In doubling, the destructive self achieves dominance within the confines of the destructive system, while still remaining connected to and aware of the primary self that operates outside the destructive system. Both automatic and conscious, doubling allows the perpetrator to function effectively within the destructive system, without sacrificing the normal self and without experiencing hesitation.

Many perpetrators in apartheid South Africa gave evidence of such doubling. During the hearings for the Heidelberg Tavern massacre, for example, Luyanda Gqomfa was asked if it made any difference if innocent civilians might be killed. In a poignant moment, Gqomfa replied, "Are you asking me as Luyanda?" When the questioner said "yes," Gqomfa paused. After considering his answer, Gqomfa then recovered, saying, "If you are given an order, it is not about how you feel or how you perceive it, you do not question orders" (Gqomfa, October 27, 1997). In this exchange, the perpetrator briefly demonstrates the doubling of the violence worker, revealing both sets of self-concepts: the primary civilian self (Luyanda) and the destructive military self (Gqomfa). A retrospective demonstration of doubling occurred in testimony during the amnesty hearings for Robert McBride. One of McBride's partners described his frame of mind after the bombing of Magoos Bar, saying "Robert is this big macho, bravado man, but he was extremely remorseful and very depressed for a very long time" (Narkedien, née Apelgren, October 7, 1999).

When confronted by their former victims during the amnesty hearings, perpetrators disclosed how they redefined their self-concepts and how they learned to accommodate their past selves. In doing so, they often revealed the experience of coexisting with two sets of self-concepts: the violent transgressor of the past and the humbled penitent giving testimony. One strategy for managing these two separate sets of self-concepts was to construct a conceptual bridge that connected the two selves but did not integrate them. In this way, the perpetrators acknowledged a link to the violent self of the past without establishing causal liability.

In some cases, perpetrators said they were different people in the past and that they could not even remember the experience of being that past person and performing those acts. In other cases, perpetrators remembered their violence-worker selves but parsed them into different characteristics, based on their roles. Captain Jeffrey Benzien described his role as a designated torturer for the SAP, while also describing himself as "a trained policeman" and "upholder of the law" (Benzien, July 14, 1997). While a sergeant in the SAP, Riaan Bellingan admitted he "coordinated everything" in the killing of seven young antiapartheid activists known as the Guguletu Seven, but he also referred to himself as a junior officer not in charge (Bellingan, November 18, 1997).

During his amnesty hearings for the murder of ANC activist Ashley Kriel, Jeffrey Benzien testified that he had killed Kriel by accident, that his gun went off during the struggle to arrest him. Several of Benzien's torture victims noted, however, that Benzien had a poster of Ashley Kriel displayed in his office with a cross marked on Kriel's face and a

caption that read: "One down . . . to go"—the elliptical bridge suggest-
ing more killings to come. Benzien was asked why he had advertised
the killing as a planned operation if, according to him, the shooting was
accidental. In his answer, Benzien separated a part of himself and exter-
nalized it: "I had a reputation to live up to when interrogating. . . . I
admit that it was surely in very bad taste to have the poster up there, but
in a certain sense it also helped with my interrogation to instill fear into
the persons I interrogated" (July 14, 1997). In this way, Benzien conceived of the torturer's reputation as a force outside of himself.

Another symptom of doubling was drunkenness. Aware that the
destructive self breached the moral principles of the primary self, perpetrators numbed the primary self with alcohol, diminishing awareness
of its connection to the destructive self. In an interview, Thapelo Mbelo
talked about his role in the ambush and killing of the Guguletu Seven: "We
didn't have feelings. It felt just like a day's work had been done. . . . You felt
nothing. The only time when you think something's going to bother you,
the thing to do was to take booze. And you stay drunk. Don't remember
nothing" (Reid and Hoffmann 2000). In some explanations of sustained
violence, emotion has been de-emphasized, with perpetrators depicted as
methodical, bureaucratized technicians, but perpetrator testimony about
the aftershocks of sustained brutality indicates otherwise.

During his hearings in front of the Amnesty Committee, Captain
Dirk Coetzee disclosed profound self-loathing for his involvement in
the murders of a decade and a half earlier, and he spoke directly to the
families he victimized. Referring to the family of Griffiths Mxenge, a
man whose murder he had ordered, Coetzee said, "I don't know how I
ever in my life would be able to forgive a man like Dirk Coetzee, if he's
done to me what I've done to them." Later Coetzee said, "Until the day I
die, my soul won't rest until the truth about the past of the apartheid era
is out to the world" (November 5, 1996). Dirk Coetzee showed genuine
remorse, his words expressing an understanding of his victims' suffering, and he was punished by that understanding.

Staub (1989, 83) proposed a further distinction: dedicated or fanatical
perpetrators who learn to value their cruelty do not need to split themselves or to compartmentalize. Three cases highlighted in this chapter
illustrate this distinction. Jeffrey Benzien and Dirk Coetzee struggled
with their past selves when giving testimony, and they experienced the

effects of having split their self-concepts. Paul van Vuuren, however, maintained his justification for torture and murder, stating that when he killed prisoners, he did so with the conviction that he was defending the country against a terrorist threat, and that he was not sorry for what he did (van Vuuren, February 25, 1997). When interviewed later, van Vuuren spoke of his discomfort at being considered a perpetrator, blaming the amnesty hearings and not the cruelty of his past actions.

Perpetration-Induced PTSD

With many perpetrators, doubling allowed them to function efficiently within their destructive system but not outside this system, within the family. Actively hiding the destructive self and its actions from one's family accrued a psychic cost. Testimony from the perpetrators supported the concept of doubling and the potential for adverse consequences, with the most extreme result being perpetration-induced post-traumatic stress disorder (PTSD) (MacNair 2002), particularly after the destructive system had been dismantled. Afterward, many perpetrators suffered at least some symptoms of PTSD because of the traumatic dividing of the self and the dominance of the destructive self when carrying out their duties.

Extensive testimony to the Amnesty Committee from Jeffrey Benzien's psychologist, Sarah Kotzé, indicated that Benzien experienced PTSD as a perpetrator within the SAP:

> He suffered from intense nightmares, with contents relating to interrogation of people. And he . . . had a few times when he actually sat on his verandah or outside, having a cigarette outside, when he had flashbacks and that he broke out into tears and had an emotional upset because of that. Because he said to me that it felt like he was there again, like he was in that circumstance again, and I considered that a valid description of a flashback. (Kotzé, October 21, 1997)

Captain Willem Mentz of the SAP gave testimony about his role in the killing of a young man suspected of divulging evidence about the SAP's illegal operations. At the time he gave testimony about the killing, Mentz had been receiving psychological therapy for three years, including treatment for PTSD (Mentz, February 24, 1997). More generally, Gibson and Haritos-Fatouros (1986) and Haritos-Fatouros (2003) documented that most of the violence workers involved with torture suffered from PTSD, reporting nightmares, depression, and excessive agitation.

It is not an inappropriate blurring of distinctions to speak of some perpetrators as victims. Certainly in apartheid South Africa, black activists in the liberation movements were both, having been exposed to the daily humiliations and deprivations of apartheid, and in many cases, harassed by the police, detained, and even tortured. Many state perpetrators also considered themselves victimized by the politicians of the National Party and by the demands of their positions, which required them to act with brutality. Archbishop Desmond Tutu, the chair of the TRC, made the then provocative statement that "even the supporters of apartheid were the victims of the vicious system which they implemented and which they supported so enthusiastically." He explained, "In the process of dehumanizing another . . . inexorably the perpetrator was being dehumanized as well" (Tutu 1999b, 103).

These observations are consistent with the findings of Grossman (1995) and Hallock (1998) with veterans of the U.S. war in Vietnam about the relationship between the direct experience of harming and killing defenseless people and later suffering from PTSD. Perpetrator testimony, however, only hints at the sources and sequelae of perpetration-induced PTSD. For an extensive introduction to this kind of PTSD, refer to MacNair's (2002) pioneering review, *Perpetration-Induced Traumatic Stress*.

Conclusions

Collective violence can be understood as having three major steps that perpetrators move through (1) a platform of personal history, consisting of collective knowledge and specific memories, (2) active priming from immediate influences and ongoing organizational directives, and (3) specific triggering events. Although the particulars and complicating factors are different, these three steps characterize violent crimes of allegiance within a mob, within an improvised group guided by political objectives, or within an established hierarchical bureaucracy. Moving through these steps, potential perpetrators perceive themselves as being guided by events, even though each step requires a clear decision and creates an interaction between the perpetrator and the organization, influencing both the individual and the group.

With sustained violence, perpetrators join their organizations, proceed through training and indoctrination, and then move incrementally from smaller, less-violent operations to increasingly lethal violations. The systemic priming in a closed professional setting encourages beliefs and actions that further maintain the collective violence: a complex of reasons for engaging in illegal activities, a belief in the goodness of one's actions, and ingenuity in conducting the specific operations. Within a hierarchical system, the trigger for violence is often not a dramatic event but rather the assignment of a specific case or operation. While actually carrying out violence, perpetrators maintain a low-level identity, focusing on the specifics of the operations. In apartheid South Africa, state violence workers involved in torture interrogation focused on inflicting as much torment as possible, as quickly as possible, to extract information without killing the victims or leaving identifiable marks. For saboteurs and killers in the liberation movements, the focus was on efficiently setting their explosives, maximizing damage, and getting away.

In addition to the routinization of violence, perpetrators are motivated by encouragement from their leadership, direct instructions from people higher up in the chain of command, social bonding within their subgroup, and rewards for missions completed. In the words of Colonel Eugene de Kock, his men were motivated by "tacit but powerful support . . . from the beneficiaries of apartheid privilege" (Gobodo-Madikizela 2003, 110). When planning and preparing their actions, managers of collective violence do not merely follow orders. A clear pattern was evident in the bureaucratic violence of apartheid South Africa: the higher the position of the perpetrator in the organizational hierarchy, the more vague the instructions; the lower the position, the more specific the instructions. In the middle, there is considerable room for initiative and creativity, dispelling the illusion of the follower as a thoughtless functionary simply obeying orders. Over time, however, many perpetrators experience inner conflict about their actions.

Multiple Truths

Regarding the study of perpetrators, the final report of the TRC voiced a caution: "In addressing motives, it is important to be mindful that reasons are likely to be pluralistic, overlapping, multi-layered and contingent on particular and local circumstances" (TRC 1999c, 283). The juxtaposition of different perpetrator testimonies and the introduction of forensic evidence provided more complete information about the crimes of apartheid but also resulted in puzzling incongruities. The confrontations between perpetrators and victims during the amnesty hearings revealed enduring insights about collective violence, but they also revealed honest and profound discrepancies between the memories of the perpetrators and the memories of the victims. These incongruities and discrepancies, in turn, created complexities in the explanations of the perpetrators' actions that could only be accommodated by the existence of multiple and contradictory truths. The following chapter examines these complexities and their implications.

4

Uncovering Truth

Confronting Perpetrators and Victims

The testimony given by perpetrators to the Amnesty Committee of the TRC revealed the kinds of explanations that people give when their very lives depend on perceived truthfulness. The perpetrators recounted their misdeeds to persuade others to grant them amnesty and to organize their past experiences so they could coexist with memories of their former selves. The hearings proceeded as a real-life suspense story: perpetrators testified before the TRC and then waited—sometimes more than a year—to hear whether or not they were granted amnesty.

This chapter analyzes the types of truth that emerged and clashed during the TRC hearings, uncovering the assumptions and implications of multiple truths. The very real consequences of the TRC and other truth commissions on people's lives argue persuasively for such an analysis. Moreover, the widespread destruction of documents by repressive governments only amplifies the urgency for understanding the qualities of testimonial truth. In South Africa, for example, three years before the TRC began its work, the National Intelligence Services of the South African government destroyed almost fifty tons of paper and microfilm records of their illegal activities during apartheid, an assault on evidence so massive that furnaces had to be used. As a result, much historical truth about the administration of apartheid now resides only in the accounts of the state perpetrators (Bundy 2000; TRC 1999a; Tutu 1999a).[1]

Two features of the South African TRC provided a distinctive opportunity to study the process of telling truths and discerning the different types of truth that constitute explanations of wrongdoing. As noted earlier, one distinctive feature of the TRC hearings was that the testimony was public, televised, and videotaped, with transcripts available on the TRC website. Second, the victims were able to confront their tormentors and ask questions, encouraging the perpetrators to analyze and to question their initial explanations.

The findings in this chapter are based on analysis of testimony from the full set of perpetrators and victims listed in the appendix, but as in the previous chapter, this chapter presents a subset of illustrative cases to exemplify the patterns of narrative truth-telling in the context of truth commissions. In particular, the chapter continues with the perpetrators highlighted previously: Captain Jeffrey Benzien of the SAP; Paul van Vuuren of the state security forces; Captain Dirk Coetzee, who commanded the security headquarters at Vlakplaas; Robert McBride of Umkhonto we Sizwe (MK)—the armed wing of the ANC; members of a mob who killed Amy Biehl; and the members of the PAC who carried out the St. James Church massacre and the Heidelberg Tavern massacre. In addition, other highlighted cases involve Captain William Mentz of the government security forces, MK unit commander John Dube, and the former president of South Africa, F. W. de Klerk.

Defining Truths

Officially, the TRC identified four types of truth in its final report: (1) factual or forensic truth, (2) personal and narrative truth, (3) social or dialogic truth, and (4) healing and restorative truth. Factual-forensic truth drew on legal, medical, and scientific evidence and focused on canonical categories of inquiry: who, what, when, where, and how—but not *why*. With regard to narrative truth, the TRC was mandated by the government to collect "people's perceptions, stories, myths, and experiences" in an effort to "restore the human and civil dignity of victims by granting them an opportunity to relate *their own accounts* of the violations of which they are victims" (TRC 1999a, 112). During the full TRC hearings, both victims and perpetrators narrated their personal experiences during apartheid.

Social or dialogic truth emerged from the interactions among participants at the hearings: judges, advocates, witnesses, victims, and perpetrators—"the truth of experience that is established through interaction, discussion, and debate" (TRC 1999a, 113). With appealing circularity, the TRC report said that social truth is "the process whereby the truth was reached" (114). So the process of revealing social truth is also social truth, with an emphasis on affirming one's dignity and integrity. Central to social truth is the idea of multiple perspectives, with the implication that they are mutually respected and valued—and potentially reconcilable. The philosopher Martin Buber (2002) locates such a dialogue in the "realm of between," which resides "on the far side of the subjective, on this side of the objective, on the narrow ridge where I and Thou meet" (243). Healing and restorative truth contributed to the reparation of damages in the past, locating "facts and what they mean within the context of human relationships" (114). The main feature of healing truth is acknowledgment: placing information on the public record and affirming that a person's suffering is real and worthy of attention. Ideally, all four types of truth had to emerge in the amnesty process, and the granting of amnesty often depended on more than one type of truth.[2]

Captain Jeffrey Benzien of the security forces eventually contributed to all four types of truth during his extensive hearings for amnesty. As described earlier, Benzien was charged with the killing of antiapartheid activist, Ashley Kriel, and the torture of prisoners during his time with the "the terrorist tracking unit" of the SAP, a unit that was responsible for finding activists and their weapons. In extended testimony, Benzien *narrated* his account of the events, providing as many *facts* as he could remember, and then faced five of his former torture victims, one at a time, revealing *dialogic* truth during the lengthy exchanges with these men. *Healing* truth emerged with Benzien's struggle to understand himself, while also acknowledging his victims, which proved necessary because Benzien often could not remember the particulars of events and was, at times, factually inaccurate (Benzien, July 14–15, 1997).

Confronting Truths

The previous chapter presented the case of Amy Biehl, the young Fulbright scholar from California who was killed by a mob in Guguletu in 1993, as South Africa was transitioning from apartheid to democracy. Four years later, the young men convicted of Amy Biehl's murder applied for amnesty and went before the Amnesty Committee. One of the main explanatory themes was that the mob had just been exhorted to violence by leaders of the Pan African Students Organization (PASO) and that they were strongly motivated to act on the words of these leaders. Although no political organizations explicitly ordered the killing of Amy Biehl, and none condoned it afterward, all four applicants received amnesty for committing a politically motivated crime.

To some, the facts of the Biehl case conflicted with the favorable amnesty decision, and the reasoning of the Amnesty Committee appeared convoluted (e.g., Jeffrey 1999; van de Vijver 2000). But such critiques focused only on factual-forensic truth and ignored the existence of narrative and restorative truths. From the perpetrators' perspective, the killing of Amy Biehl was a direct result of the political pressures at the time and the unlikely appearance of a young white woman in Guguletu. The decisive moment in this case occurred at the end of the hearings, when Amy Biehl's parents rose to address the Amnesty Committee and the perpetrators. They spoke about their daughter's energetic optimism, her commitment to South Africa, and her strong belief in social justice. They concluded their statements by saying that they did not oppose amnesty, adding that if Amy had not been killed, she would have embraced the amnesty process (Biehl and Biehl, July 9, 1997). In this case, the subsequent decision to grant amnesty to the killers of Amy Biehl elevated healing-restorative truth—at the expense of factual-forensic truth. In fact, many of the dilemmas faced by the TRC arose from the conflict between gathering forensic truth and collecting narratives to promote reconciliation, which could lead to intractably different interpretations (Simpson 2002, 238).

Robert McBride applied for amnesty for setting off a car bomb outside a crowded nightclub, killing three young women and seriously injuring sixty others. With McBride and his associates, narrative truth and dialogic truth appeared most pertinent: the opportunity for the victims and their families to tell their stories and to confront the perpetrators. During the McBride hearings, consensus was not reached—far from it. There was no meeting of minds and no healing. Both sides gave their perspectives, sometimes with considerable insult. The hearings went on for two weeks, and near the end, the daughter of one of the slain women said that Robert McBride's testimony had changed her position from supporting amnesty to opposing it (van der Linde, October 13,

1999). In this case, narrative and dialogic truth conflicted with healing-restorative truth. Robert McBride was also granted amnesty.

The cases of Amy Biehl and Robert McBride highlight a fundamental question that the TRC never addressed: What happens when different types of truth contradict each other? To borrow the strong words of Derrida (1998), the different categories of truth may create "a series of cleavages that will incessantly divide every atom of our lexicon" (1).[3]

Parallax Truth

The confrontation of multiple truths during the TRC hearings can be interpreted through the principles of *parallax*. In physics, parallax is the apparent displacement of an object against its background, caused by a change in the position of the observer. A star, for example, appears to be in a different position depending on the location of the astronomer. Moreover, by observing parallax and performing the appropriate calculations, one can precisely specify the position of the distant object. In other words, parallax creates two different perceptions of the same distant object, *and* it can be used to locate the object in question. In fact, only by considering the different perceptions can we know the nature of the elusive object.

The physical principles of parallax can be transposed to the problem of multiple truths, creating the concept of parallax truth. This concept can then be applied to characterize the discrepant perspectives narrated in testimony, while also revealing their irreconcilable differences. In fact, parallax truth *requires* multiple accounts of the same events in order to support judgments about the veracity of the accounts. Although parallax truth arises from confrontation, it differs from dialogic truth in that its defining feature is the unbridgeable gap among different perspectives. Indeed, there is parallax in the concept of parallax truth. In one sense, parallax provides a method for arriving at a version of truth, but in another sense, parallax is a difference in perspectives that is never reconciled and will never go away (Žižek 2006). Did Jeffrey Benzien *plan* to kill Ashley Kriel, as his sisters testified, or was the killing the result of reflexive judgments during a physical struggle, as Benzien testified? The facts and the narratives suggested both. In truth commissions, events often remain unreconciled, and judges must agree on a satisfactory version of the events, often within the space between the discrepant accounts.

The social psychologist Roy Baumeister has referred to the discrepancy between perpetrators and victims as the *magnitude gap* (Baumeister 1997; Baumeister, Stillwell, and Wotman 1990). For the prisoner being interrogated through torture, there is nothing else but the body in torment (Améry 1980). For the conscientious perpetrator, there are other considerations: extracting information, not leaving identifiable marks, staying within time constraints. From the victim's perspective, the violence is incomprehensible and senseless. From the perpetrator's perspective, it is rational and motivated.[4] Jeffrey Benzien, for example, described his relationship with one of his torture victims in the following way: "Apart from those two occasions where I questioned him in an unconventional way, we built up an excellent rapport" (Benzien, July 14, 1997). The victim did not agree.

Niclo Pedro, a former prisoner of Benzien's, testified that he told Benzien he had swallowed a letter with important information about his contacts in South Africa. Pedro then said Benzien tried to retrieve the letter by inserting a stick into his anus, telling Pedro he would extract the letter from his stomach. Earlier, however, when confronted by Pedro's advocate, Benzien adamantly denied doing anything invasive with the prisoner's anus. He testified that he took Niclo Pedro to a bathroom, encouraged him to defecate on some newspaper, and then searched through the feces on the newspaper (Benzien, July 15, 1997; Pedro, October 20–21, 1997). Aside from disclosing the unglamorous aspects of security work, this incident revealed an obvious gap between the remembered experience of the victim and that of the perpetrator. Although there was no method for closing the gap, one can discern narrative truth by characterizing the *contours* of the gap. Based on Benzien's narrative and the conflicting narrative of his victim, Niclo Pedro, we know that Benzien engaged in *some* kind of unusually intrusive act with the prisoner's feces following interrogation. Ultimately, the Amnesty Committee decided that although Benzien's memory was faulty, he fully disclosed what he was able to remember about the events that day.

The hearings for Robert McBride revealed the clash of narrative truths during the confrontations between McBride and the family members whose relatives were killed in his car bombing of Magoos Bar. To Sharon Welgemoed, McBride was a terrorist who blew up a bar filled with innocent young people who had nothing to do with enforcing apartheid. To the ANC, McBride was a freedom fighter who adhered to the principle of not harming children by bombing a nightclub and who hastened the end of apartheid by bringing violence into the white areas of South Africa (McBride, October 12, 1999; Welgemoed, October 12–13, 1999).

Consider the magnitude gap in the case of Paul van Vuuren, the member of the security forces who specialized in torture interrogation of prisoners through the use of electrical shocks. One of the prisoners he tortured was Scheepers Morudu, who eventually testified against van Vuuren at his amnesty hearings. Van Vuuren admitted to torturing Morudu, and he carefully described his methods, but he also said that he could not remember where he applied the shocks to Morudu, proposing that it was probably the hands and legs. The *first* point Morudu made under oath was that the shocks were applied not to his hands or his legs but to his genitals.

The case of van Vuuren also provides an illustration that narrative truth does not arise from just any narrative account. If an accounting of events is appropriately structured but missing central actions, it can be in narrative form without providing narrative truth. Van Vuuren described his interrogation of Scheepers Morudu but insisted that Morudu was not detained after the torture interrogation (van Vuuren, February 25, 1997). Morudu said he was beaten and tortured by Paul van Vuuren, and then detained for two months (Morudu, February 26, 1997). Factual evidence and other narrative accounts revealed that Morudu had been detained for at least one week after the torture. Van Vuuren's account that Morudu was not detained at all, therefore, fell *outside* the contours of parallax truth, as defined by factual evidence, Morudu's testimony, and the accounts of others involved in the incident. Situated beyond these established contours, van Vuuren's account could reasonably be judged as not contributing to narrative truth.

Serious discrepancies between the memories of perpetrators and the memories of victims occurred throughout the amnesty hearings of the TRC. As the hearings proceeded, in one instance after another, the memories of the perpetrators came into direct conflict with the memories of the victims. For example, as Jeffrey Benzien's former victims listened to his sworn testimony about his illegal activities during apartheid, they became increasingly distressed about his description of their torture interrogations. Also distressing to his former victims was what Benzien could not remember. In two days of testimony—in free recall and in answering questions—Benzien cited his inability to remember more than sixty times (Benzien, July 14–15, 1997). He could not remember who helped him during his interrogations, the length of time he interrogated prisoners, or the particular methods (beatings, repeated suffocation, or suspending prisoners in handcuffs so their feet could not touch the ground). Each of his former victims expressed deep suspicion at Benzien's version of the interrogations and his failure to recall events that they considered central to their mistreatment.

In his controversial minority report, TRC Commissioner Wynand Malan criticized the bias in favor of the victim's point of view, saying, "Exaggeration is a natural consequence of human suffering" (TRC 1999c, 441). Malan's statement is oddly insensitive but also informative. What exactly is exaggerated? It is not experiential, narrative truth, but factual information: the duration of an incident, the number of shots fired, the number of people involved. Malan was referring to the magnitude gap of Baumeister but giving primacy to the perspective of those who had not physically suffered. The majority response of the TRC to Malan's minority statement created its own gap in the assessment of the Amnesty Committee when it declared Malan's statement to be "impertinent and startlingly inappropriate" (459), even though they cited the work of Baumeister (1997), who also cautioned against automatically accepting the recall of victims without critical analysis. In fact, we cannot rely solely on the narratives of the victims *or* the perpetrators. We need both to define parallax truth, which only occurs during the confrontation between victim and perpetrator. During the amnesty hearings, as the victim questioned and the perpetrator answered, a gap appeared that did not close, and this gap revealed its contours through the dialogue. As observers of the confrontation, we gain a greater understanding of the events through the memory lapses of the perpetrator and the memory sharpness and elaboration of the victim.

The TRC managed such conflicts case by case, yet often the four truths created an unstated implication: factual-forensic truth maintained a separate status from the other three types of truth. The specifics of who, what, when, where, and how remained essential elements of a comprehensive history: the identities of the perpetrators, the specific events themselves, the dates and times of the events, the sequence, the locations, and the methods. The testimony of Captain Willem Mentz illustrated the separate status of factual truth in the form of medical evidence. Mentz was an officer in the government security forces who applied for amnesty for the murder of Brian Ngqulunga, a man he suspected of spying on the security forces and providing information to the armed wing of the ANC. Mentz told of going with several of his men to abduct Ngqulunga and to transport him to the site where he would be shot and his body disposed of. He described sitting on top of Ngqulunga with the other men, while Ngqulunga lay facedown in the back of the vehicle. When they reached their destination, Mentz said they hit Ngqulunga "to make him lose consciousness as quickly as possible" (Mentz, February 25, 1997).

Near the end of Mentz's testimony, Judge Wilson of the Amnesty Committee compared the forensic medical evidence describing Ngqulunga's injuries to Mentz's narrative description of forcefully restraining Ngqulunga during his transport and then quickly knocking him out. Using the rhetorical strategy of the list, Judge Wilson described the condition of Ngqulunga's body before he was shot: fractures of the first, second, and third ribs on both sides of the body, fractures of both clavicles, a collapsed lung, a lacerated upper lobe of the left lung, a ruptured heart, ruptured small intestines, and a ruptured bladder. Judge Wilson then averred that the factual-forensic evidence contradicted Mentz's narrative of an efficient operation of abduction and execution and supported a narrative of a torture-beating that preceded the murder (Wilson, February 25, 1997).

Perpetrators themselves need to confront the narratives of victims in order to learn about their own explanatory narratives. When Jeffrey Benzien was asked what kind of man tortures other human beings, his answer, which was the truth for him, was that he had asked himself that question many times and that ultimately *he did not know*. But as the hearings proceeded, the men he tortured let him know, narrating their own accounts and challenging Benzien's narratives in the process, defining the contours of the space between Benzien's narratives and theirs (Benzien, July 14–15, 1997).

In general, the narratives of perpetrators disclosed how they redefined their self-destructed lives and how they learned to coexist with their past selves through new self-narratives. One dominant strategy for the perpetrators of apartheid was to construct *two* separate self-narratives, one for the violent transgressor of the past and one for the humbled penitent giving testimony, with a *bridge narrative* connecting the two selves but not integrating them. Such a strategy appears to follow the literary counsel of A. B. Yehoshua (2003) that "if a story has the right ending, it can be about anything" (301).

Explaining Truth

In his book *Why?* (2006), Charles Tilly discussed four overlapping categories of reasons that people invoke to explain themselves: conventions, stories, codes, and technical accounts. *Conventions* are well-accepted, abbreviated reasons for transgression or misfortune, offering cryptic, causal explanations: "My train was late," "I didn't get much sleep last night," "Traffic was terrible," and the ubiquitous, "It's all for the best."[5] We accept conventions for small matters but find them analytically unsatisfying for unusual events. In Tilly's framework, *stories* are explanatory narratives, integrating a causal explanation for one's behavior, often for unusual or distinctive events. Stories maintain chronology, simplify cause and effect, and concentrate on a few central characters and actions. People expand reasons into stories when conventions are not appropriate or adequate. *Codes* are specialized sets of categories: procedures, rules of interpretation, and diagnostic categories. In medicine, codes catalog symptoms, provide standardized vocabularies, establish relations between diagnosis and treatment, and set standards for good practice. An explanation based in medical code, for example, would tell how symptoms fit a diagnosis and how the chosen treatment plan for the diagnosis conforms to accepted practice. Reasons make reference to codes by citing their conformity to these codes, invoking the logic of appropriateness. *Technical accounts* provide causal explanations rooted in a body of knowledge, such as medicine, engineering, or psychology, providing causal explanations within a systematic, specialized discipline. Of the four categories of reasons, only stories provide motivations and only stories address morality; conventions, codes, and technical accounts do not.

Tilly's four reasons can be superimposed on the four types of truth codified by the TRC. Factual-forensic truth consists of facts, medical and legal codes, and technical accounts. Narrative truth consists of elaborated stories, which are more comprehensive than standard stories. Narrative truth, which may begin as a standard story, needs to account for incremental decisions, secondary actors and actions, motivations, mistakes, and pertinent details in order to satisfy the requirements of full disclosure. Perpetrators could not get by on standard narratives alone because narratives reduce, and full disclosure requires more.[6] Conventions are offered when participants want to avoid the intimacy of personal narratives. Dialogic truth and healing truth consist of competing and cooperating elaborated stories that directly influence the relationships among the participants.

Why do some explanations fail to convince? In Tilly's terms, one reason is that a convention is offered when a story is expected. During the amnesty hearings, explanations for complex events were often judged inadequate when they consisted primarily of conventions. For example, in telling why he attacked the St. James Church, killing eleven worshippers, Bassie Mkhumbuzi said simply, "This attack would bring down the spirit of the oppressors" (Mkhumbuzi, July 9, 1997). To justify the Heidelberg Tavern massacre, Luyanda Gqomfa opined, "In every war there are casualties" (Gqomfa, October 27, 1997). Captain Jeffrey Benzien explained his torture of prisoners conventionally: "Due to my unorthodox conduct, we made a big difference in the combating of terror" (Benzien, July 14, 1997). Adriaan Vlok, the former minister of law and order, justified the illegal bombing of a community center in the middle of Johannesburg by saying, "We were in a war situation" (Vlok, July 21, 1998). Each of these conventional explanations was then challenged by the Amnesty Committee as inadequate, and each perpetrator was asked to provide more testimony, primarily in the form of a personal narrative.

In some cases, explanations fail when they *violate* commonly held conventions. Jeffrey Benzien's psychologist, Sarah Maria Kotzé, encountered resistance from the TRC when she tried to explain Benzien's memory lapses as resulting from PTSD, as a victim.

> I think he became a victim when he was moved from a position as a very successful policeman where he did an excellent job into a position where he had to do things that he didn't like doing. I think that is when his

inner turmoil started. . . . It victimized him in the sense that he had to go home every day and live a normal life with his family and he could not tell his family what he had done the whole day, or what he was involved in. He became secretive, he couldn't talk about things, he became a victim of his job. (Kotzé, October 21, 1997)

Kotzé's explanation was forcefully challenged by Judge Bernard Ngoepe and Judge Andrew Wilson of the Amnesty Committee because she violated a convention especially pertinent to the Committee: that state perpetrators were not victims.

In addition, by basing her reasons on clinical practice and social science, Kotzé compounded the difficulty of violating conventions. Unlike the natural or physical sciences, social science faces the distinctive problem of having to explain processes that nonspecialists already explain through conventions and stories. Many nonpsychologists possess what they consider to be an adequate understanding of love, guilt, anger, grief, trauma, and memory. To complicate matters, social science may go beyond offering a specialized account and may actually contradict the prevailing conventions and stories, thereby encountering even more conflict and disbelief (Tilly 2006).

The reasons given by Amy Biehl's killers were challenged because they violated conventions about mob violence. The evidence leader Robin Brink expressed one of these conventions when he described the mob as a single, unthinking mass—"a pack of sharks smelling blood" (Brink, July 8, 1997). The perpetrators rejected such a characterization, stating that they were active members of PASO following the instructions of their leaders, that they were aware of their actions, and that they were responding in part to an unprovoked assault by the SAP on some of their friends. Indeed, as the mob attacked Amy Biehl, Mongesi Manqina paused to assess the situation and to ask another person for a knife.

When Captain Dirk Coetzee of the security forces provided a flat description of the murder of ANC activist Sizwe Khondile and the disposal of his body afterward, his narrative violated restorative truth because of its very flatness. Observers often look for honest emotion to validate narrative truth, and when it is absent, the narrative becomes suspect. If the testimony conveys that the perpetrator is ashamed or even distraught, the narrative takes on more value as a form of confessional truth.

Narrative Limits

Truth commissions are often mandated to promote national unity, which is then extrapolated into a mandate for a unity of truths—even though an agreement of different narratives is incompatible with multiple truths, which exist simultaneously and in contradiction. In an effort to unify the narrative themes, truth commissions generally limit the individual narratives in three distinct ways: with binary distinctions that do not account for complexity and overlap, with macronarratives that categorize the individual stories, and with frames that inhibit narrative flux.

With the TRC, the moral binary of victim and perpetrator limited the narratives by resisting the possibility of being both, simultaneously. Yet in complex, systemic violations of human rights, participants may be perpetrators as well as victims, although not in equal portions. Moreover, responsibility for these violations of human rights is not either-or and cannot be clearly assigned to the foot soldiers or the managers or the political leaders. Responsibility is distributed in ways that can only be discovered through multiple narratives.

In its effort to characterize the responsibility of President F. W. de Klerk during the final years of apartheid, the TRC graphically illustrated the shortcomings of binary distinctions, failing to consider the discrepancy in narratives as a source of narrative truth. President de Klerk professed no role in fomenting violence among different liberation groups, in the funding of death squads, and in the condoning of torture. Well-informed commanders on the ground, however, disagreed. Most notably, Colonel Eugene de Kock narrated an account of de Klerk as being directly involved in overseeing the planned violence, the death squads, and the torture of antiapartheid activists (de Kock 1998, 277–283; de Kock, July 29–30, 1998). The original findings of the TRC about President de Klerk were blocked by a court injunction, in part, because they emphasized unambiguously the commanders' narratives of de Klerk's direct responsibility, while ignoring de Klerk's narrative. Instead of specifying a version of narrative truth, the gap in the discrepant narratives appeared only as a solid black surface covering two-thirds of a page in the final volume of the 1999 TRC report, a somber Rothko signifying only incompleteness (TRC 1999c, 225).

In analyzing bias, simple binaries also do not apply. With the TRC, an analysis of the amnesty applications, the testimony, and the amnesty decisions revealed that the overall process did not favor black applicants over white applicants or vice versa—nothing so simply specified. Instead, the analysis revealed a complex bias in favor of narratives that invoked well-structured organizations, chains of command, and defined missions and against narratives of smaller organizations, loose alliances, and spontaneity.

More broadly, judgments of narrative truth are often shaped in accordance with existing (and unquestioned) macronarratives. With the TRC, prevailing political and religious themes transfigured the particulars of the individual narratives. As summarized by televised reports of the TRC hearings, the human rights violations in apartheid South Africa fit neatly into a global narrative of national wrongdoing, a narrative that could also account for human rights violations in Soviet-dominated Eastern Europe. In addition, the TRC was presided over by an archbishop of the Anglican Church and infused with the desire for Christian forgiveness, with an assumed macronarrative of confession, repentance, and redemption (Posel and Simpson 2002b).

Finally, the pressure to establish an acceptable story made it difficult for the TRC to deviate from a narrative outline once it had been established. Consider the case of Sicelo Dlomo, a young antiapartheid activist assassinated in January 1988 and left under a tree on the outskirts of Soweto. For nine years, it was assumed he was killed by the Security Police, and he was regarded in the liberation movement as a hero of the antiapartheid struggle. In early 1997, however, the TRC investigation unit uncovered shocking news: Sicelo Dlomo was killed by four members of his own ANC-MK unit, and the MK members who applied for amnesty said they killed him because he was a police informer (Pigou 2002b). The main applicant, MK unit commander John Dube, presented his story to the TRC, condemning Dlomo. During the hearings, however, it was disclosed that no one in the ANC ordered the killing of Sicelo Dlomo, that Dlomo was missing a large amount of cash after John Dube killed him, that Dube was himself a police informer, and that there was no evidence to support that Dlomo was cooperating with the pro-apartheid police (Dube, February 16–17, 1999; Makhubu, February 17–18, 1999; Tshabalala, February 18, 1999; Zungu, February 18, 1999). Instead, it appeared that John Dube decided to kill Dlomo for his own, unspecified reasons. The Amnesty Committee, however, decided *not* to include the new narrative outline that emerged as a result of forensic evidence and the conflicting personal narratives, choosing instead the unsupported version of events that Dube proposed in order to gain amnesty, which he received.[7] The double turn of events in the case of Sicelo Dlomo's murder challenged the strategy of interpreting narratives as inflexible frames, instead of interpreting them as reverberating interactions among participants (Harris 2007). As the dissenting TRC Commissioner Wynand Malan pointed out, "A shared understanding of our history requires an understanding of different perspectives, not the building of a new national myth" (TRC 1999c, 442).

Parallax Truth Revisited

How, then, do we gather the diverse, individual stories from truth commissions and weave them into coherent national narratives for reformed countries? One answer comes from the integrative concept of parallax truth, which recognizes the unbridgeable gap among conflicting narratives and addresses the tension between coherence and multiplicity. Parallax truth eliminates the binary opposition of conflicting narratives and replaces it with a description of the contours of the gap and the overlap among the narratives. A telling example of parallax truth is revealed in the *second* version of the findings on President de Klerk's responsibility during the last years of apartheid. In this later version, the contours and overlap in the conflicting narratives are specified. Four years after the initial five-volume TRC report was published, volume 6 still depicted the gap in narratives as a flat black surface covering an entire page (TRC 2003a, 59) but then followed this image with a set of specific findings characterizing the conflicting narratives of President de Klerk and the field commanders (60–62). Indeed, the depicted gap created parallax with these subsequent findings, with the inconsistency of the two representations accurately reflecting the truth-finding process and narrative truth itself.

One stated goal of the TRC was to elicit "as much truth as possible about past atrocities" (TRC 1999a, 120), but the most enduring result of the TRC may be the documentation of what was *not* true. Truth commissions function as national lie detectors, as polygraphs using multiple measures to identify falsehoods in mainstream national narratives (Posel 2002). After the TRC, for example, the National Party could no longer claim that police hit squads did not exist, that torture was carried out by only a few delinquent members of the security forces, that only terrorists were targeted by the apartheid government, and that the state was not involved in fomenting violence among different liberation groups. On a national level, detecting what is not truth may be a more realistic goal of truth commissions than finding truth (Ignatieff 1996). Within the gap in narratives, we can make judgments and try to locate truth through principles of parallax. Or we can characterize truth by describing the contours of the gap among narratives, and leave it at that. But if a narrative lies *outside* the gap, we can state clearly that it does not represent narrative truth. Without the TRC, it is quite possible that falsehoods generally accepted by the white minority would continue to be debated to this day. As a result, one of the TRC's greatest achievements was to discredit the apartheid regime in the eyes of its beneficiaries (Mamdani 2000), fundamentally reshaping how apartheid will be construed by future generations of South Africans.[8]

Looking toward Reconciliation

During the amnesty hearings, as perpetrators and victims offered new facts and narratives about the crimes of apartheid and as the confrontations between victims and perpetrators defined the contours of acceptable discrepancies, a new collective memory of apartheid South Africa coalesced (Gibson 2004). In this way, reconciliation began. Confronting testimony promoted reconciliation by encouraging the perpetrators to understand the pain and humiliation caused by their crimes, while allowing victims to hear directly from the perpetrators about their own motivations and responsibilities.

Confronting testimony could also block reconciliation. Incomplete disclosure, intractable differences in narrative truths, the predictable occurrence of the magnitude gap, the clash of different kinds of truth, and the inconsistent emphases applied to these different kinds of truth all combined to create impediments to reconciling. Focusing on personal reconciliation between perpetrators and victims and within the individuals themselves, the following chapter addresses the complexities of reconciliation, analyzing the testimony that promoted reconciliation and the testimony that blocked it.

5

Reconciling Testimony

A Work in Progress

The most resonant conclusion about reconciliation from the amnesty hearings is as fraught as it is direct: sincere disclosure is necessary for reconciliation. In testimony after testimony, when victims and their families responded to the perpetrators during the amnesty hearings, they reiterated the need to know who perpetrated the destructive acts, who gave the orders, what was done, and why. When perpetrators who were directly implicated in the crimes failed to testify or when those who testified failed to make sincere disclosure, victims and their families rejected reconciliation and recommended against amnesty.

The parliamentary act that created the TRC showed foresight in joining truth and reconciliation in the title of the commission and in placing truth first. Without institutional requirements to enforce truth gathering and without diligent efforts from the perpetrators to provide truth, it is unreasonable, even inhumane, to expect reconciliation from the victimized. For victims to begin the process of reconciling with the perpetrators, they needed to perceive the perpetrators' efforts as honest—and difficult. The testimony could be flawed and missing critical details, but if victims witnessed a sincere attempt at full disclosure, then reconciliation became possible. Contrition, however expressed by the perpetrators, also promoted reconciliation. Denial, protective revisions, and an unwillingness to confront transgressions were destructive to the process of reconciliation.

With its limited time frame and mandate, the TRC focused on promoting the beginnings of reconciliation, encouraging further work by individuals and organizations in parallel with the hearings and afterward. The TRC was acutely aware of its limitations in bringing about reconciliation, describing the hearings as "beacons of hope," "signposts on the long road," and "warnings of pitfalls," but not as a means for completing the reconciliation process (TRC 1999c, 350). As the hearings proceeded, the chair of the TRC, Archbishop Desmond Tutu, repeatedly reminded his fellow South Africans that the TRC was mandated to *promote* national unity and reconciliation, not to *achieve* these goals (Tutu 1999b). The TRC did not provide a forum for reconciliation so much as a platform to initiate efforts for reconciling that would then continue outside the amnesty hearings.

During the amnesty hearings, the confrontations between victims and perpetrators were uniquely revealing about the requirements and possibilities of reconciliation. In ordinary life when we are wronged, we want our day in court—to confront the person or groups who perpetrated the injustice against us. The TRC institutionalized this confrontation. To be considered for amnesty, perpetrators were required to face any of their former victims who chose to confront them. This confrontation promoted reconciliation by encouraging the perpetrators to understand the pain and humiliation caused by their crimes, while allowing victims to hear directly from the perpetrators about their own motivations and responsibilities.

This chapter analyzes the testimony provided by perpetrators during the amnesty hearings and the interactions between the perpetrators and their former victims as they sought to understand each other and the crimes that had been committed. The primary source materials for this analysis were seventy-two hours of videotaped testimony and a complete set of transcripts from twelve major cases decided by the Amnesty Committee, with testimony from thirty-four perpetrators and thirty-seven victims (Table 5.1). This analysis informs the process of reconciliation between perpetrators and victims, as well as the individual efforts made by perpetrators to reconcile their past selves and their present lives. The primary focus is on personal reconciliation between victims and perpetrators: the interactions that promoted reconciliation during the amnesty hearings and the obstacles that blocked it.

TABLE 5.1: *Specific Cases Studied in the Qualitative Analysis of Reconciling Testimony*

CASE 1, PART 1: Killing of Griffiths Mxenge and Sizwe Khondile Hearings: November 5–7, 1996, Durban
    Applicant: Dirk Coetzee
    Victim: Charity Khondile, mother of Sizwe Khondile, as represented by her advocate

CASE 1, PART 2: Killing of Griffiths Mxenge
    Hearings: January 20–21, 1997, Johannesburg
    Applicants: Dirk Coetzee, David Tshikalanga, Almond Nofomela
    Victim: Akanyang Daniel Maponya

CASES 2 AND 3: Killing of Joe Tsele; killing of Brian Ngqulunga and interrogation of Scheepers Morudu
    Hearings: February 24–26, 1997, Cape Town
    Applicants: Brigadier Jan Hattingh Cronje, Captain Jacques Hechter, Captain Willem Mentz, Warrant Officer Paul van Vuuren
    Victims: Legina Mabela, Tholakele Catherine Ngqulunga (wife of Brian Ngqulunga), Scheepers Morudu

CASE 4: Murder of Amy Biehl
    Hearings: July 8 and 9, 1997, Cape Town
    Applicants: Mongesi Manqina, Easy Nofemela, Ntombeki Peni, Vusumzi Ntamo
    Victims: Parents of Amy Biehl, Linda Biehl and Peter Biehl

CASE 5: St. James Church massacre
    Hearings: July 9–10, 1997, Cape Town
    Applicants: Bassie Mkhumbuzi, Thobela Mlambisa, Gcinikhaya Christopher Makoma
    Victims: Lorenzo Victor Smith, David Jacobus Ackerman

CASE 6, PART 1: Killing of Ashley Kriel and torture of activists
    Hearings: July 14–16, 1997, Cape Town
    Applicant: Captain Jeffrey T. Benzien
    Victims: Tony Yengeni (demonstration of "wet bag" torture), Ashley Forbes, Gary Kruse, Bongani Jonas, Peter Anthony Jacobs, Michelle Ashua (sister of the late Ashley Kriel)

CASE 6, PART 2: Killing of Ashley Kriel and torture of activists
    Hearings: October 20–21, 1997, Cape Town
    Applicants: Captain Jeffrey T. Benzien, Major General Johannes Griebenauw
    Victim: Niclo Pedro
    Psychologist expert witness: Sarah Kotzé
    Additional victim testimony: August 5, 1996, Melanie Adams

CASE 7: Mduduzi Gumbi and Robert Zuma
    Hearings: July 28–29, 1997, Pietermaritzburg
    Applicants: Mduduzi Gumbi and Robert Zuma
    Victim: Recoria Judith Dlamini

CASE 8: Bheki Mbuyazi
    Hearings: August 1, 1997, Durban
    Applicant: Bheki Mbuyazi
    Victims: Unnamed family members related to the killed victims

TABLE 5.1: *(continued)*

CASE 9: Heidelberg Tavern massacre
    Hearings: October 27–28, 31, 1997, and January 14, 1998, Cape Town
    Applicants: Luyanda Gqomfa, Vuyisile Madasi, Sola Prince Mabala
    Witness: Bennet Sibaya
    Victims: Franciso Cerqueira, Andrea Langford, Jeanette Anne Fourie, Quentin
        Cornelius, Michael January, Roland Palm, Benjamin Brode, Mr. Fourie (father of
        Linda Anne Fourie, who was killed), Gary Atkinson

CASE 10: Murder of Sicelo Dlomo
    Hearings: February 16–19, 1999, Johannesburg
    Applicants: John Dube, Sipho Tshabalala, Clive Makhubu, Precious Wiseman Zungu
    Witnesses: Dr. Klepp, Ramatale Joseph Thwale, Ntombi Mosikare, Puleng Zwane
    Victims: Dlomo family, Sylvia Dlomo-Jele

CASE 11: Robert McBride hearings
    Hearings: September 29–October 13, 1999, Durban
    Applicants: Aboobaker Ismail, Ernest Pule, Robert McBride, Zahrah Narkedien (née
        Greta Apelgren), Edward Pearce, Marcel Andrews, Matthew Lecordier
    Victims: Claire Burton, Jonathan Jeffers, Helen Kearney, Cher Gerrard, Sharon Wel-
        gemoed (née Gerrard), Candice van der Linde, Ms. Erwin

CASE 12: Bombing of Alexandria Health Clinic
    Hearings: November 27–29, 2000, Johannesburg
    Applicant: Paul Erasmus
    Victims: Dr. Timothy Wilson, Beauty Tsoeunyane, Violet Ramhitshana

---

Defining Reconciliation

In evaluating critiques of the TRC, James L. Gibson (2004) pointedly identified one main implication: "No one seems to know what 'reconciliation' is" (202). Even after many analyses of the TRC, there remains a lack of clarity about the meaning of reconciliation and about the process of reconciling. In fact, much of the confusion about reconciliation arises from the conflation of reconciliation and the related concept of forgiveness. To define reconciliation, then, it is also necessary to define forgiveness, clearly distinguishing the two as separate processes.[1]

Forgiveness begins when victims devote themselves to renouncing anger, resentment, and revenge. It is a private act, arising from a strong belief system—often religious—and a sincere acceptance of flawed human nature (Hamber 2007, 2009). Forgiveness proceeds by reinterpreting one's pain and suffering away from a singular connection with the person who caused the original injuries and toward a broader perspective that pain and suffering are experiences that all human beings share. To forgive, people must move away from defining themselves in direct relation to the perpetrators, and away from defining perpetrators only in terms of the injuries they caused (Rowe et al. 1989).

Molly Andrews (2000) drew a clear distinction between what she termed *unilateral* forgiveness and *negotiated* forgiveness. According to Andrews, unilateral forgiveness is "contained entirely within an individual" in private consultation with one's beliefs, with no response required of the perpetrator (76). Negotiated forgiveness transpires through dialogue between the perpetrator and the victim, with the perpetrator disclosing the crimes and taking responsibility, and the victim contextualizing the behavior of the perpetrator and trying to understand the perpetrator's world. Thus, victims and perpetrators need each other to accomplish negotiated forgiveness. Mellor, Bretherton, and Firth (2007) described negotiated forgiveness as "reaching out to others and looking into oneself" (18).

With regard to truth commissions, this distinction between unilateral forgiveness and negotiated forgiveness should be maintained—but relabeled. In the context of truth commissions, unilateral forgiveness is *forgiveness,* and negotiated forgiveness is *reconciliation.* During truth commissions, forgiveness appears as an internal disengagement from the perpetrator, independent of the actions of the perpetrator. In contrast, reconciliation is a dialectical process of acceptance, involving direct interactions between perpetrators and victims. Perpetrators disclose their crimes, accept responsibility, and acknowledge the suffering of the victims; victims gain an understanding of the perspectives of the perpetrators.

This distinction between forgiveness and reconciliation addresses an unsettling development that arose during the amnesty hearings: victims could forgive perpetrators but at the same time *not* support reconciliation or amnesty.[2] Consider the case of Philemon Maxam, introduced in chapter 3. In an attempt to steal weapons from a white-owned farmhouse, Maxam killed the housekeeper and the gardener who worked at the farm. During the amnesty hearings, the son of the slain housekeeper made his views known through a statement from his legal representative: "He feels that it is his Christian duty to forgive the people, and he has said so. But by the same token, he feels that this Act has specific requirements, and if the applicants apply for amnesty, they should meet these requirements. And he feels they do *not* meet them" (Swart, July 7, 1997). In this case, the son of the slain housekeeper *forgave* Maxam, but he did not reconcile with Maxam's murderous actions, and he did not support amnesty.

David Ackerman and his family were worshipping in the St. James Church in Kenilworth when three members of the PAC attacked the congregation, killing eleven people and seriously wounding another fifty-eight. After the attack, Ackerman found his mortally wounded wife and rushed her to the hospital, where she died soon afterward. Four years later, during the amnesty hearings of the TRC, Ackerman told all three perpetrators, "I want you to know that I forgive you unconditionally." Yet even with Ackerman's sincere forgiveness, when asked if the perpetrators deserved amnesty, he replied, "My subjective answer is *no,* I don't think that I've heard everything. I think there might yet be something more" (Ackerman, July 10, 1997).

Michael January suffered serious injuries to his leg and pelvis in the attack on the Heidelberg Tavern, also carried out by the PAC. In his testimony, January summarized his path to forgiveness. "I have continually prayed to God to give me strength to face these hardships and the courage to forgive the men who inflicted this disaster on my family. This forgiveness did not come easily, and for many years I dreamt of vengeance." He then spoke directly to the Amnesty Committee about the attackers: "I unconditionally forgive them for what they have done to me personally." But when it came to amnesty, he stated clearly, "I am opposed to amnesty" (January, October 31, 1997).

Forgiveness can take place without reconciliation because forgiveness is a separate and private process. With the TRC, statements of forgiveness did not originate from the amnesty hearings but from years of thought and preparation between the commission of the crimes and the hearings. When victims and their families explicitly forgave perpetrators during the amnesty hearings, the state of forgiveness had already been achieved before the hearings began, accomplished through careful and personal consideration of one's beliefs. No response was required of the perpetrator, except to listen to and acknowledge the statement of forgiveness from the victim. Analysis of testimony revealed that forgiveness almost always originated in religious belief, unrelated to the specifics of the crimes or the testimony.

Importantly, people forgave *the whole person* but reconciled with the *specific destructive acts* of that person. During the amnesty hearings, when victims offered unilateral forgiveness to the perpetrators, they still withheld reconciliation until after they had witnessed the hearings or participated in direct interactions with perpetrators. Reconciliation demanded specifics from the perpetrator: Exactly what was done, by whom, and for what reasons?

A clear moral distinction is evident. Forgiveness begins with efforts by the victim in private. Reconciliation begins with specific actions by the perpetrator and continues with interactions between the perpetrator and the victim. Reconciliation cannot proceed unless perpetrators acknowledge their wrongdoing, accept responsibility for their crimes, and recognize the suffering of their victims. Without these efforts by the perpetrator, victims should not be expected to reconcile.

During the amnesty hearings, acknowledgment of the crimes against each victim and of the victim's suffering was public and official. This acknowledgment came individually from the perpetrators applying for amnesty and collectively from the TRC. In fact, when victims sought reparations, they did so more as a demonstration of the government's sincerity than as a way of putting things back in their places. After the public hearings, the permanent form of official acknowledgment was the final volume of the TRC report, which served as a biblio-memorial for the victims, listing all the victims identified by the TRC (TRC 2003b). As with the Vietnam Veterans Memorial in Washington, DC, this final volume explicitly named what people collectively forget: each individual whose life was damaged or destroyed by widespread violence.

For the victims, to reconcile is to bring oneself to accept the explanations of another person who has committed wrongdoing. In short, victims must work toward reconciliation. Andrea Langford, whose daughter was killed in the Heidelberg Tavern massacre, talked of the difficult work of reconciliation, not only in recovering from her personal tragedy but also in facing the testimony of the perpetrators, which revived the initial memories of the tragedy:[3]

> Regardless of how I feel, regardless of the three years and ten months that I thought I put behind my back and that I thought I had dealt with quite well, that was brought back to me because of your application for

amnesty. It just brought back *everything*. It put me right back to where I
had thought I had gone past. (Langford, October 31, 1997)

Although testimony was painful, most victims and their families were
grateful for the opportunity to tell of their suffering in public, to remember loved ones they lost in the violence, and to receive acknowledgment
from the TRC and from the perpetrators. Recalling their suffering in
public allowed the victims to maintain their memories, while also relin-
quishing sole responsibility for these memories. Documenting the memories of the crimes in public lessened the painful obligation of remembering and diminished the fear and guilt associated with victimization.

Ultimately, reconciliation requires mutual understanding among people about responsibility and loss—who bears the responsibilities and who
bore the losses (Kriesberg 2000). In the broadest sense, to reconcile with
another person is to understand the actions and experiences of that person.

Promoting Reconciliation

Testimony during the amnesty hearings demonstrated that reconciliation requires perpetrators to come forward and provide detailed
descriptions of their crimes and their reasons for these crimes. Victims
must then be given an opportunity to confront the perpetrators in a
safe environment, challenging their accounts of the crimes and telling
of the suffering they endured. Disclosure of undocumented crimes was
valuable not only for uncovering truth but also for promoting reconciliation, clearly demonstrating the sincerity of the perpetrator.

Humanizing the Perpetrator

For those who watched the amnesty proceedings and for those who
participated, the testimony humanized and particularized the perpetrator. As perpetrators gave testimony, they divulged their crimes, but they
also revealed themselves as flawed and understandable human beings.
They spoke to the Amnesty Committee of their own doubts and private
sufferings about the crimes they committed, as they were shaped and
rewarded by their violent organizations (Kraft 2007, 2011). Perpetrators
explained the beliefs that motivated their violence, the coercion from

their commanders and peers, their thoughts while committing their crimes, and their reactions afterward: the motivating affirmations, the denials, the rationalizations, the regrets, and the shame.

With its bracing immediacy and vivid detail, perpetrator testimony discouraged simplification. The testimony presented perpetrators as multifaceted human beings: complex individuals with distinctive patterns of speech, facial expressions, personal mannerisms, and emotional responses. Honest accounts of abhorrent actions were almost certainly repellent, and the initial responses to these accounts moved some victims and their families away from reconciliation. Over time, however, the difficulty of the disclosures and the sincerity of the perpetrators served to promote reconciliation. In some cases, a begrudging appreciation of the perpetrators' efforts brought about a change in the willingness of victims and their families to understand the perspectives of the perpetrators.

In a reinterpretation of Jacques Lacan, Slavoj Žižek discusses the *virtual imaginary* in the context of what we can know about another person, pointing out that we do not know—or even think about—the personal or bodily concerns of the famous or notorious other (Wright 2004). After the initial documentation of the perpetrators' crimes and before the amnesty hearings, the people of South Africa knew the perpetrators primarily through their destructive actions. In short, they knew their work. During testimony, however, these perpetrators could also become more than professional violence workers and more than Žižek's virtual imaginary; they could be known as biological humans. In the late afternoon of his first day of testimony, Jeffrey Benzien showed brief, undeniable poignancy and physical humanity when he looked to the members of the Amnesty Committee and inferentially implored them to adjourn: "I don't know how to approach the court at this moment. (He pauses.) I have been sitting here and I have gone through a jug of water" (Benzien, July 14, 1997).

Testimony as Punishment

Given the profound consequences of the amnesty hearings and the confrontation by victims and their families, many applicants to the Amnesty Committee considered giving testimony as a form of punishment. After Paul van Vuuren testified in front of an audience that included the mothers and wives of the men he tortured and killed, he said, "I felt as though I was the one being tortured" (Pauw 1998, 21). After describing the damage to his reputation and the real dangers to his family of testifying before the Amnesty Committee, Jeffrey Benzien declared, "As God is my witness, believe me, I have also suffered" (Benzien, July 14, 1997). In many cases, the shaming of the public amnesty hearings and the official publication of those who were granted amnesty were experienced as punishments by the perpetrators (Simpson 2002). In fact, as a form of immediate justice, the shame of disclosure served to promote reconciliation between victims and perpetrators. With Jeffrey Benzien, the visible torment of giving testimony supported his case for amnesty. His struggle to remain faithful to his former self while also committing diligently to the amnesty hearings created a confused dignity that convinced others of his sincerity, however inaccurate his memory for details.

Transmitted Trauma

As Yvonne Khutwane spoke in front of the TRC, telling how she was sexually humiliated and violated by several young soldiers in the South African Army, Pumla Gobodo-Madikizela, a member of the TRC, had to choke back tears as she listened (TRC 1999c, 352–353). At the end of the hearings, Khutwane found Gobodo-Madikizela and told her how healing it had been to see her show of emotion, that seeing clear signs of her trauma being transmitted at an emotional level to a member of the TRC had been restorative (Gobodo-Madikizela 2003, 91–93).

To begin reconciliation, victims and their families needed to hear specifics of the crimes, but they also sought out qualities outside the facts and the narratives. Victims and their families rejected cliché in the apologies and admissions of regret. They looked for sincerity, even when the perpetrator was factually inaccurate. Similarly, when the victimized communicated their suffering to the perpetrators and when perpetrators honestly confessed difficulties in coming to terms with their past actions, the transmission of emotional truth often promoted the reconciliation process.

Obstacles to Reconciliation

Incomplete Disclosure

Disclosure that is obviously incomplete hinders reconciliation. During the amnesty hearings, victims and their families sought this missing truth and demanded the withheld testimony. In one case involving an operation that killed several ANC activists, the commanders gave testimony, but the man who actually carried out the killings, Joe Mamasela, did not. Mamasela was involved in separate and lengthy trial procedures, and his lawyers did not want to jeopardize his legal appeals with testimony to the TRC. This refusal by Mamasela to disclose the facts of the actual killings blocked efforts to reconcile. The wife of one of the murdered men, Legina Mabela, made this clear in her exchange with the evidence leader for the Amnesty Committee, Advocate Mpshe (Mabela, February 24, 1997; Mpshe, February 24, 1997).

> LEGINA MABELA: We cannot forgive them unless we can know the truth from Mr. Mamasela. To know what they have done and what was his part in the incident. Then we will be able to think how we can forgive them. If you know the truth, you are able to forgive. We don't know whether what they have told us is the truth or not.
>
> MPSHE: Your own feelings about reconciliation, what kind of feelings do you have about reconciliation and forgiveness?
>
> MABELA: I want to know the truth.
>
> MPSHE: Is there anything you want to say?
>
> MABELA: I want to know the truth only. I want to know the truth.

The importance of complete disclosure was highlighted in the amnesty hearings for the perpetrators of the Heidelberg Tavern killings. In an effort to gain attention and increase their leverage in the negotiations between the ANC and the National Party, the PAC ordered a deadly attack on the Heidelberg Tavern, a popular night spot for students from the University of Cape Town. In December 1993, three members of APLA, the armed wing of the PAC, shot into the crowd of customers at the tavern, killing three young women and critically injuring scores of others. Four years later, during the amnesty hearings for the perpetrators of the Heidelberg Tavern attack, the victims gave their own accounts and confronted the three men who actually carried out the attack.

Two of those who confronted the perpetrators and gave testimony were Andrea Langford and Jeannette Fourie, both of whom lost their daughters in the attack. In her testimony, Langford pointedly questioned the absence of the men who ordered the killings: "These are the perpetrators of gross human violations. They say . . . that they were acting under orders. . . . Why have their instructors not been brought before this Commission? And if we as the victims have to reconcile, then the truth of the matter is we will never know who was behind the hideous atrocity and we will leave this place with a half truth" (Langford, October 31, 1997). Jeanette Fourie reiterated Langford's concern: "We came here hoping to hear the truth about who the people in high command were who organized this whole dastardly affair. I am not convinced that that truth has come out, and until it does, I am not happy that you [the three amnesty applicants] could just disappear" (Fourie, October 31, 1997).

A related obstacle to reconciliation is that perpetrators may offer explanations that are inappropriate for healing. Elaborated narratives are necessary for reconciliation because they provide personal details and moral commentary. In terms of Tilly's (2006) framework introduced in chapter 4, conventions are inappropriate because they are too simple and too impersonal, sounding like uncaring excuses for brutal acts. Similarly, although technical accounts provide detailed descriptions, they are also inappropriate because they do not explain motives or establish emotional truth. When perpetrators explained their violent actions in the form of conventions or technical accounts instead of narratives, victims and their families often came away from the hearings more distant from reconciliation than when they arrived.

The Magnitude Gap

Another major obstacle to reconciliation is the *magnitude gap*—as discussed in the previous chapter: the predictable discrepancies between what the victims remember and what the perpetrators remember about the same events (Baumeister 1997; Baumeister, Stillwell, and Wotman

1990; Schütz and Baumeister 1999; Zechmeister and Romero 2002). Consistent with the experimental literature on the magnitude gap, testimony given to the TRC revealed dramatic and predictable discrepancies between the memories of the perpetrators and those of the victims (TRC 1999c). Perpetrators bracketed the criminal incidents within a narrow time frame; victims encoded the incidents as part of a series of events, with abuses before and after remembered as parts of the incidents. Perpetrators placed their wrongdoing within the context of doing their jobs; victims did not recall mitigating factors that might lessen the severity of the crimes. From the perpetrator's perspective, the violence was justified—even if it was recognized later as morally wrong. From the victim's perspective, the violence was often incomprehensible and senseless (Kraft 2009).

During the hearings for the car bombing of Magoos Bar, when the victims and their families confronted Robert McBride and his associates, a dramatic magnitude gap appeared. The perpetrators recalled the justifications for their acts and the specifics of the operations, bracketing the incidents, whereas the victims recalled the suffering caused by the acts, the meaning of the events, and the emotional aftermath. Differences in memory were most extreme in the case of torture, but even with torture, the perpetrator remembered the situational constraints. After describing his "unorthodox" interrogation procedure involving wet bag water torture, Jeffrey Benzien implored the Amnesty Committee "to think of it in the context of the time we were living in then," concluding, "I hope the people here could see the predicament that I was in" (Benzien, July 14, 1997).

The magnitude gap between individual perpetrators and victims can be exacerbated by larger divisions in collective memory, as represented in the popular media, textbooks, films, memorials, and national commemorations. These collective memories can differ from one group to another when sizable groups choose different events to memorialize or when they attach different meanings to the same events. For example, to black South Africans, the Sharpeville massacre was the slaughter of sixty-nine unarmed men, women, and children protesting the extension of the restrictive pass laws. To the supporters of the National Party, the Sharpeville massacre was a justifiable use of force against a hostile crowd of 20,000 people that could easily have become violent. These differences in the collective memory for historical events further wid-ened the magnitude gap between individual victims and perpetrators during the amnesty hearings.

Ultimately, many victims simply did not *believe* the discrepancies between their own personal memories and the memories of the perpe-trators, and they went on record stating that the perpetrators had failed to disclose fully their involvement in the crimes. In part, this assertion arises from the discrepancy in the way the gap itself is experienced. Per-petrators accept the gap more readily, whereas victims are less willing to acknowledge its validity (Hamber 2007, 2009). Not only do victims experience the offenses with greater magnitude, they also experience the magnitude gap itself more acutely than the perpetrators. Given that perpetrators were required to provide honest and comprehensive dis-closure in order to receive amnesty, the discrepancy in recall between the perpetrators and the victims could potentially block efforts to gain amnesty.

The magnitude gap also brought up a fundamental question of applied metacognition: Given the gap in remembering, what criteria do people use to judge the comprehensiveness and honesty of memory descriptions? (Bond and DePaulo 2006; Ekman and O'Sullivan 1991; Ekman, O'Sullivan, and Frank 1999; Scoboria et al. 2004). With regard to this question, Judge Bernard Ngoepe of the TRC amnesty commit-tee offered a discerning observation during the final day of hearings for Captain Jeffrey Benzien:

> How do you reconcile the ability not to remember certain things with the ability to remember not having done certain things? In other words, the person says he has forgotten about certain things, he has blocked them out of his mind, but when other things are put to him he says, "No, I remember very well, it did *not* happen." I think that's what the problem is: he's *able* to remember that such and such a thing did *not* happen, but at the end of the same breath, he's saying, "I am not able to remember that, I've lost my memory or part of it, I am not able to say whether cer-tain things did or did not happen." (Ngoepe, October 21, 1997)

Part of the answer to Ngoepe's question comes from action identifi-cation theory, as described in chapter 3. Perpetrators are more likely to encode the technical aspects of interrogation and less likely to attend to personal or moral considerations of their acts. Consistent with the predictions of action identification theory, the perpetrator's low-level identity leads to representations primarily of contextual factors, whereas the victim's high-level identity leads to memory representations of personal considerations (Vallacher and Wegner 1987; Wegner and Vallacher 1986). Another part of the answer comes from recognizing and identifying the specific characteristics of the magnitude gap.

No Redemption

One belief held by some victims was that for reconciliation to occur, one's victimization must be superseded by personal recovery and success. Victims and their families then looked to a better life as a way of vindicating their suffering, and if their life had not improved, reconciliation could be thwarted. This belief contributed to Charity Khondile not forgiving Captain Dirk Coetzee for planning the murder of her son, Sizwe Khondile. "It is easy for Mandela and Tutu to forgive," she said. "They lead vindicated lives. In my life nothing, not a single thing, has changed since my son was burnt by barbarians . . . nothing. Therefore, I cannot forgive" (Pauw 1998, 25). Quentin Cornelius lost the use of his legs as a result of being shot in the spine during the attack on the Heidelberg Tavern. At the hearings for the perpetrators of this attack, Cornelius stated directly, "I oppose this request for amnesty." He then gave one reason for his opposition: "the humiliation of trying to adjust back into a very unforgiving society as an invalid" (Cornelius, October 31, 1997). This belief in tangible compensation for one's suffering could block reconciliation if compensation of some sort did not occur.

When Quentin Cornelius gave testimony, he was twenty-four years old and confined to a wheelchair because of the Heidelberg Tavern attack. When confronting the three attackers and considering amnesty, Cornelius looked for equity in a hypothetical choice:

> I would like to have each of the perpetrators look me in the eye and choose whether they would not mind having a rifle stuck in their spines and the trigger being pulled on them in cold blood, to leave them emotionally and physically scarred and disabled as I have been or would they

rather stay in jail and serve their sentences for the crimes that they committed? (Cornelius, October 31, 1997)

Contributing to the perception of failed redemption was the fundamental asymmetry in the TRC's response to perpetrators and victims (Hamber 2009). As in the criminal justice system, the relationship between the TRC and the perpetrators was more developed than the relationship between the TRC and the victims. For the TRC, the decision about the perpetrators was clear and unequivocal: to grant amnesty or to refuse it. If granted, amnesty meant the perpetrator was immediately protected from all legal and civil liability. Victims had their day in court, but beyond that, the benefits of testifying were unclear. Amnesty was typically decided within a year, while reparations took considerably longer and were appreciably smaller than originally planned—if they were allocated at all.

Obstacles Overcome: Forms of Reconciliation

During the hearings, most victims did not directly support amnesty. The most frequent favorable response of victims to amnesty was negative acceptance: victims and their families *did not oppose amnesty.* In almost all of these cases, victims stated that they would accept the decision of the Amnesty Committee.

Reconciling the Magnitude Gap

In psychology, the debate continues about the role of personality *traits* versus situational *states* in the behavior of perpetrators: internal dispositional characteristics versus strong external influences that lead people to behave badly. This theoretical debate became actualized in the confrontations between victims and perpetrators during the amnesty hearings. In general, those who gave testimony to the Amnesty Committee interpreted their own behavior in terms of situational states and their adversary's behavior in terms of dichotomous traits (e.g., good versus evil). Victims perceived the perpetrators as powerful individuals, able to choose between right and wrong, whereas perpetrators saw themselves as functioning within a powerful system, carrying out their necessary duties.

For victims to reconcile the magnitude gap, they needed to shift the general explanation for the perpetrators' actions away from personality traits and toward situational states. During the amnesty hearings, most of the victims began as trait theorists, assuming satanic perpetrators—who else could torture and murder?—but as the hearings proceeded, some of the victims became more willing to accept a partially situationist perspective, with the perpetrator's behavior influenced by the state of the situation. When reconciliation began, it was partly due to the victim's recognition of the perpetrator's world through an understanding of the magnitude gap and a willingness to reconsider the version of events remembered by the other person.

Reconciling with the Process

The writer Gillian Slovo confessed that although she supported the TRC, the amnesty hearings actually increased her feelings of contempt for the perpetrators. Slovo's mother, Ruth First, was a prominent antiapartheid journalist and activist assassinated by a mail bomb sent by members of the security forces. Slovo attended the amnesty hearings for the men involved in killing her mother, including her mother's assassin, Craig Williamson, a commander in the security forces. After the hearings, she characterized the perpetrator's testimony as "displaced responsibility" and "empty justifications." Taken as a whole, however, Slovo found value in the amnesty hearings, saying, "Although they didn't *tell* the truth, I did discover this truth." Ultimately, she reconciled in her own way, concluding, "The reconciliation that I experienced was with what happened, not with the perpetrators" (Slovo 2002, 6).

During the hearings for Robert McBride's car bombing of Magoos Bar, although the exchanges between McBride and members of the victims' families were hostile and at times insulting, they revealed a dialogic truth: that there was anger, that there were profoundly divergent attitudes about McBride's lethal actions, that these attitudes would remain unresolved, and that no words could justify the killing of three young women. Nevertheless, speaking face-to-face, forcefully and nonviolently, led to a begrudging courtroom coexistence that acknowledged the influences acting on the perpetrators and the suffering of the victims' families (McBride, October 12, 1999).

Less appropriately, the McBride hearings resulted in coercive reconciliation. Sharon Welgemoed, the sister of one of the women McBride killed with his car bomb, was forcefully challenged under cross-examination by McBride's legal advocate and scolded for not forgiving McBride. At that point, Judge Pillay, the chair of the amnesty hearings for McBride, intervened and said, "Let the process proceed and see what happens. You can't ask for a commitment on that score." But later, it was Judge Pillay who suggested to Sharon Welgemoed that she "consider forgiving those who cause the heartbreak," concluding that "it's important to this country" (Pillay, October 13, 1999). After listening to the two admonitions to reconcile, Sharon Welgemoed spoke of reconciliation not in terms of acceptance but as a form of *resignation:*

> I want this to be the end for me. It has been a lingering thing, I've had to deal with a lot traumatically. I lost my son previously to losing my sister. I had two deaths to contend with and it's taken me psychiatrists and medication and hospitalization to come to terms with this, to be able to sit here today and even talk across the table to you as I am now. I want this to come to an end. I don't want to read about it in the papers again, I don't want to hear any more about it again, I want it to end. I want the past to be put in the past where it belongs. (Welgemoed, October 13, 1999)

Perpetrators Reconciling with Themselves

The testimony of perpetrators disclosed how they redefined their self-concepts and how they learned to accommodate their past selves. Striking individual differences arose in how perpetrators adapted to giving testimony about their wrongful acts. Some perpetrators radically changed their ideology. Others maintained their ideology but adapted it to the new, democratic South Africa, translating their ideology into acceptable political beliefs. In some cases, there was an epiphany of shame; in others a realization more gradual than an epiphany. Some amnesty applicants described the punishment of confronting their own destructiveness as perpetrators and realizing more fully the implications of this destructiveness (Coetzee, November 5, 1996; Gobodo-Madikizela 2003; de Kock 1998). When perpetrators realized how their actions shattered the lives of the victims and their families, it was punishment *and* a way of acknowledging the crimes against the victimized (Gobodo-Madikizela 2003).

During the TRC hearings, some members of the SAP described changing their perception of the ANC activists from evil terrorists bent on the destruction of South Africa to courageous soldiers struggling for their freedom. These members of the SAP, particularly, were forced to confront the faultiness of the very ideology that gave meaning to their past lives. For SAP perpetrators, this change in the perception of the ANC from villainous to heroic created a need to reconcile with their past professional identities. As these state perpetrators faced the testimony of ANC activists at the amnesty hearings, they fundamentally altered their way of thinking about their former victims and in turn painfully revised their own self-concepts. During his testimony, Captain Dirk Coetzee showed genuine remorse, expressing understanding and empathy for those he victimized and condemnation of his own past destructiveness (Coetzee, November 5, 1996).[4]

During the exchanges with their former victims, many perpetrators talked about coexisting with two sets of self-concepts. In some cases, perpetrators would say that they were different people in the past and that they could not recall the experience of their former selves. Other perpetrators were able to remember their violence-worker selves, parsing them into different characteristics, based on their roles. As discussed in chapter 4, another dominant strategy for the perpetrators was to construct two separate sets of self-concepts, one for the past self and one for the present, with a conceptual bridge connecting the two selves without integrating them.

The case of Bheki Mbuyazi illustrated the powerful desire to reconcile with one's own actions, with reconciliation occurring in a single dramatic moment that resulted in Mbuyazi unexpectedly withdrawing his application for amnesty in exchange for an opportunity to reconcile. Bheki Mbuyazi's crimes originated in the deadly clashes between the Inkatha Freedom Party (IFP) and the ANC during the final years of the apartheid system. When he was a teenager, Mbuyazi joined the ANC and began a relentless struggle with members of the IFP in his community. His home was attacked three times by the IFP, and during the third attack, members of the IFP burned down his house and killed his oldest brother. Afterward, he and his father reported the assault to the police at the Kangwana station, but according to Mbuyazi, the police came only "to collect the corpses" and then left. Mbuyazi testified, "After that, we decided that we should attack our attackers . . . because we realized that if we sit back and do nothing and fold our hands, we might be attacked again" (Mbuyazi, August 1, 1997).

In taking action, Mbuyazi broke into the house of a local leader of the IFP, looking for the men who brutalized his family. Once inside the house, he did not find the men he was looking for, but instead found three women in hiding. In his testimony, Mbuyazi described his state of mind when he found the three women: "At that time I wasn't in the human sense—because my mind was confused when all this was happening." He then stabbed all three women to death, believing they were IFP members, as well. Shortly afterward, as an eighteen-year-old member of the ANC, Mbuyazi was arrested, tried, and convicted on three counts of murder and sent to prison in September 1991, remaining there ever since.

After Mbuyazi gave testimony during his amnesty hearing, there was a short adjournment, followed by a surprising development. Mbuyazi withdrew his application for amnesty and instead requested to meet with the relatives of the murdered women. Fully aware that this withdrawal was a permanent decision that would send him back to prison, Mbuyazi expressed his realization that his murderous actions did not deserve amnesty and that the only way to reconcile was to accept his prison sentence and meet with the surviving family. Chairs were set up, and Mbuyazi met with the male relatives of the victims. The men talked for twenty minutes before the impromptu meeting ended, with apparent reconciliation—all filmed silently by the SABC cameras after the adjournment of the hearings. Following this meeting, Bheki Mbuyazi returned to prison to serve out his original sentence (Mbuyazi, August 1, 1997).

After months of preparing his amnesty application, Mbuyazi began his testimony with clarity and certainty, but as he described his reasons for killing the three women, he seemed hesitant and unsure. He could not remember his perspective at the time of his attack, and his explanation faltered—in the presence of the women's surviving relatives. At this point, he may have judged his own reasons for the killings to be inadequate and insincere. As questioning proceeded, Mbuyazi's testimony indicated a fuller realization of the magnitude of the crimes and their enduring effects on the grieving families. Motivated by the desire to reconcile with his own past actions, Mbuyazi then chose to reconcile with the victimized families in the most meaningful way, foreclosing his opportunity for amnesty but opening the possibility of sincere reconciliation.

Committing to Coexistence

In most cases, when reconciliation was acknowledged during the hearings, it was confined to the hearings, without an extended agreement to work together after the hearings. In several noteworthy cases, however, the amnesty hearings led to a long-term commitment between perpetrators and victims to work together, actively promoting interactive coexistence.[5] In these cases, the process began with a bold initiative by either the victimized or the perpetrators, which motivated the participants to arrange meetings to discuss their perspectives and to attempt reconciling outside the hearings of the TRC.

In the case of Amy Biehl's murder, it was the surviving parents who initiated long-term reconciliation by committing to help the impoverished community in which the perpetrators grew up. The hearings themselves began the reconciliation process, with recognition of the strong political influences on the young perpetrators and with the acknowledgment of Amy Biehl's compassion and courage in the struggle for a democratic South Africa. Amy Biehl's parents accepted the amnesty process and entered into a mutual agreement with the young men who killed their daughter to work with the communities in the area to help educate young people and raise their standard of living.

In the case of the Trust Feed killings, it was the perpetrator, Brian Mitchell, who made the initial commitment and the Trust Feed community who accepted him. Mitchell's crimes began when he was a young police captain violently opposing the ANC-backed United Democratic Front (UDF) in KwaZulu-Natal. As station commander in a district that included the village of Trust Feed, Mitchell recruited and deployed special constables from the IFP to target and destroy the houses of UDF activists. On the night of December 2, 1988, Mitchell ordered a small group of IFP constables to assault a house suspected of being a safe house for the UDF. As it happened, the constables attacked the wrong house and killed eleven members of an Inkatha family who were holding a memorial service, an incident that later became known as the Trust Feed killings (Mitchell, October 16, 1996). The transcript of the judgment in the eventual Trust Feed trial stated that the constables meant "to kill all the people in the house" and that they shot "anyone they saw moving." One defendant testified that he saw "a head rising" and shot it (Wilson 1989).

Eight years after the Trust Feed killings, Captain Brian Mitchell gave testimony before the Amnesty Committee, fully disclosing his role in the killings and offering sincere apologies for the murders he planned and supervised. Toward the end of the hearings, the advocate representing the Trust Feed community stated that the people of Trust Feed were willing to meet with Mitchell to discuss his offer to help rebuild the community (Kajee, October 16, 1996). Over a period of months, Mitchell met with the families who had lost relatives in the killings and with representatives from the IFP and ANC. At these meetings, Mitchell detailed his commitment to serve the community of Trust Feed, which he then carried out over a period of years, building a successful coalition of coexistence that Deputy President Jacob Zuma (now president) called "a lesson for us all about the power of reconciliation and the results of full disclosure before the TRC" (Zuma 2003).

6

Beyond the TRC

Negotiating the Aftermath of Collective Violence

But then, once in a lifetime
The longed-for tidal wave
Of justice can rise up,
And hope and history rhyme.
　　Seamus Heaney, *The Cure at Troy*[1]

To focus solely on the deep and persisting societal divisions in South Africa today is to ignore the reverberating example set by the TRC as a national institution for gathering truth and promoting reconciliation after decades of violent conflict. Even with its setbacks and limitations, the TRC stands today as an enduring example of the potential for restorative justice on a national scale and a prototype for other national truth commissions.[2]

Over a span of six years following the end of apartheid, the achievements of the TRC's amnesty hearings sent several resonant messages throughout South Africa: truths about widespread human rights violations will be uncovered, secrets of illegality will be disclosed, government crimes will be illuminated, and perpetrators will be held publicly accountable for their crimes. By describing and generalizing the goals of the Amnesty Committee and the procedures and concepts that supported these goals, the distinctive achievements of the TRC's amnesty hearings can be applied to future efforts in negotiating the aftermath of collective violence.[3] In the process, broader contributions of the amnesty hearings to restorative justice can be identified and elaborated, including the consideration of a truth commission in the United States.

Goals and Procedures of the Amnesty Committee

The idea of implementing conditional amnesty to help South Africa recover from the pervasive destructiveness of apartheid began in the South African Parliament with the Promotion of National Unity and Reconciliation Act. While conceptualizing the requirements for a truth commission, South African officials recognized that reconciliation could only be achieved by uncovering comprehensive truths about human rights violations and that an official investigation was necessary to uncover these truths (TRC 1999a; Tutu 1999b; Boraine 2000). They also realized that this investigation depended on extensive testimony from the perpetrators involved in the crimes of apartheid.

The mandate of the Amnesty Committee was to consider amnesty for perpetrators of politically motivated violations of human rights and to grant or refuse amnesty to these perpetrators based on their testimony. The three primary goals of conditional amnesty were to uncover truth about the crimes of apartheid, to establish accountability for the perpetrators, and to promote reconciliation. While working toward these goals, the Amnesty Committee sought to maintain openness during the proceedings and to follow the rule of law to the greatest extent possible (Minow 1998). The following sections summarize these goals and offer recommendations for future truth commissions.

Uncovering Truth

During the amnesty hearings, the uncovering of truth involved discovering, detailing, and publicly acknowledging past abuses, overcoming official denial of the abuses, and documenting a history of human rights violations, what Hayner (2002) referred to as "sanctioned fact finding" (24). A major accomplishment of the Amnesty Committee was the use of perpetrator testimony to collect evidence that would not be recoverable in criminal proceedings and to discover hidden crimes, identifying the perpetrators and documenting the details of these crimes. For crimes that involved disappearances, multiple murders, the destruction of evidence, and the planting of false evidence to implicate innocent people, perpetrator testimony was the only source of information. Prior to the amnesty hearings, knowledge about such cases consisted only of well-motivated suspicions and educated guesses. Even with surviving witnesses and available forensic evidence, perpetrator testimony contributed necessary information about the human rights abuses of apartheid.

Notably, victims and perpetrators were permitted to tell their own stories, unconstrained by the procedures of a courtroom. In the process, the TRC produced a history of apartheid more comprehensive and an education of the public more thorough than if the South African government had endeavored to prosecute a selected group of perpetrators in criminal trials (Hayner 2002; Verwoerd 2003).[4] Overall, more than 1,600 perpetrators and 22,000 victims told their stories, creating a massive archival record of the crimes and sufferings of apartheid (Posel and Simpson 2002a; TRC 2003a; Verdoolaege 2008). With prosecutions, the history of events is typically only a by-product of the legal adversarial process of examination and cross-examination. The witnesses (victims) tell their stories within the narrow range of the charges against the defendants (perpetrators), and the defendants answer only those questions they are asked (Landsman 1996; Minow 1998). Indeed, truth commissions and criminal trials have been characterized as contradicting one another, with truth commissions focusing on truth, and courts of law focusing on traditional, retributive justice (Rosenbaum 2004). In addition, when perpetrators admitted their guilt during the amnesty hearings, they resolved the uncertainties that can occur in trials when offenders maintain their innocence even after a guilty verdict (Ntsebeza 2000).

RECOMMENDATIONS

As with the TRC, future truth commissions should obtain documents and collect oral testimony. To obtain documents, truth commissions need subpoena power, access to pertinent information from governmental organizations, and the power of search and seizure, within the mandate of the commission. To go beyond documentation, truth commissions need to collect testimony from victims and perpetrators, with perpetrators giving testimony under oath.

Accountability

Against the backdrop of criminal trials and civil cases, the TRC enforced accountability for the perpetrators through conditional amnesty: the granting of complete amnesty for full disclosure under oath and the rejection of amnesty for incomplete or dishonest disclosure. Of those applications that met the TRC's requirements, amnesty was refused when disclosure was judged to be incomplete or dishonest (TRC 2003a). For those who chose not to participate, traditional legal and civil consequences could be applied. As stated in the TRC final report, "the 'stick' of prosecutions and civil claims was combined with the 'carrot' of amnesty to encourage perpetrators to testify about gross violations of human rights" (TRC 1999a, 53). In this way, the TRC placed restorative justice in the context of the existing judicial system, recognizing that although the truth commission was quasi-legal, the emphasis was as much on *legal* as it was on *quasi*. The specific rules and conditions for conditional amnesty are discussed in detail in chapter 2.

RECOMMENDATIONS

A meaningful form of accountability for offenders must be in place for any truth commission, although the particular form can vary. Other effective forms of accountability in truth commissions include public declarations of the crimes, public apologies, professional penalties (e.g., disbarment for lawyers and losing one's license for doctors and mental health professionals), removal of people from the positions in which they harmed others, and bans from holding official office, known as lustration (Bronkhorst 2006; Crocker 2000, 2003; Eyal 2004; Hayner 2002; Mayer 2009; Minow 1998). In all cases, future truth commissions need to require an effective form of accountability, with testimony from perpetrators given under oath and with victims able to confront the perpetrators and ask questions. Those perpetrators who do not participate may be subject to investigation through existing legal and civil procedures.

Reconciliation

The amnesty hearings promoted reconciliation by encouraging full disclosure from the perpetrators and by providing a safe environment for the victims and their families to confront the perpetrators, ask questions, and consider reconciliation without being directly pressured (in most cases).

The direct confrontation with former victims focused the perpetrator on each victim's experience of events and the long-term damage to the victim and to the lives of family members. The magnitude gap that occurred during confrontations between victims and perpetrators, however unsettling, provided an opportunity for individual perpetrators to learn directly of the victim's experience of suffering. Similarly, victims learned of the systemic influences within the perpetrators' violent organizations and the reasons that motivated their violent actions. Ideally, confronting the magnitude gap allowed perpetrators and victims to see each other's humanity more fully and in more detail.

It is noteworthy that the Amnesty Committee did not promise or enforce reconciliation; rather, it promoted individual reconciliation through its hearings and encouraged national reconciliation through its public display of civility and fairness. In fact, Verdoolaege (2008) proposed that promoting a culture of reconciliation was the most enduring legacy of the TRC, and one that would continue long after the hearings ended.

RECOMMENDATIONS

Reconciliation is most urgent when large numbers of people have perpetrated crimes against even larger numbers of victims, creating a fundamental need to accommodate and reconcile across a broad spectrum of the population. In South Africa, for example, 40 million people (approximately 90 percent of the population) suffered under the institutions and laws of apartheid, and the violations of these laws. For smaller groups of victims, an effort should be made to include nearly all surviving victims and their families in safe proceedings that are specifically designed to foster direct dialogue with perpetrators.[5] In all cases, future truth commissions should begin the process of reconciliation through civil confrontation between victims and perpetrators in a setting that is supportive and safe for both—as with the amnesty hearings—and continue to provide support for conciliatory meetings after the hearings.

Openness

The TRC announced its schedule of hearings, held its hearings in or near the communities most affected by the events addressed in the hearings, provided public space for an audience, recorded and broadcast the hearings on national television, and posted transcripts on the TRC website. With these procedures, the TRC demonstrated the value of such hearings, with the process and the outcomes fully accessible. As a result, the populace learned about the specific crimes of apartheid, while also receiving a psychological education in understanding the emotional aftermath of past atrocities (Verdoolaege 2008).

RECOMMENDATIONS

Wherever possible, future hearings should be open to the public and to the media, with broadcasts, podcasts, and recordings, and with transcripts available online. Televising, streaming, and recording the proceedings not only establish openness and accountability in the contentious and potentially threatening atmosphere of giving testimony but also promote safety and trust among the participants. Afterward, the recorded testimony can be permanently housed in video archives, serving the dual purpose of memorializing the events and supporting future research.

The Rule of Law

Any quasi-legal commission will inevitably have conflicts between the *quasi* and the *legal*. Regarding the rule of law, the Amnesty Committee endeavored to balance the rights of victims, the requirements of conditional amnesty, and traditional principles of due process. The balance between comprehensive truth and traditional justice, however, necessitated exceptions to principles of due process. In most cases, the amnesty applicants (the perpetrators) were not allowed to cross-examine their accusers (the victims), most statements by the victims were not given under oath (more than 90 percent), and many victim statements described violations told to them by others, which would be considered inadmissible in the courtroom as hearsay (Crocker 2000, 2003; Jeffrey 1999). Most distinctively, all of the perpetrators necessarily waived protection against self-incrimination, giving testimony under oath and submitting to cross-examination.

RECOMMENDATIONS

To the extent possible, the rule of law should be followed to be consistent with international standards and to ensure due process and procedural fairness (Bronkhorst 2006). For future truth commissions, the balance among the rule of law, the humane treatment of victims, and the testimony from perpetrators would depend on the type of accountability imposed on perpetrators. If the commission adopts conditional amnesty in exchange for full disclosure, then applicants need to acknowledge that applying for amnesty waives their right against self-incrimination and that their accusers (the people they victimized) can provide unsworn testimony and can confront them without cross-examination. If the truth commission is mandated to gather information for later prosecutions, then the hearings need to conform to established legal principles. If other forms of accountability are implemented (professional penalties, public apologies, removal from present positions, and lustration), these forms replace the threat of prosecution, and applicants should be granted immunity from legal and civil trials. In general, a truth commission should follow procedures that are congruent with the form of accountability for the offenders, balancing the adherence to the established rule of law, the humane treatment of victims, and the process of effective truth gathering.

Conceptual Requirements

During the amnesty hearings, four general concepts were advanced that helped South African society come to terms with the historic destructiveness of apartheid: the existence of multiple truths, the recognition of perpetrator testimony as both humanizing and punishing, the need for representative diversity on truth commissions, and the integration of psychology throughout the process.

Multiple Truths

As analyzed in detail earlier, the TRC anticipated the existence of multiple truths and the magnitude gap, specifying four types of truth, each with different characteristics and different functions (factual or forensic truth, personal and narrative truth, social or dialogic truth, and healing and restorative truth). The Amnesty Committee accommodated multiple truths by defining them, identifying them, questioning disagreements during their deliberations, and allowing minority opinion to accompany the majority report. It did not, however, devise documented strategies for managing the clash of these truths, and instead made decisions case by case. Chapter 4 introduces the concept of parallax truth to accommodate the necessary disagreements among different versions of the same events and to distinguish those versions that convey narrative truth and those that do not.

RECOMMENDATIONS

Future truth commissions need to anticipate and accommodate multiple truths that corroborate and also conflict with each other. They must also be aware of magnitude gaps between perpetrators and victims that can interfere with reconciliation and complicate the process of constructing historical narratives. Multiple truths can be reported at a level of generality that stays above the areas of conflict or by issuing a majority report accompanied by minority reports, as with the TRC (Crocker 2000). Multiple versions of the same events can be reported in two parts: areas of consensus and areas of disagreement. In all cases, the comprehensive final report of a truth commission must faithfully represent conflicting versions of events, while also addressing the tension between multiplicity and coherence.

Perpetrator Testimony as Humanizing and Punishing

Despite the severity of their crimes and the fallibility of their memories, when perpetrators gave testimony with sincerity—and some difficulty—they came across less and less as caricatures of brutality and more as flawed human beings, unquestioningly devoted to the violent goals of their organizations. Extensive testimony from perpetrators revealed the orders, the incentives, and the policies that guided their illegal activities, resulting in a greater understanding of these activities and of the perpetrators themselves (Kraft 2007, 2011). At the same time, full disclosure exacted a high price, particularly for government perpetrators. Such disclosure was punishing not only because the perpetrators publicly admitted their brutal misconduct but also because they were talking at all, breaking the vow of secrecy to their organizations. Ultimately, the difficulty of seeking amnesty can be traced back to a time before the amnesty hearings, back to the original crimes of apartheid.

RECOMMENDATIONS

Future truth commissions should take measures to provide a safe environment for perpetrators whose testimony can be emotionally punishing and potentially endangering. These commissions should also prepare the interested public for perpetrator testimony that contextualizes the crimes and makes them more understandable, although no less heinous. Those considering the relative benefits of prosecutions and truth commissions should be aware that the shame of public confession can act as a powerful and humane deterrent to organized criminal violence.

Maintaining Diversity

The Amnesty Committee operated within South Africa just after the end of apartheid, endeavoring to investigate the crimes of apartheid and to bring about reconciliation. While operating during this highly emotional and politically charged time, it was essential for the Committee to establish and maintain ethnic and lingual diversity. This diversity then contributed to the perception of fairness and the lack of documented bias along two major fault lines in South African society: Black versus White and liberation movements versus security forces.

Even so, subtle biases may have emerged in the amnesty process. Members of the Amnesty Committee were judges and advocates trained in legal principles and accustomed to the order of the courtroom. As a result of this training and experience, the Committee appeared more receptive to testimony from applicants who had been members of well-structured organizations, such as the ANC and the SAP—organizations with charters and understandable chains of command. In contrast, many applicants from the IFP were unable to describe the organization of their paramilitary groups or delineate the chain of command, primarily because there was little structure in the IFP and no clear hierarchy of leadership below the top level. As a result, these applicants could seem bewildered and disorganized, which may have hurt their chances for amnesty in front of a committee that favored structure and resisted improvisation and spontaneity.

RECOMMENDATIONS

In an effort to bridge social divides and reduce bias, members of truth commissions should represent as many ethnic and cultural groups as possible within a society. They should also be vigilant about congruence—or lack of congruence—between the committee granting amnesty and the applicants seeking it, helping to minimize any resulting bias in the amnesty decisions.

Integrating Psychology

The psychological well-being of the participants in the TRC hearings was a central concern, from the founding act of Parliament through the completion of the final report. Even before the TRC began its work, the preamble to the South African Constitution referenced memory and suffering, encouraging a psychologically literate truth commission (Fagan 1998). During the hearings of the TRC, psychology was accepted as an integral discipline for understanding and managing truth gathering and reconciliation. To ensure psychological expertise, a clinical psychologist was appointed to the HRV Committee, and psychologists were consulted throughout the hearings. The lengthy analysis of perpetrators in the final report integrated research psychology into the interpretation of the results (TRC 1999c), citing the work of social psychologists Roy Baumeister (1997), John Duckitt (1992), Stanley Milgram (1974), Ervin Staub (1989), and Neil Kressel (1996) and clinical psychologist Robert Lifton (1986). Psychology also entered directly into the *decisions* of the Amnesty Committee. Crucial to amnesty for Jeffrey Benzien, for example, was the testimony of his psychologist, who gave elaborate testimony explaining Benzien's specific memory lapses as well as general principles of trauma and forgetting (Kotzé, October 21, 1997).

RECOMMENDATIONS

Psychologists should be officially represented on all future truth commissions, advising on the effects of extended trauma, providing therapeutic assistance for those who testify, following up with all those who participate, and contributing to the writing of the final report (Cornejo, Rojas, and Mendoza 2009; Minow 1998). Concurrently, truth commissions should educate the general public about the aftermath of victimization and the necessity of support networks conducted by mental health professionals. Another potential application of psychology would be in the preparation for a truth commission. Comprehensive survey research could be conducted to identify public expectations for a truth commission, thereby shaping the mandate for the commission (Mullet, Neto, and Pinto 2008). In this way, psychology would be integrated into the truth-gathering process right from the beginning.

The TRC and Restorative Justice

One prominent example of the TRC's influence on implementing principles of restorative justice at the national level is the ongoing Truth
and Reconciliation Commission of Canada. Drawing on South Africa's
TRC as its model, the new TRC in Canada is endeavoring to investigate
and repair the damage inflicted by more than 120 years of the Canadian
government's program of Indian Residential Schools. Established in the
late nineteenth century, these schools maintained strict control over the
education of First Nations Métis and Inuit children, cutting off family
involvement and forbidding the children from speaking their language
and practicing the traditions and rituals of their cultures—with as yet
untold cases of violence against these First Nations children. The effects
of this forced education have resounded through the generations,
including an estimated 80,000 former students living today.

As with the South African TRC, the Canadian TRC will receive voluntary testimony from the former students, their families, and other
members of the affected communities. Consistent with the goals of the
South African TRC, the Canadian TRC intends to construct a thorough historical record of the policies and operations of the residential
schools, promote awareness of the Indian Residential School program,
support commemoration of the former students, establish a national
research center, and complete a public report of their findings, with recommendations for helping the affected communities. (For more information on the TRC of Canada, refer to its website: www.trc.ca/.)

The TRC has also encouraged nongovernmental organizations to
adapt and elaborate its concepts, applying them to their specific community-based programs. As Colvin (2000) noted, "The TRC provided
both the impetus and the model for many of the parallel and subsequent
projects in civil society that have tried to add to, complement, extend
and critique the work initiated by the TRC" (2). One such example is
the Centre for the Study of Violence and Reconciliation (CSVR) in
South Africa. Founded in 1989, the CSVR rose out of the ashes of apartheid, with a multifaceted approach to healing the traumas of the past
in a way that also prevents further trauma. It then grew considerably
in conjunction with the hearings of the TRC, operating programs in
six different areas of restorative justice: criminal justice, gender-based

violence, peace building, transitional justice, trauma and transition, and the prevention of youth violence.

One specific principle of the TRC that generalizes to community-based programs of restorative justice is the necessity of perpetrators and victims to engage each other safely and *directly*. Another generalizable principle is that *truth gathering* is required for reconciliation, that moving beyond the violence of the past cannot occur until the violence is made known and discussed. With the TRC, testimony functioned as palimpsest, with memories of past violations of human rights informing ongoing efforts to reconcile. Coker (2002), in fact, has advocated for a restorative justice model in cases of domestic abuse that integrates the truth-gathering process of the TRC with the comprehensive community-based practices of Navajo peacemakers.

Community-based restorative justice programs have also learned from what the TRC did *not* specifically implement. To carry out restorative justice on a national scale, the TRC needed to attend to circles of influence larger than those in community-based programs of restorative justice, which focus more on the smaller circle of perpetrators, victims, and judges and experts facilitating the proceedings. As mandated, the TRC required the *state* to provide reparations, instead of encouraging the perpetrators themselves to provide material and personal reparations. In contrast, many community-based programs of restorative justice emphasize that the offenders must genuinely believe that what they did was wrong and in violation of the principles of their civil society. These offenders must also participate meaningfully in the reparations to the individuals who were harmed and to their communities (Perry 2002; van Ness and Strong 2010; Zernova 2007).

In Navajo peacemaking, for example, when one individual violates another, this violation is treated as a failure of the entire community to educate and enculturate the offender appropriately. The injured person makes a demand that the offender repair the damage, and the offender is then requested to participate in the efforts to resolve the dispute. Reparations go beyond material compensation to a repairing of the relationship among the individuals and the entire community (Johnstone 2002; Lobb 2010).[6] Community-based restorative justice programs also encourage emotional honesty, which the TRC achieved with the victims of apartheid—and, in a few newsworthy cases, with members of the TRC—but not as much with the perpetrators (Johnstone 2002; van Ness and Strong 2010).

In general, the amnesty hearings of the TRC vivified several ideas essential for restorative resolution of violent conflicts: the accommodation of multiple truths, the safe and civil confrontation between perpetrators and victims, the clear and specific sanctification of diversity, the embrace of complexity, and the integration of psychology into the institutions of justice. In fact, one lasting influence of the TRC is as an exemplar of civility and restorative practice, competing with ideological platforms that vilify designated groups of people and demand violent retribution for past injustices.

Considering a Truth Commission in the United States

Successful truth commissions will necessarily operate in different forms and with different particulars, depending on the country and its histories. But all truth commissions share an emphasis on uncovering truths, listening to the victims, creating detailed accounts of wrongdoing, establishing full accountability for those responsible for human rights abuses, maintaining openness and documentation of the proceedings, obeying the rule of law, accepting the existence of multiple perspectives, and promoting reconciliation (Amnesty International 2009; Bronkhorst 2006; Cornejo, Rojas, and Mendoza 2009; Crocker 2000, 2003; Hayner 1994, 2002; Minow 1998; Mullet, Neto, and Pinto 2008; U.S. Institute of Peace 2009; Verwoerd 2003).

Given these requirements, it may seem impractical or even unnecessary to consider truth commissions in established democracies, such as the United States. But this consideration is not unprecedented. Just five years ago in the United States, there were ongoing public discussions about truth commissions to investigate the programs of enhanced interrogation and extraordinary rendition, procedures at Abu Ghraib and Guantánamo, and alleged violations of fundamental rights of habeas corpus and privacy in the aftermath of the attacks on September 11, 2001. Cogent appeals for a truth commission were heard from several sources, including the chairs of the Senate Judiciary Committee (Leahy 2009), the House Judiciary Committee (Conyers 2009), and the Senate Armed Services Committee (Kingsbury 2009; Levin 2005; Mayer 2009); prominent journalists (Ambinder 2009; Kristof 2008, 2009a, 2009b; Rutten 2009); leaders of human rights organizations (Cox 2009; Malinowski 2008); legal scholars (Cole 2009; Martinez 2009); and a coalition of more than 200 religious groups (Salmon

2009). There was also a growing investigative literature studying abuses at Guantánamo (Margulies 2007; Worthington 2007) and Abu Ghraib (Danner 2004; Greenberg and Dratel 2005; Hersh 2005), with extraordinary rendition and black sites (Conyers 2009; Mayer 2009), with operations in the Department of Justice (Iglesias 2008), and with the program of warrantless wiretapping (Fine et al. 2009).

A constitutional rebuttal to calling for a truth commission in the United States would identify those institutions for finding truth that are already in place and cite existing checks and balances designed to prevent or expose criminal acts in the government. A political rebuttal would opine that partisan positions are too polarized to agree on the specifics of such a commission. A historical rebuttal would aver that the preferred method of official inquiry is the fact-finding commission, with prominent examples being the Warren Commission, the Kerner Commission on Race, the Commission on the Internment of Japanese-Americans during World War II, and the 9/11 Commission.

A reply to these rebuttals would show that serious constitutional abuses can occur even with established oversight, that political consensus can be reached in the case of serious violations of human rights, and that fact-finding commissions are not the same as truth commissions. Regarding fact-finding commissions, they are typically not centered on listening to the victims, they do not impose consequences on the offenders, their work is mostly private—other than a public report—and although they may take testimony, the testimony is not necessarily public or under oath. With the 9/11 Commission, for example, President George Bush, former president Bill Clinton, Vice President Dick Cheney, and former vice president Al Gore testified privately and not under oath, President Bush and Vice President Cheney took the unusual step of testifying together, and Condoleezza Rice, the national security advisor during the attacks of 9/11, did not testify at all.

Even though public discussions about truth commissions in the United States are nonexistent in today's political discourse, now that the idea of a truth commission has entered the cultural lexicon, and now that it has engendered serious political debate, it may reemerge in the future as a suggested solution to large-scale violations of constitutional rights. If so, applying the distinctive achievements of the South African TRC while avoiding its identified shortcomings would provide a valuable beginning for such a process.

Conclusions

Learning from the Violence of Others

The amnesty hearings of the South African TRC provided an unprecedented opportunity to study perpetrators of political violence and the difficulties and intricacies of reconciling in the wake of this violence. The Amnesty Committee of the TRC granted complete amnesty to the violent perpetrators of apartheid South Africa in exchange for full and public disclosure of their political crimes and the reasons for committing these crimes. Perpetrators were also required to answer all questions from the Amnesty Committee and to confront their victims and members of the victims' families. All the amnesty hearings were videotaped and transcribed, which ultimately created the most extensive collection of testimony from violent perpetrators ever assembled. Analysis of this testimony then made it possible to learn directly from the people involved how ordinary human beings manage to commit extraordinary brutality in the service of a political cause and how victims and perpetrators attempt to reconcile in the aftermath.

Regarding Perpetrators of Collective Violence

Individuals transform into violence workers in a stepwise process. An initial set of influences constitutes a *platform* that encourages violent behavior, beginning with a selective set of beliefs that demonizes other groups of people and deifies one's own group and culminating in a devoted commitment to follow through on the goals of a violent organization. Once inside a violent organization, perpetrators are *primed* through strategic indoctrination and tactical training, a progression in the destructiveness of the assigned operations, the maintenance of tight cohesiveness and strict secrecy, and the invocation of *war* as the ultimate justification. Within violent organizations, members progress incrementally and quickly across different levels of involvement, with each new level of violence more destructive than the last and with acclimation to each level serving both as a barrier to stepping back and as preparation for the next level of violence. Ultimately, many perpetrators find themselves at a level of violence where they harass, torture, and murder their designated enemies.

Within violent organizations, individuals and their organizations influence each other reciprocally to engage in bolder and even more ambitiously destructive operations. Managers of collective violence are not thoughtless bureaucrats, passively shaped by their responsibilities. Instead, they willingly accept the destructive strategies of their organizations, creatively developing and refining their own methods of destruction. In their violent organizations, perpetrators display ambition and ingenuity, dispelling the illusion of the follower.

Within the binding norms of violent organizations, expectations shift so radically that torture and murder can be assimilated into one's repertoire and maintained through social conformity and rationalization. In turn, members of these organizations can cite clear reasons for each act of violence and unquestioned beliefs in the virtue of their organizations and their specific operations. In apartheid South Africa, for example, setting lethal car bombs, blowing up community buildings in downtown Johannesburg, and torturing prisoners with electric shocks were all justified as necessary and morally appropriate actions at the time. Comprehensive ideologies are not necessary for maintaining sustained violence. An abbreviated ideological rationale reinforces motivation and justification—supported in some cases by simple, deadly slogans.

Testimony from perpetrators during the amnesty hearings demonstrated convincingly that once an organization begins to implement its violence, it is very difficult to prevent *triggering events* that initiate even more violence. Once primed, violent actions need only a momentary trigger to set them in motion. During the height of the political violence in South Africa, only a highly unexpected event could shock the combatants into pausing, as with the murder of Amy Biehl, when leaders of the warring organizations broke with their long-standing traditions of unrelenting antagonism.

Given these findings, initial efforts to prevent collective violence or attenuate ongoing violence should focus on the establishment of *competing platforms* of openness and nonviolence.[1] Such platforms are most effective before partial ideologies of hatred and violence become prevalent, but they are also effectively established in opposition to hateful beliefs, even after their rise to official prominence.[2]

The next step would be to *minimize priming* within potentially violent organizations. Given that sovereign countries will not willingly relinquish their security agencies or dismantle their militaries, independent investigative offices within these organizations should make regular and concerted efforts to reassess their ongoing operating procedures. In addition, as testimony from the amnesty hearings strongly suggested, the potential for collective violence can be appreciably reduced with more openness in existing security agencies and more flexibility in bureaucratic hierarchies that engage in covert operations, with provisions for questioning policies and directives and for reporting violations of the law.[3]

In light of the amnesty testimony, a focused effort should also be made to educate members of secret governmental agencies specifically about the cultures and histories of countries and organizations that are the targets of these agencies. During the hearings for the Trust Feed killings, for example, Captain Brian Mitchell spoke of being "shrouded in a cocoon of ignorance" and living within "a capsule of indoctrination and beliefs," which encouraged him to carry out his murderous security operations against the ANC (Mitchell, October 16, 1996). Notably, high-ranking state perpetrators in South Africa traced their single-minded focus on eradicating the liberation movements back to personal histories of never coming in contact with ideas other than those of the pro-apartheid National Party and the Dutch Reformed Church (Coetzee, November 5, 1996; de Kock, July 29, 1998; Erasmus, November 27, 2000; van der Merwe, July 22, 1998; Vlok, July 21, 1998).

These general recommendations may seem obvious, especially from a reflective distance, but the very pervasiveness of hateful messages in a dominant culture can mask how truly unusual they are—relative to historic norms. Radical messages of fear and intolerance can saturate the public media to such an extent that cultural norms shift and particular violations of human rights move dramatically from the execrable to the acceptable. In the United States, for example, after September 11, 2001, various forms of torture that had been condemned for years were openly discussed and officially approved as valuable tactics against designated enemies in the war on terror. In fact, truth commissions themselves can provide a powerful corrective to years of corrupting messages that normalize systemic injustice and condone deadly abuses of human rights.

Promoting Reconciliation

Reconciliation begins with sincere disclosure. Perpetrators convey the specifics of their crimes and victims tell of the suffering they experienced. Reconciliation proceeds when perpetrators acknowledge the suffering of the victims and victims work to understand the conditions that influenced the destructive actions of the perpetrators. Reconciliation demands that *both* sides of the conflict bridge the gap between their different perspectives. The perpetrator accepts what the victim says about the pain, humiliation, and long-term suffering caused by the perpetrator's crimes; the victim accepts what the perpetrator says about the situational constraints and personal weaknesses that led to the commission of these crimes. With continued effort, perpetrators can understand the victims' suffering, as the victims discern the perpetrators' humanity. To reconcile, in the words of Cynthia Ozick (2010), people need to achieve "a knowledge beyond the commonplace" (93).

In reconciliation, both sides shift their perspectives. One-sided efforts do not work. Captain Dirk Coetzee fully disclosed his role in the murder of Sizwe Khondile and offered sincere regret for his ideology and his murderous actions, but Khondile's mother did not participate in the hearings and could not justifiably reciprocate. Candice van der Linde participated in the amnesty hearings for Robert McBride, stating that she was open to reconciliation for the car bombing death of her mother. When she left the hearings, however, she said she was more distant from reconciliation than before. According to van der Linde, Robert McBride's testimony lacked contrition, avoided the admission of mistakes, and neglected the perspectives of the victims, thereby failing the minimal requirements for a perpetrator to achieve reconciliation (van der Linde, October 13, 1999).

One surprising development during the amnesty hearings was that victims could forgive perpetrators but at the same time *not* support reconciliation or amnesty. Analysis of the exchanges between victims and the perpetrators and between victims and members of the

Amnesty Committee helped explain this difference, showing that forgiveness and reconciliation are two separate processes. When victims and their families explicitly forgave perpetrators, forgiveness had already been achieved in private before the amnesty hearings began. Victims stated that they based their forgiveness in their own belief systems, renouncing anger and revenge against the perpetrators and accepting their own pain and suffering as part of the human condition. During the amnesty hearings, forgiveness appeared as an internal disengagement from the perpetrator. No response was required of the perpetrator, except to listen to and acknowledge the statement of forgiveness from the victim.

In contrast, reconciliation is an iterative process, requiring direct interactions between perpetrators and victims. Perpetrators describe their crimes, take responsibility, and acknowledge the suffering of the victims. Victims then work toward understanding the perspectives of the perpetrators. Reconciliation requires specifics from the perpetrator: What was done, by whom, and for what reasons? During the amnesty hearings, victims and their families forgave the whole person but reconciled with the specific destructive acts of that person.

Obstacles to reconciliation appeared during the confrontations between perpetrators and victims, with the primary obstacle being incomplete disclosure by the perpetrators. If disclosure appeared insufficient, victims and their families strenuously sought more testimony and refused to reconcile unless the testimony was forthcoming. Another major obstacle to reconciliation is the magnitude gap— the predictable discrepancies between how victims and perpetrators remember the same events, with victims experiencing stronger emotions and more intense and vivid personal involvement. Perpetrators bracket their criminal incidents within a narrow time frame, whereas victims remember the incidents as part of a series of events with a longer duration. Perpetrators place their wrongdoing within the context of doing their jobs, whereas victims do not recall mitigating factors that might lessen the severity of the crimes. From the perpetrator's perspective, the violence is justified; from the victim's perspective, the violence is incomprehensible and senseless. Victims perceive perpetrators as powerful individuals, able to choose between right and wrong, whereas perpetrators see themselves as having functioned within a powerful system, carrying out their necessary duties.

One powerful influence in overcoming the magnitude gap and moving toward reconciliation during the amnesty hearings was the testimony itself, which humanized and particularized the perpetrator. Before the amnesty hearings, victims knew the perpetrators exclusively through their destructive actions, their work. During testimony, however, perpetrators became more than professional violence workers, revealing themselves as flawed and understandable human beings—with distinctive mannerisms, personal weaknesses, and emotional responses. A final influence toward reconciliation was the punishment of disclosure, with testimony serving as a form of immediate justice for the perpetrators.

Ideally, efforts to reconcile include sincere disclosure by the perpetrators, public acknowledgment of those who suffered and those who inflicted the suffering, a recognition of humanity in both the victims and the perpetrators, redress for the victims, and an expectation of civil relationships among former adversaries. With continued efforts, reconciliation can then lead to coexistence, which involves a long-term commitment to live together without animosity and to accommodate full participation from all parties in the institutions and daily activities of public and private life.

Final Observations

This book ends with guarded hopefulness. In countries with histories of focused injustice and violent conflict, it is surprisingly easy to shape people to commit violence for a cause—to kill and torture other human beings without regard for their suffering. In apartheid South Africa, for example, some special training was necessary for the managers of collective violence, but not elaborate training. With foundational principles of restorative justice in place, however, it is also possible to reshape violent offenders and to encourage understanding between former enemies. Based on traditions in different parts of the world—the healing circles of Hollow Water, the peace-building approaches of the Navajo, the southern Africa worldview of Ubuntu—the concepts underlying restorative justice can be effectively applied on a national scale with truth commissions trying to repair the damage from widespread political violence and on a more local scale with community-based programs facilitating reconciliation between individual offenders and victims (Amnesty International 2009; Bronkhorst 2006; Hayner 2002; Johnstone 2003; Perry 2002; van Ness and Strong 2010).

The TRC was a temporary institution mandated to gather truth and promote reconciliation but not to resolve long-standing divisions in South African society. Nonetheless, as a temporary institution, the TRC derived permanence from its six years of focused investigations and hearings on the crimes of apartheid, from the lessons and strategies it conveyed to ongoing and future programs in restorative justice, and *most tangibly* from the videotaped and transcribed testimony of its hearings.

Violence to conquer and enforce oppression of other people and violence to gain freedom from this oppression have been prevalent for millennia, but direct and detailed accounts from the violent oppressors and from those fighting for their freedom are something distinctive and new. The testimonies from the amnesty hearings provide a rare view of the interior life of violent perpetrators and of their efforts to regain their humanity after the violence and reconcile with those they have victimized.

By recording, transcribing, and collecting the testimony of violent perpetrators, the Amnesty Committee created both a memorial of apartheid and an archive to be used for future research. In one testimony after another from the amnesty hearings, perpetrators reveal their specific memories of the crimes, their thoughts while committing these crimes, and their reasons for committing them. Moreover, each videotaped testimony presents a face and a voice that would otherwise not be seen or heard, providing information that could not be gathered from documents or represented in the broad strokes of statistics. The words, the gestures, the intonations, the hesitations, the emotional distress, the painful insights, the struggle to explain what previously appeared inexplicable are all immediate and available in the videotaped testimony of the amnesty hearings.

Studying a collection of perpetrator testimonies imparts a valuable synthesis of the psychological and the historical, revealing the actions of the individual within broader patterns of past events. Testimony from the amnesty hearings allows us to study many perpetrators, one at a time, divulging their crimes in public—in safe, communal spaces and in direct, civil confrontations with the people they once victimized. This very testimony about the torment and destruction of other human beings teaches us about collective violence but also about restoring individuals and rebuilding communities in the aftermath of this violence. The testimony allows us to see violent perpetrators not as inscrutable villains or enigmatically robotic bureaucrats but as flawed and destructive individuals trying to account for their past transgressions, as human beings who can be listened to and contemplated—and ultimately understood.

APPENDIX

List of Analyzed Testimonies from the TRC Amnesty Hearings:
Perpetrators, Victims, and Witnesses

PERPETRATORS (APPLICANTS FOR AMNESTY)

NAMES, DATES, LOCATIONS, AND INFORMAL LABELS OF THE HEARINGS

Andrews, Marcel: October 8, 1999, Durban, "Robert McBride Hearings"

Bellingan, W. Riaan: November 17–19, 1997, Cape Town, "Guguletu Seven"; July 30, 1998, Pretoria, "Khotso and COSATU House Bombings"

Benzien, Jeffrey T. (captain): July 14–16, 1997, and October 20–21, 1997, Cape Town, "The Killing of Ashley Kriel and the Torture of Activists, Parts 1 and 2"

Coetzee, Dirk (captain, commander of Vlakplass): November 5–7, 1996, Durban, and January 20–21, 1997, Johannesburg, "The Killing of Griffiths Mxenge, Parts 1 and 2"

Cronje, Jan Hattingh (brigadier): February 24–26 and March 7, 1997, Pretoria, "Killing of Joe Tsele; Killing of Brian Ngqulunga and Interrogation of Scheepers Morudu"; March 11, 1997, Cape Town, "Torture and Murder of Activists"

de Kock, Eugene (colonel, commander of Vlakplass): July 29–30, 1998, Pretoria, "Khotso and COSATU House Bombings"; October 1, 1997, Port Elizabeth, "Killing of Motherwell 4"; January 29, 1998, Bloemfontein, "Various Killings"

Dube, John: February 16–17, 1999, Johannesburg, "Murder of Sicelo Dlomo"

Dumakude, Lester: September 29, 1999, Durban, "Robert McBride Hearings"

Erasmus, Paul (Security Police): November 27–29, 2000, Johannesburg, "Bombing of Alexandria Health Clinic"

Goosen, Eric (sergeant): May 3, 1999, Pretoria, "Kidnapping and Assault"

Gqomfa, Luyanda: October 27–28, 1997, and January 14, 1998, Cape Town, "Heidelberg Tavern Massacre"

Griebenauw, Johannes (major general): October 20, 1997, Cape Town, "The Killing of Ashley Kriel and the Torture of Activists, Part 2"

Gumbi, Mduduzi: July 28–29, 1997, Pietermaritzburg, "Gumbi and Zuma"

Hechter, Jacques (captain): February 24–26 and March 3 and 6, 1997, Pretoria, "Killing of Joe Tsele; Killing of Brian Ngqulunga and Interrogation of Scheepers Morudu"; March 11, 1997, Cape Town, "Torture and Murder of Activists"

Hlengwa, Vusi: August 7, 1997, Durban, "Murder of Masulele Makanja"

Hlope, Msizi: August 4, 1997, Durban, "Double Murder"

Ismail, Aboobaker (ANC commander): September 28 and October 7, 1999, Durban, "Robert McBride Hearings"; May 6, 1998, Johannesburg, "ANC Bombers"

Jodwana, Mncedisi: May 27, 1999, East London, "Bisho Massacre"

Kolela, Mthetheli: May 25, 1999, East London, "Bisho Massacre"

Kondile, Zandisile: October 12, 1998, "Katlehong Massacre"

Kulman, Luvoyo: April 16–17, 1998, East London, "Killing of Donné and Mike Meyers"

Lecordier, Matthew: October 11, 1999, Durban, "Robert McBride Hearings"

le Roux, Johan (general): July 29, 1998, Pretoria, "Khotso and COSATU House Bombings"

Mabala, Sola Prince: October 28, 1997, and January 14, 1998, Cape Town, "Heidelberg Tavern Massacre"

Madasi, Vuyisile: October 28, 1997, and January 14, 1998, Cape Town, "Heidelberg Tavern Massacre"

Makhubu, Clive: February 17–18, 1999, Johannesburg, "Murder of Sicelo Dlomo"

Makoma, Gcinikhaya Christopher: July 9–10, 1997, Cape Town, "St. James Church Massacre"

Mani, Mabitana: May 25, 1999, East London, "Bisho Massacre"

Manqina, Mongesi: July 8, 1997, Cape Town, "The Killing of Amy Biehl"

Maxam, Philemon: July 7, 1997, Cape Town, "Killing of Rholian-Anne Foster and John Geyser"

Mbelo, Tikapela: November 18, 1997, and February 3–4, 1998, Cape Town, "Guguletu 7, Parts 1 and 2"

Mbuyazi, Bheki: August 1, 1997, Durban, "Bheki Mbuyazi"

McBride, Robert: October 5–7, 1999, Durban, "Robert McBride Hearings"

Mentz, Willem (captain): February 24–25, 1997, Pretoria, "Killing of Joe Tsele; Killing of Brian Ngqulunga and Interrogation of Scheepers Morudu"; March 12 1997, Cape Town, "Torture and Murder of Activists"

Mitchell, Brian (police commander): October 15–16, 1996, Pietermaritzburg, "Trust Feed Killings"

Mkhumbuzi, Bassie: July 9–10, 1997, Cape Town, "St. James Church Massacre"

Mkosana, Vakele: February 3, 2000, East London, "Bisho Massacre"

Mlambisa, Thobela: July 9–10, 1997, Cape Town, "St. James Church Massacre"

Mnisi, Johannes: September 29, 1999, Durban, "Robert McBride Hearings"; May 8, 1998, Johannesburg, "ANC Bombers"

Momberg, Willem (lieutenant, Security Police): May 3, 1999, Pretoria, "Kidnapping and Assault"

Motaung, Sipho: July 29, 1997, Pietermaritzburg, "Pietermaritzburg Hearings"

Mthembu, Dumisani: July 31, 1997, Pietermaritzburg, "Attempted Murders"

Mthembu, Victor: July 6, 1998, Sebokeng, "Boipatong Massacre"

Myeza, Thulani: March 26, 1998, Durban, "Massacres and Assassinations at KwaZulu-Natal in the Early 1990s"

Narkedien, Zahrah (née Greta Apelgren), October 7, 1999, Durban, "Robert McBride Hearings"

Ndinisa, Crosby: July 7, 1997, Cape Town, "Killing of Rholian-Anne Foster and John Geyser"

Ndlovu, Mkanyiso: March 26, 1998, Durban, "Massacres and Assassinations at KwaZulu-Natal in the Early 1990s"

Ngcobo, Goodman: March 23, 1998, Durban, "Massacres and Assassinations at KwaZulu-Natal in the Early 1990s"

Ngqunge, Bafo: May 25, 1999, East London, "Bisho Massacre"

Nieuwoudt, Gideon (colonel, Security Police): September 30, 1997, Port Elizabeth, "Killing of the Motherwell 4"; March 30, 1998, Cape Town, "Death of Mr. Biko"

Nofemela, Easy: July 8, 1997, Cape Town, "The Killing of Amy Biehl"

Nofomela, Almond: January 20–22, 1997, Johannesburg, "The Killing of Griffiths Mxenge"

Ntamo, Vusumzi: July 9, 1997, Cape Town, "The Killing of Amy Biehl"

Nzimande, Mafoeka: July 30, 1997, Pietermaritzburg, "Gengeshe Murders of September 1992"

Pearce, Edward: October 8, 1999, Durban, "Robert McBride Hearings"

Peni, Ntombeki: July 8, 1997, Cape Town, "The Killing of Amy Biehl"

Poswa, Mandlenkosi: July 30, 1997, Pietermaritzburg, "Gengeshe Murders of September 1992"

Pule, Ernest: September 29, 1999, Durban, "Robert McBride Hearings"

Schoon, W. F. (brigadier): July 23, 1998, Pretoria, "Khotso and COSATU House Bombings"

Shaik, Mohamed A.: May 6–7, 1998, Johannesburg, "ANC Bombers"

Sibisi, Nhlanhla: July 29, 1997, Pietermaritzburg, "Pietermaritzburg Hearings"

Sithole, Johannes: July 29, 1997, Pietermaritzburg, "Pietermaritzburg Hearings"

Thembu, Nimrod: March 24, 1998, Durban, "Massacres and Assassinations at Kwa-Zulu-Natal in the Early 1990s"

Thutha, Zama: April 16–17, 1998, East London, "Killing of Donné and Mike Meyers"

Tisana, Madoda: July 7, 1997, Cape Town, "Killing of Rholian-Anne Foster and John Geyser"

Tshabalala, Sipho: February 18, 1999, Johannesburg, "Murder of Sicelo Dlomo"

Tshikalanga, David: January 20–21, 1997, Johannesburg, "The Killing of Griffiths Mxenge"

van der Merwe, Johannes (general and police commissioner): July 22 and 28, 1998, Pretoria, "Khotso and COSATU House Bombings"

van Rensburg, Nicholas (general and divisional commander): September 29, 1997, Port Elizabeth, "Killing of the Motherwell 4"; February 25, 1998, Port Elizabeth, "Crad-dock 4"

van Vuuren, Paul (warrant officer): February 25–26 and March 6, 1997, Pretoria, "Killing of Joe Tsele; Killing of Brian Ngqulunga and Interrogation of Scheepers Morudu"; March 11 1997, Cape Town, "Torture and Murder of Activists" van Zyl, Johan (colonel): February 23, 1998, Port Elizabeth, "Craddock 4"

Vlok, Adriaan (government minister of law and order): July 20, 22, and 27, 1998, Pretoria, "Khotso and COSATU House Bombings"

Zuma, Robert: July 28–29, 1997, Pietermaritzburg, "Gumbi and Zuma"

Zungu, Precious Wiseman: February 18, 1999, Johannesburg, "Murder of Sicelo Dlomo"

VICTIMS

Ackerman, David Jacobus: July 10, 1997, Cape Town, "The St. James Church Massacre"

Adams, Melanie: August 5, 1996, Cape Town, "The Killing of Ashley Kriel"

Ashua, Michelle (the sister of the late Ashley Kriel): July 16, 1997, Cape Town, "The Killing of Ashley Kriel and the Torture of Activists, Part 1"

Atkinson, Gary: October 31, 1997, Cape Town, "Heidelberg Tavern Massacre"

Biehl, Linda: July 9, 1997, Cape Town, "The Killing of Amy Biehl"

Biehl, Peter: July 9, 1997, Cape Town, "The Killing of Amy Biehl"

Brode, Benjamin: October 31, 1997, Cape Town, "Heidelberg Tavern Massacre"

Burton, Claire: October 12, 1999, Durban, "Robert McBride Hearings"

Cerqueira, Franciso: October 31, 1997, Cape Town, "Heidelberg Tavern Massacre"

Cornelius, Quentin: October 31, 1997, Cape Town, "Heidelberg Tavern Massacre"

Dlamini, Recoria Judith: July 28–29, 1997, Pietermaritzburg, "Gumbi and Zuma"

Dlomo family: February 19, 1999, Johannesburg, "Murder of Sicelo Dlomo"

Dlomo-Jele, Sylvia: February 19, 1999, Johannesburg, "Murder of Sicelo Dlomo"

Erwin, Diane: October 13, 1999, Durban, "Robert McBride Hearings"

Forbes, Ashley: July 14, 1997, Cape Town, "The Killing of Ashley Kriel and the Torture of Activists, Part 1"

Fourie, Jeanette Anne: October 31, 1997, Cape Town, "Heidelberg Tavern Massacre"

Fourie, Johann: October 31, 1997, Cape Town, "Heidelberg Tavern Massacre"

Gerrard, Cher: October 13, 1999, Durban, "Robert McBride Hearings"

Jacobs, Peter Anthony: July 15, 1997, Cape Town, "The Killing of Ashley Kriel and the Torture of Activists, Part 1"

January, Michael: October 31, 1997, Cape Town, "Heidelberg Tavern Massacre"

Jeffers, Jonathan: October 12, 1999, Durban, "Robert McBride Hearings"

Jonas, Bongani: July 15, 1997, Cape Town, "The Killing of Ashley Kriel and the Torture of Activists, Part 1"

Kearney, Helen: October 12–13, 1999, Durban, "Robert McBride Hearings"

Khondile, Charity: November 5, 1996, Durban, "The Killing of Sizwe Khondile"

Kruse, Gary: July 14, 1997, Cape Town, "The Killing of Ashley Kriel and the Torture of Activists, Part 1"

Langford, Andrea: October 31, 1997, Cape Town, "Heidelberg Tavern Massacre"

Mabela, Legina Ngqulunga (mother of Brian Ngqulunga), February 24, 1997, Cape Town, "Killing of Brian Ngqulunga"

Maponya, Akanyang Daniel: January 21, 1997, Johannesburg, "The Killing of Griffiths Mxenge"

Morudu, Scheepers: February 26, 1997, Cape Town, "Interrogation of Scheepers Morudu"

Palm, Roland: October 31, 1997, Cape Town, "Heidelberg Tavern Massacre"

Pedro, Niclo: October 20–21, 1997, Cape Town, "The Killing of Ashley Kriel and the Torture of Activists, Part 2"

Ramhitshana, Violet: November 29, 2000, Johannesburg, "Bombing of Alexandria Health Clinic"

Smith, Lorenzo Victor: July 10, 1997, Cape Town, "St. James Church Massacre"

Tholakele Catherine (wife of Brian Ngqulunga), February 25, 1997, Cape Town, "Killing of Brian Ngqulunga"

Tsoeunyane, Beauty: November 29, 2000, Johannesburg, "Bombing of Alexandria Health Clinic"

Unnamed family members related to the killed victims: August 1, 1997, Durban, "Case of Bheki Mbuyazi"

van der Linde, Candice: October 13, 1999, Durban, "Robert McBride Hearings"

Welgemoed (née Gerrard), Sharon: October 12–13, 1999, Durban, "Robert McBride Hearings"

Wilson, Timothy (doctor): November 29, 2000, Johannesburg, "Bombing of Alexandria Health Clinic"

Yengeni, Tony (demonstration of "wet bag" torture with Jeffrey Benzien): July 14, 1997, Cape Town, "The Killing of Ashley Kriel and the Torture of Activists, Part 1"

WITNESSES

Klepp (doctor): February 18, 1999, Johannesburg, "Murder of Sicelo Dlomo"

Kotzé, Sarah: October 21, 1997, Cape Town, Psychologist and expert witness in the hearings for Captain Jeffrey Benzien.

Loots, Flip (colonel): February 28 and March 3, 1997, Cape Town.

Mosikare, Ntombi: February 18, 1999, Johannesburg, "Murder of Sicelo Dlomo"

Sibaya, Bennet: October 28, 1997, Cape Town, "Heidelberg Tavern Massacre"

Siubulena, Jabulani (colonel): March 5, 1997, Cape Town, "Assault of Richard Motasi"

Tlhwale, Ramatala Joseph: February 18, 1999, Johannesburg, "Murder of Sicelo Dlomo"

Zwane, Puleng: February 19, 1999, Johannesburg, "Murder of Sicelo Dlomo"

NOTES

NOTES TO INTRODUCTION

1. *Regarding the Pain of Others* by Susan Sontag. © 2003 by Susan Sontag. Reproduced by permission of Farrar, Straus and Giroux, LLC. and Penguin Books, Ltd.
2. Martin S. Holocaust Testimony (T-641), Fortunoff Video Archive for Holocaust Testimonies, Yale University Library.

NOTES TO CHAPTER 1

1. The SABC televised the hearings throughout the week and then assembled a one-hour special report to be broadcast every Sunday (Thloloe 1998). These reports contained a broad range of programming: educational documentary footage, interviews, private reconciliations, special hearings, and excerpts of testimony from the Human Rights Violations Committee, the Reparation and Rehabilitation Committee, and the Amnesty Committee—with footage of testimony from perpetrators applying for amnesty. A complete collection of the eighty-four special reports broadcast by the SABC is housed in the South African TRC Videotape Collection of the Yale Law School Lillian Goldman Library (www.law.yale.edu/trc). The full collection of videotaped footage is housed in the National Archives of South Africa, established by the National Archives and Records Service of South Africa Act (Act No. 43 of 1996, as amended).
2. Although eleven languages were spoken at the hearings, the five most frequently used languages accounted for most of the testimony and dialogue (English, Afrikaans, Xhosa, Zulu, and Sotho). All the translators were provided by the Unit for Language Facilitation and Empowerment of the University of the Free State (TRC 2003a, 748–751).
3. Within the security forces, managers were located in the middle ranks of captain, warrant officer, and (depending on one's responsibilities) sergeant. If a captain was in charge of a large operation, that person would be considered an upper-level manager in the organizational hierarchy (e.g., Captain Dirk Coetzee, in charge of an entire operation at Vlakplaas). Commanders were generals and colonels, and executives were people in the civilian ranks of the apartheid government in charge of particular departments, including cabinet ministers. Foot soldiers in the security forces were low-ranking enlisted personnel.

In the liberation forces, managers were those people in charge of particular cells or specific operations planned by the larger organization. Commanders or executives were literally given the title of commander and were in charge of formulating policies and strategies. Foot soldiers were those people in the liberation forces who took orders to carry out specific operations.

The bulk of testimony came from the managers in the security forces and the liberation movements, even though all three levels of perpetrator were well represented. Although all perpetrators talked of their thoughts and motivations, in terms of detailed organizational information, commanders were knowledgeable about political strategies and chains of command, managers were knowledgeable about justifying, planning, and carrying out specific operations, and foot soldiers primarily focused on implementation of specific operations.

4. Volume 5 of the TRC final report states, "To be even-handed in understanding the motives of perpetrators also requires full recognition that violence of the powerful, the South African state, was not necessarily equal with violence of the powerless, the disenfranchised, oppressed and relatively voiceless black majority" (TRC 1999c, 276).

5. One general limitation of this methodology is that influences not described in the testimony were not available for analysis. With the perpetrator testimony, the most notable omission involved gender-related norms. The vast majority of perpetrators who applied for amnesty were male, and although gender-related norms were a pervasive influence within the violent political organizations of apartheid South Africa, the very ubiquity of these norms made them invisible to these male perpetrators (TRC 1999c). All the perpetrators in this study but one were male, so the invisibility of gender-related norms meant that concepts of masculinity were not brought up in the testimony and were not subject to analysis. Another mostly unmentioned influence was the Cold War. Even though the Communist Party in South Africa was aligned with the ANC, the Cold War was rarely mentioned in the testimony—except by a few senior officials in the apartheid security forces—because it was such a distant influence on the perpetrators and because the Communist Party of South Africa focused on apartheid and not on the wider issues of the Cold War or the Soviet Union.

6. In addition, unlike phenomenological studies that gather data through interviews, I did not directly engage with the participants. I studied each videotaped testimony in the third person. With this method, I could attend closely to the words, the intonations, and the gestures of the people giving testimony, to the questions and statements from the Amnesty Committee and other participants, and to the reactions of the audience—without intruding on the proceedings. Those involved in the amnesty hearings were unaffected by my appearance or my mood or my facial expressions or my spontaneous, unintentional remarks or how much time I spent observing each testimony.

7. In the second step, as Wertz (2011) has described, the ideas or "meaning units" can vary in size, from a phrase to longer expressions. With analysis of transcribed text,

Giorgi and Giorgi (2003) specifically used what they called "meaning transitions" to separate the different meaning units, placing a dividing line between adjacent passages whenever there was a shift of topic (33). For my analysis, I identified ideas (meaning units) by adapting procedures originally developed by cognitive psychologists Walter Kintsch and Jean Mandler for parsing connected discourse into individual propositions and narrative units (Kintsch and van Dijk 1978; Kintsch 1985; McKoon 1977; Mandler and Johnson 1977). I also noted the type of reasoning used in each segment of testimony, drawing on standard categories of figurative language (Corbett 1990). Finally, with the videotaped testimony, I noted nonlinguistic factors: pauses, facial expressions, hand gestures, and eye contact.

8. The third step involved differentiating and combining the ideas identified in the testimonies. After studying and analyzing a subset of testimonies, taking overviews and identifying ideas, I compared exemplified ideas across different testimonies, grouping similar exemplified ideas into categories and building a comprehensive set of categories with particular instances in each category. According to Wertz (2011), this step is the most difficult because it entails understanding the relations among constituents and "thematizing recurrent modes of experience, meanings, and motifs" (132).

9. The world hypothesis underlying progressive qualitative analysis is *formism,* with its root metaphor of similarity (Pepper 1942). That is, the analysis assumed that there were commonalities in the influences, motivations, and experiences of violent perpetrators and that by comparing many testimonies, these common-alities could be identified. Supporting the basic assumption of formism was the shared defining experience for the perpetrators in this study: active participation in a violent political organization fighting against a designated enemy. In fact, the powerful abnormality of the perpetrators' experience often resulted in similar or even identical language in the testimony, especially in the stated reasons and moti-vations for committing illegal violence against others. This verbatim commonality was helpful in identifying the patterns of influence, motivation, and experience.

The world hypothesis of formism can be contrasted with *contextualism,* which would view each testimony as a distinct whole, emphasizing the individuality of experience and not the shared patterns of influence, motivation, and experience. A contextualist approach would then lead to an analysis that presented a set of individual narratives, with each narrative distinct from the others. With contex-tualism, one event may have details of texture in common with other events, but taken as a whole, its combination of details is unique and not comparable to other events. As an example, the main, middle section of *The Theatre of Violence: Narra-tives of Protagonists in the South African Conflict* (Foster, Haupt, and de Beer 2005) can be considered a contextualist analysis of perpetrator narratives, featuring the individuals and not the commonalities across different narratives.

10. The operational definitions of these categories involved eighteen types of killing, thirteen types of torture, sixteen types of severe ill-treatment, and two types of abduction (TRC 1999c).

NOTES TO CHAPTER 2

1. One of the foundational principles of apartheid was the establishment of a single nation for the white racial group (those of European ancestry who spoke either Afrikaans or English) and multiple nations for the different black ethnic groups and other nonwhites, making the white nation the largest in the country (Thompson 2000). To divide the black communities and disenfranchise them from the larger South Africa, the apartheid government created distinct *homelands* for nonwhites, based what it considered to be the dominant ethnicity in each designated homeland. In addition, the government fragmented each homeland into different areas, separated by more economically desirable white-owned areas. To implement the homelands system, the apartheid government deported millions of nonwhites and forced them to live in a land area totaling only 13 percent of the larger South Africa—leading to intense overcrowding and its associated problems of poverty, violent crime, economic hardship, inadequate basic services, and loss of community. Eventually, the apartheid government designated ten such homelands, with the idea of encouraging them to work toward independence, thereby isolating the homelands from the larger South Africa. Four homelands were granted nominal independence (Transkei, Bophuthatswana, Venda, and Ciskei), while the other six, including KwaZulu, ended up with various levels of independence. In addition, the apartheid government created *townships* on the outskirts of South African cities, forcibly deporting nonwhites living in the cities to these peripheral areas. In the process, the government took away the rights of South African citizenship from the inhabitants of the homelands and the townships.

2. One of the most notorious urban relocations occurred in 1955, when the government removed all black South Africans from Sophiatown near the center of Johannesburg, rezoned it for white South Africans, renamed it Triomf, and resettled the black residents into a collection of townships twelve miles from Johannesburg, which became known as Soweto (standing for South Western Townships).

3. Historical, cultural, and linguistic influences in South Africa can lead to multiple spellings of names. One provocative example is the spelling of *Guguletu* or *Gugulethu,* an area near Cape Town. The spelling during the TRC hearings and the official spelling when this book was written was *Guguletu,* so I chose that spelling. The historically accurate spelling, however, is *Gugulethu.* For instance, as of June 2013, street signs were spelled *Guguletu,* but publications discussing those street signs used the spelling *Gugulethu.* By the time this book is published, the official spelling may, in fact, be changed to *Gugulethu.*

   Surnames may also have more than one spelling in English because of choices made in translating the names from another language, most often isiZulu, isiXhosa, or Afrikaans—the three largest languages in South Africa. With multiple spellings, my strategy was to spell names as they were spelled by the TRC during its hearings. This strategy was not without complications, however, because the TRC could use different spellings during different hearings. For example,

Almond Nofomela was referred to as *Nofomela* but also *Nofemela*. W. Riaan Bellingan's surname was spelled *Bellingan* and *Bellinghan,* and also *Bellingham. Nofomela* and *Bellingan* were most frequent, so I chose those spellings.

I realize that selecting a particular spelling is not merely an orthographic choice. In making my choices, I assessed the available information and strived for consistency, even though the results could have unintended personal and political implications.

4. Beyond the numbers on violence, the statistics comparing opportunities for black and white South Africans in post-apartheid South Africa are stark. Consider just two comparisons. In 1996, after forty-six years of apartheid and two years of the ANC government, unemployment was 42.5 percent among black South Africans and only 4.5 percent among white South Africans, an unemployment rate differing by a factor of 10. In that same year, nearly a quarter of black South African adults had *no* schooling at all, whereas the percentage of white South African adults with no schooling was barely 1 percent, a clear reflection of the enforced denial of education by the apartheid government (Thompson 2000, 299).

5. On March 21, 1960, several thousand black people gathered in the township of Sharpeville to protest the "pass laws" that required Blacks to carry passports to travel within their own country. The police fired on the nonviolent protesters, ultimately wounding 186 and killing 69.

6. Some victims and family members have justifiably criticized the amnesty hearings they were personally involved in, charging the perpetrators with uncooperative and misleading testimony (e.g., Slovo 2002), but these charges do not negate the value of testimony from those perpetrators who sincerely—and fallibly—disclosed their crimes and answered the questions of the victims. The general criticism that the testimony from the amnesty applicants was "scripted" (e.g., Chapman 2007, 65) applies primarily to the opening statements of some of the amnesty applicants and not to the bulk of testimony, which occurred during later examination by the applicant's counsel, during cross-examination by the evidence leader of the Amnesty Committee and by the counsel for the victims and their families, and during questioning by the victims themselves.

7. The videotaping of the testimony changed over the six years of the amnesty hearings. Each of the earlier hearings was videotaped by one producer and two camerapersons from the South African Broadcasting Corporation (SABC), with the producer watching a monitor, directing the cameras, and choosing which camera shot to broadcast and record. With two cameras, the video shots alternated between the questioner and the applicant for amnesty. When the applicant was addressed by a member of the Amnesty Committee, one camera filmed the committee member and the other filmed the applicant. When the amnesty applicant was questioned by his former victims, the alternating shots were equivalent head-and-shoulder shots in medium close-up of the applicant and the questioner. As the exchange proceeded, both shots often became

tighter close-ups, showing mostly the face (e.g., Benzien, July 14–15, 1997). In later amnesty hearings, the SABC used a single camera that focused mainly on the amnesty applicant in medium shots, with the camera occasionally panning quickly to the questioner, often the evidence leader of the Amnesty Committee (e.g., McBride, October 5–6, 1999).

8. In the sections describing the process of giving testimony to the Amnesty Committee, I refer to the perpetrators as *amnesty applicants* or simply *applicants*. These terms are explicitly used to maintain consistency with the official procedures of the amnesty process.

9. Specifically, the amnesty hearings followed a particular sequence: (1) introductions of the chair of the Amnesty Committee, the evidence leader, the counsel for the applicant, and the counsel for the victims and their families; (2) swearing in of the amnesty applicant; (3) an opening statement by the applicant; (4) testimony from the applicant, led by the applicant's counsel; (5) cross-examination of the applicant by opposing counsel and by the evidence leader; (6) testimony from available witnesses; (7) questions and testimony from the victims and members of the victims' families; and (8) reexamination by counsel for the victims and their families and by the evidence leader. With more than one applicant at a hearing, counsel was introduced for all the applicants at the beginning, and then each applicant went through the entire process one at a time. Occasionally, before beginning the proceedings, members of the Amnesty Committee discussed the sequence of applicants and witnesses, the notification of victims and their families about the hearings, the logistics of transporting applicants who were in prison, and the distribution of materials to the various participants.

10. This informative bluntness is illustrated in the following exchange between the chair of the Amnesty Committee and Captain Dirk Coetzee, former commander in the security forces at Vlakplaas. The focus of the exchange is Coetzee's assertion that he never questioned the directives given to him (Mall, November 6, 1996; Coetzee, November 6, 1996).

JUDGE MALL, CHAIR OF THE AMNESTY COMMITTEE: So because of the position you occupied and the role you played, you didn't think that you had to verify whether the person you were going to eliminate, that the decision to do so, was based on reliable information concerning that individual?

DIRK COETZEE: Coming from my superior I accepted it as reliable, and if I had ever questioned it, or any other commander before or after me would have, they wouldn't have been in that position very long, they would have been transferred. The security culture is not formally taught, you grow into it, and your direction of specialization is then determined by your attitude toward the ANC and your skills.

JUDGE MALL: It must have come to your knowledge at some stage during your activities that you were busy eliminating people who were being eliminated perhaps on information which was not good. Innocent people might be eliminated.

DIRK COETZEE: No.

JUDGE MALL: Did it never come to your knowledge, did it never concern you?

DIRK COETZEE: It never concerned me.

11. Abrahamsen and van der Merwe (2005) studied a sample of twenty-seven amnesty applicants from the liberation movements, mostly the ANC and affiliated groups. One overriding theme from their study was the deep sincerity on the part of the applicants to reveal what they had done and to reconcile with their victims. The majority of the applicants wanted to meet the victims of their crimes, so they could explain their own actions and seek their victims' reactions. Moreover, the presence of the victims and their families was the key factor in the applicants' experience of reconciliation, overshadowing the influence of the larger audience. The most prominent idea that the applicants conveyed was that their violent actions were more motivated by the circumstances at the time and less motivated by personal choice.

12. A brief thought experiment can help evaluate the influence of external conditions on the content of the testimony. How would the testimony change, for example, if perpetrators gave unsworn statements to independent researchers in private or sworn depositions with only lawyers present? In unsworn statements for researchers, perpetrators would most likely experience less anxiety in providing testimony but also less motivation to disclose details of their crimes, given no reward for full disclosure. In sworn depositions with opposing attorneys, perpetrators would stay sharply focused on only those questions asked by the deposing attorney, offering little or no additional information about their thoughts or motivations or social pressures. Public testimony in front of the Amnesty Committee, however, was subject to questioning and commentary by a number of different participants and motivated by the requirements of conditional amnesty. It is reasonable to assume that such conditions would create more stress than private interviews or sworn depositions but would also encourage more varied and more thorough testimony.

13. According to the research of the TRC, the IFP was the main perpetrator of killings on a national scale, responsible for more than 4,500 killings, compared with 2,700 attributed to the SAP and 1,300 to the ANC (TRC 2003a, 232–233).

14. In any discussion of veracity, some of the responsibility should be assumed by the critics of the testimony. That is, what testimonies have been shown to be knowingly false? Certainly, there are such cases (chapter 4 describes a poignant example of false, self-interested testimony in the Sicelo Dlomo case), but the *documentation* of falsehoods has been rare. The more sustainable criticism concerns incompleteness, but even that does not dismiss the validity of testimony as a valuable source of information about the perpetrators' thoughts and motives. As long as the perpetrators made an honest effort to remember the violent events and to answer the questions during examination and cross-examination, the TRC testimony represents the primary source of information about the perpetrators' experiences of committing their crimes and the influences and choices that led to them.

15. Of the 157 countries and territories investigated in the 2009 Amnesty International Report on human rights, at least 20 fit the category of repressive countries with strong central governments, large bureaucracies, developed infrastructure, active participation in the global economy, and organized opposition forces. Such countries that were singled out as distinctively repressive include *Myanmar* (forced labor, torture, and killings—with more than 140,000 state killings since 2005); *Nigeria* (killings and torture by security forces); *Brazil* (extrajudicial executions, torture, abuse, and death squads composed of state agents); *North Korea* (a widespread manipulated famine, forced labor, and torture); *Saudi Arabia* (jailing of political dissidents and the oppression of women and migrant workers); *Russia* (arbitrary detention and torture); and *China* (systematic oppression of Tibetan-populated regions and increased repression of human rights activists, journalists, and ethnic minorities). Scores of other countries were documented to have committed widespread human rights abuses, including the United States (Amnesty International 2009).

NOTES TO CHAPTER 3

1. Identifying these requisite influences requires Ockham's razor to slice away those influences that may be present in some violent organizations but not necessary for the maintenance of collective violence. The South African Police, for example, did not need the extensive and violent indoctrination identified in some military dictatorships to train people to torture members of the opposition or to kill political activists (Haritos-Fatouros 2003; Huggins, Haritos-Fatouros, and Zimbardo 2002).

2. The concept of priming is drawn directly from the cognitive psychological literature on attention and memory: an immediate experience that increases the likelihood of a particular set of responses. The trigger is analogous to another concept in the cognitive psychological literature on memory: a retrieval cue for remembering a designated item.

3. For descriptions of early influences, it is best to consult case studies of individuals (e.g., Foster, Haupt, and de Beer, *The Theatre of Violence: Narratives of Protagonists in the South African Conflict* [2005]); autobiographies (e.g., Eugene de Kock, *A Long Night's Damage* [1998]; Nelson Mandela, *Long Walk to Freedom* [1995]); and biographies (e.g., Bryan Rostron's biography of Robert McBride, *Till Babylon Falls* [1991]; Pumla Gobodo-Madikizela's account of interviews with Eugene de Kock, *A Human Being Died That Night* [2003]).

4. Consider two examples. Colonel Eugene de Kock's choice of words in his autobiography, *A Long Night's Damage,* revealed a rationalizing righteousness and self-centeredness. He spoke of two colleagues, Almond Nofomela and Dirk Coetzee, with great disdain for having divulged the truth about Vlakplaas, saying that Nofomela "chirped like a canary" (40) and that Coetzee "sung like a canary" and "spilled the beans" (203), whereas when de Kock himself began

"giving evidence," he "pulled back the covers on the whole miserable story of our dirty war" and "decided to let it rip" (de Kock 1998, 273–274). Another example of diligent self-interest came just as Captain Jeffrey Benzien was about to demonstrate the wet bag method of torture interrogation in front of the Amnesty Committee. His main concern was not its offensiveness or its immorality, but rather his diminished agility in carrying it out.

5. An extensive collection of pamphlets, runs of journals, and posters that document specific, reverberating events during apartheid is housed in the Bodleian Library of Commonwealth and African Studies in Rhodes House at Oxford University.

6. Brian Mitchell was a young police captain and police station commander in Natal in the district of New Hanover, which included the village of Trust Feed. He was specifically trained to carry out clandestine operations in small black communities like Trust Feed for the purpose of interfering with the political gains made by the UDF. In an operation designed to gain advantage over the UDF in Trust Feed, Mitchell ordered an attack on a house suspected of being a safe house for the ANC. As it happened, the constables attacked the wrong house and killed eleven members of an Inkatha family who were holding a memorial service. This murderous incident later became known as the Trust Feed killings.

7. The words of Ashley Forbes echoed those of Nelson Mandela, who famously said, "The time comes in the life of any nation when there remain only two choices: submit or fight" (Mandela 1961).

8. In *Buda's Wagon* (2007), Davis recounts the history of the car bomb, beginning with an account of a horse-drawn carriage bombing on Wall Street in September 1920 carried out by Mario Buda as revenge for the arrest of his comrades, Nicola Sacco and Bartolomeo Vanzetti. The blast left 40 dead and more than 200 injured, serving as a powerful example for other anarchists and future revolutionaries of how one person could deliver large quantities of explosives to a designated target with considerable destruction.

9. In general, to provide lexical support for its own impartiality, the TRC chose neutral terminology: *operative* rather than *freedom fighter, terrorist,* or *guerrilla; former government* rather than *regime* or *apartheid state; killings* rather than *murders,* which is consistent with other truth commissions (Cherry, Daniel, and Fullard 2002, 22).

10. On July 14, 1986, McBride and his two associates, Mathew Lecordier and Greta Apelgren, participated in the car bombing on the Marine Parade near two of Durban's most popular taverns, Magoo's Bar and the Why Not Bar. Apelgren secured the parking spot with her car, waited for McBride, and then left her spot and waited down the street so McBride could park his car bomb. McBride's vehicle was loaded with fifty kilos of TNT in the trunk and a limpet mine in the center to set it off. At the conclusion of his trial, on April 7, 1987, McBride was found guilty of murdering Angelique Pattendon, Marchelle Gerrard, and Julie

van der Linde, who were in Magoos Bar the evening of the car bombing, and he was sentenced to death (Rostron 1991).

NOTES TO CHAPTER 4

1. In an eight-month period in 1993, at the headquarters of the National Intelligence Services (NIS), forty-four tons of paper and microfilm records were destroyed. As a result, no documentary evidence has been found for the National Security Management System (NSMS) or the Civil Cooperation Bureau (CCB), including the people who staffed it, how it was financed, and what it did (Bundy 2000, 16).

2. Although the TRC officially acknowledged four categories of truth, the oath it used did not. The prototype oath included the familiar phrase "The evidence you're about to give to this committee will be the truth, the whole truth, and nothing but the truth." In fact, the oath should have read, "The evidence you're about to give will be in accordance with factual, narrative, dialogic, and healing truths, from your particular perspective."

3. Outside the crucible of the truth commission, conflicts among the four kinds of truth can occur in everyday human interactions. We may be able to offer factual truth or even narrative truth, yet refrain from doing so for the purposes of social or restorative truth. For instance, in order to avoid damaging a relationship, we may withhold hurtful criticisms of a friend or choose not to scold a colleague—even when we believe we are factually or narratively accurate. That is, putting aside one type of truth can result in a different type of truth. Not telling facts that might damage a relationship can contribute to social truth; altering a narrative that is consistent with one's experience but hurtful to another can contribute to restorative truth.

4. Students of narrative may be aware that the magnitude gap is partially responsible for the acceptance of *disproportionate revenge*—in news events and also in popular entertainment (Žižek 2006, 160–161). In the standard plot of a revenge story, the roles of victim and perpetrator are reversed, and the victims end up carrying out revenge against the original perpetrators. The victims' distinctive perspective of their own suffering creates a narrative of crime and punishment that can lead them to exact revenge that far exceeds the original transgression. If a movie is structured to encourage close identification with the victims, then the excessive punishment justified by the magnitude gap is applauded by the audience.

5. In the amnesty hearings of the TRC, the subtext for many victims and perpetrators consisted of *competing conventions:* for victims, the conventions were "Never forget" and "Never again"; for perpetrators, "Let bygones be bygones" and "What's past is past."

6. The official summaries of events in the TRC database constitute synoptic narratives, abbreviated outlines of the people involved and the events, but no more. Consider, for example, the official description of the St. James Church massacre, as quoted in Buur (2002, 82):

At about 19h30 on Sunday 25 July 1993, two APLA operatives burst into the evening service at St. James' Church in Kenilworth. They fired machine guns and threw two hand-grenades covered with nails at a congregation of over a thousand people. Eleven people were killed and fifty-eight injured. The attackers escaped in a waiting car which had been hijacked earlier. The congregation was racially mixed and those killed included four Russian sailors.

7. The transcripts of the hearings regarding Sicelo Dlomo are a matter of record and can be examined for many contradictions and unsubstantiated charges. The killing of Dlomo and the testimony of John Dube, in particular, can be found on the TRC website, documenting the four days of amnesty hearings held in Johannesburg, beginning February 16, 1999 and running through February 19. A key witness, Hein Grosskopf, later appeared for his own amnesty hearing on November 21, 2000 and testified that he had never been informed of the Dlomo assassination by Dube, which contradicted Dube's sworn testimony. All three co-applicants depended on the word of John Dube in the assassination of Dlomo.

8. See Bilali, Tropp, and Dasgupta (2012) for a focused empirical study of how attributions of responsibility for mass violence shape the way individuals remember this violence and alter its representation in historical accounts.

NOTES TO CHAPTER 5

1. In addressing the general confusion about the meaning of reconciliation, Gibson (2004) offered a contextualized definition of reconciliation, specifically pertinent to post-apartheid South Africa: "People of different races getting along better with each other" (202). He then elaborated "getting along better" as more communication, greater understanding, and increased appreciation of racial diversity. Gibson's concept of reconciliation is rooted in South Africa but applicable elsewhere: equal treatment of all races, with acceptance, dignity, and respect. Gibson operationalized reconciliation in terms of nine statements having to do with treating individuals in other racial groups as individuals worthy of understanding, friendship, respect, trust, appreciation, generosity, and tolerance (205).

2. Reconciliation could also occur without forgiveness. Victims and their families could understand the political reasons for specific acts of violence and accept the general need for amnesty, while also believing that the perpetrators actively and enthusiastically (and unforgivably) chose to inflict suffering. Responses to the perpetrators' testimony from victims and their families could be structured in the form of a two-by-two diagram, with all four cells filled in: forgiveness (yes or no) and reconciliation (yes or no).

3. Personal memory is represented at two distinct levels: core memory and narrative memory. Personal events are initially stored as core memories: representations of the original phenomenal experience in the form of visual images, sounds, smells, tastes, emotions, and bodily sensations. Narrative memories are

then constructed from the images in core memory and shaped in accordance with narrative conventions. Narrative memory calls upon existing knowledge to organize the images in core memory, forming coherent representations designed to communicate with one's conscious self and with other people. When people think about and describe traumatic events, they may begin by accessing narrative memories. With continued probing, however, they can move into the lower level of core memories, reexperiencing the original images, emotions, and bodily sensations (Kraft 2002, 2004).

4. Going on record with one's crimes could also have the practical effect of encouraging threats from members of the offended community. After Captain Dirk Coetzee originally gave testimony about the illegal operations at Vlakplaas, he described having to move thirty-eight times with his two sons to stay ahead of those who might harm him (Coetzee, November 5, 1996). Jeffrey Benzien also testified directly about his efforts to combat harassment: barricading his windows, keeping a damp blanket in the bathroom to protect his children against the aftermath of grenade attacks, and being transferred away from his job.

5. According to Kriesberg (2000), coexistence can be defined by what it is *not*: a relationship between people or groups "in which none of the parties is trying to destroy the other" (183). Within this absence of mutual destruction, coexistence entails that formerly hostile groups interact with each other in meaningful ways and that none of the groups maintain dominance or subservience. Volume 5 of the TRC final report summarized six noteworthy cases as examples of reconciliation that led to coexistence between victims and perpetrators after the hearings. One case was the dramatic reconciliation between Neville Clarence and Aboobaker Ismail. As a commander in the armed wing of the ANC, Ismail ordered an attack against the South African Air Force headquarters in Pretoria, which permanently blinded Clarence, who was an air force captain at the time. After the hearings, the two men met with each other and spoke at length, ultimately reconciling. Another case was that of Beth Savage. During an attack by APLA in November 1992, Savage was almost killed after sustaining serious injuries to her heart, intestines, and legs. Six years later, she attended the amnesty hearings for Thembelani Xundu, the APLA commander responsible for ordering the attack that nearly killed her. After the hearings, Savage met with Xundu and spoke directly about her suffering and her desire to reconcile. As a result, Savage said that the nightmares and emotional disturbances from her long ordeal of recovering from her injuries went away. The TRC report highlighted the reconciliatory attitude by quoting Cynthia Ngewu, whose son was one of the Guguletu Seven killed by the South African Police. Ngewu stated, "We do not want to return evil by another evil. We simply want to ensure that the perpetrators are returned to humanity" (TRC 1999c, 366).

NOTES TO CHAPTER 6

1. *The Cure at Troy: A Version of Sophocles'* Philoctetes by Seamus Heaney. © 1990 by Seamus Heaney. Reprinted by permission of Farrar, Straus and Giroux, LLC. and Faber and Faber, Ltd.

2. To accept and apply the principles and accomplishments of the TRC, it is crucial to reject the meme that war is the natural state of humankind and that we have been at peace for only a handful of years in recorded history (e.g., Waller 2002). In fact, most people have been at peace most of the time. Studying the frequency of violent conflicts down through history and concluding that our natural state is war is like studying statistics on traffic fatalities and concluding that the natural state of driving is to be in serious accidents. As with traffic fatalities, war is far too frequent, but that does not mean it is our desired state.

3. The chapter does not present a comprehensive guide to designing truth commissions or a thoroughgoing critique of the TRC. Rather, it focuses on the generalizable accomplishments of the amnesty hearings, basing its conclusions on the analyses in the previous chapters.

4. During the HRV hearings, victims of apartheid had an opportunity to document their narratives, receive acknowledgment of their suffering, and help restore their dignity (Minow 1998; Mullet, Neto, and Pinto 2008), with a subset of "window cases" selected for the public hearings. Acknowledgment was codified by the TRC and published in volume 7 of the TRC final report: a comprehensive, alphabetized list of all the identified victims and the crimes committed against them, which now serves as a biblio-memorial to those who were victimized by apartheid (TRC 2003b).

5. Over the past thirty years, the scope of truth commissions has varied widely, depending on the needs of the countries involved. The South African TRC was large in scope, covering the period from 1960 to 1994, collecting more than 20,000 victim statements and more than 7,000 applications for amnesty. The 2007 truth commission in Ecuador was of medium scope, covering human rights abuses perpetrated between 1984 and 1988 and finding that 150 individuals were forcibly disappeared and approximately 500 were tortured or arbitrarily detained. South Korea's truth commission that began in 2000 was likewise of medium scope, investigating suspicious deaths from 1975 to 1987 under the government of General Chun Doo Hwan and finding that the government was responsible for 52 suspicious deaths. Truth commissions in Côte d'Ivoire and Peru were far more tightly focused in their content and time frame. The truth commission in Côte d'Ivoire investigated the postelectoral violence that occurred over a three-day period in late October 2000 that claimed 171 lives. The 1986 Peru truth commission focused on the execution of detainees in three prisons on two nights in June 1986 (U.S. Institute of Peace 2009).

6. Consider an example of Navajo justice in the case of sexual assault, which was settled when the offender compensated his victim through a gift of livestock. The repair was accomplished not only by the material compensation but also by

the symbolic meaning of the gift, which validated the guilt of the offender and acknowledged the innocence of the victim (Johnstone 2002).

NOTES TO THE CONCLUSIONS

1. One provocative example of such a platform is President Barack Obama's speech in Cairo in 2009, which described a platform of international cooperation and diplomacy for achieving democracy in many countries in the Arab world. Several months later, the president received the Nobel Peace Prize for advancing this alternative platform—for which the Nobel Committee and the president received substantial criticism in the national media. Yet even though the new administration was short on accomplishment, its efforts to construct a new platform of cooperation and diplomacy to replace the existing one of antagonism and war represented a dramatic change that may have contributed to the mass political movements two years later, known as the Arab Spring.

2. Many platforms of nonviolence and tolerance that successfully replaced existing platforms of systemic injustice are storied, including the guiding ideologies and actions of Mohandas Gandhi in India, Martin Luther King Jr. in the United States, Lech Wałęsa in Poland, Corazon Aquino in the Philippines, Václav Havel in Czechoslovakia, and Aung San Suu Kyi in Burma. In addition, Joaquín Chávez (2012) and Nelson Portillo (2012) reported on one prominent institution whose ideology of peaceful resistance brought about social change under repressive regimes in El Salvador. These articles described the work at the Central American University (which became known as the University for Social Change) begun by Jesuit scholars to promote fundamental societal change on the platform of liberation psychology.

3. One potential intervention for the United States would involve more vigilant oversight of the Western Hemispheric Institute for Security Cooperation (formerly called the School of the Americas) and regular review of its curriculum, decreasing its potential to promote human rights abuses in Latin America (Hodge and Cooper 2004).

BIBLIOGRAPHY

Abrahamsen, T., and H. van der Merwe (2005). "Reconciliation through Amnesty? Amnesty Applicants' Views of the South African Truth and Reconciliation Commission." Centre for the Study of Violence and Reconciliation, Johannesburg, South Africa, www.csvr.org.za/.

Ackerman, D. (1997, July 10). Testimony provided to the Amnesty Committee of the Truth and Reconciliation Commission, Cape Town.

Adam, H. (1997). "Africa's Nazis: Apartheid as Holocaust?" *Indicator SA* 14(1): 13–16.

Alba, J. W., and L. Hasher (1983). "Is Memory Schematic?" *Psychological Bulletin* 93(2): 203–231.

Ambinder, M. (2009, January 6). "Torture and a Truth Commission." *Atlantic.* Retrieved June 15, 2009, from http://marcambinder.theatlantic.com/archives/2009/01/torture_etc.php/.

American Heritage Dictionary of the English Language (1996). 3rd ed. Boston: Houghton Mifflin.

Améry, J. (1980). *At the Mind's Limits.* Translated by Sidney Rosenfeld and Stella P. Rosenfeld. Bloomington: Indiana University Press.

Amnesty International (2009). *Amnesty International Report 2009: The State of the World's Human Rights.* London: Amnesty International Publications.

Andrews, M. (2000). "Forgiveness in Context." *Journal of Moral Education* 29(1): 75–86.

Arendt, H. (1994). *Eichmann in Jerusalem: A Report on the Banality of Evil.* New York: Penguin Books.

Asmal, K., L. Asmal, and R. S. Roberts (1998). *Reconciliation through Truth: A Reckoning of Apartheid's Criminal Governance.* New York: St. Martin's Press.

Bandura, A., B. Underwood, and M. E. Fromson (1975). "Disinhibition of Aggression through Diffusion of Responsibility and Dehumanization of Victims." *Journal of Personality and Social Psychology* 9(4): 253–269.

Baumeister, R. F. (1997). *Evil: Inside Human Violence and Cruelty.* New York: Holt.

Baumeister, R. F., A. Stillwell, and S. R. Wotman. (1990). "Victim and Perpetrator Accounts of Interpersonal Conflict: Autobiographical Narratives about Anger." *Journal of Personality and Social Psychology* 59(5): 994–1005.

Bellingan, W. R. (1997, November 17–19; July 30, 1998). Testimony provided to the Amnesty Committee of the Truth and Reconciliation Commission, Cape Town and Pretoria.

Benzien, J. T. (1997, July 14–16). Testimony provided to the Amnesty Committee of the Truth and Reconciliation Commission, Cape Town.

Biehl, L., and P. Biehl. (1997, July 9). Testimony provided to the Amnesty Committee of the Truth and Reconciliation Commission, Cape Town.

Bilali, R., L. R. Tropp, and N. Dasgupta. (2012). "Attributions of Responsibility and Perceived Harm in the Aftermath of Mass Violence." *Peace and Conflict: Journal of Peace Psychology* 18(1): 21–39.

Bond, C. F., and B. M. DePaulo (2006). "Accuracy of Deception Judgments." *Personality and Social Psychology Review* 10(3): 214–234.

Boraine, A. (2000). *A Country Unmasked: Inside South Africa's Truth and Reconciliation Commission.* Cape Town: Oxford University Press.

Brink, R. (1997, July 8). Comments provided to the Amnesty Committee of the Truth and Reconciliation Commission, Cape Town.

Bronkhorst, D. (2006). *Truth and Justice: A Guide to Truth Commissions and Transitional Justice.* 2nd ed. Amsterdam: Amnesty International.

Browning, C. R. (1998). *Ordinary Men: Reserve Police Battalion 101 and the Final Solution in Poland.* New York: HarperCollins.

Buber, M. (2002). *Between Man and Man.* Translated by Ronald Gregor-Smith. New York: Routledge Classics.

Bundy, C. (2000). "The Beast of the Past: History and the TRC." In *After the TRC: Reflections on Truth and Reconciliation in South Africa,* edited by W. James and L. van de Vijver, 9–20. Claremont, South Africa: David Philip Publishers.

Buur, L. (2002). "Monumental Historical Memory: Managing Truth in the Everyday Work of the South African Truth and Reconciliation Commission." In *Commissioning the Past: Understanding South Africa's Truth and Reconciliation Commission,* edited by D. Posel and G. Simpson, 66–93. Johannesburg: Witwatersrand University Press.

Camic, P. M., J. E. Rhodes, and L. Yardley, L., eds. (2003). *Qualitative Research in Psychology: Expanding Perspectives in Methodology and Design.* Washington, DC: American Psychological Association.

Centre for the Study of Violence and Reconciliation. www.csvr.org.za/.

Chapman, A. R. (2007). "Truth Commissions and Intergroup Forgiveness: The Case of the South African Truth and Reconciliation Commission." *Peace and Conflict: Journal of Peace Psychology* 13(1): 51–69.

Chapman, E., and J. A. Smith (2002). "Interpretative Phenomenological Analysis and the New Genetics." *Journal of Health Psychology* 7(2): 125–130.

Charmaz, K. (2003). "Grounded Theory." In *Qualitative Psychology: A Practical Guide to Research Methods,* edited by J. A. Smith, 81–100. Thousand Oaks, CA: Sage.

Chávez, J. M. (2012). "The University for Social Change and the Legacy of Ignacio Martín-Baró, S. J." *Peace and Conflict: Journal of Peace Psychology* 18(1): 68–76.

Cherry, J., J. Daniel, and M. Fullard (2002). "Researching the 'Truth': A View from Inside the Truth and Reconciliation Commission." In *Commissioning the Past: Understanding South Africa's Truth and Reconciliation Commission,* edited by D. Posel and G. Simpson, 17–36. Johannesburg: Witwatersrand University Press.

Coetzee, D. (1996, November 5–7). Testimony provided to the Amnesty Committee of the Truth and Reconciliation Commission, Durban.

Coker, D. (2002). "Transformative Justice: Anti-subordination Processes in Cases of Domestic Violence." In *Restorative Justice and Family Violence,* edited by H. Strang and J. Braithwaite, 128–153. New York: Cambridge University Press.

Cole, D. (2009, March 2). "Room for Debate: A Truth Commission for Bush Era?" *New York Times.* Retrieved March 2, 2009, from www.nytimes.com/pages/opinion/index.html/.

Coleman, M. (1998). *A Crime against Humanity: Analysing the Repression of the Apartheid State.* Johannesburg: Human Rights Committee.

Colvin, C. J. (2000). "'We Are Still Struggling': Storytelling, Reparations and Reconciliation after the TRC." *Centre for the Study of Violence and Reconciliation.* Johannesburg, South Africa. www.csvr.org.za/.

Conyers, J. (2009). *Reining in the Imperial Presidency.* Washington, DC: U.S. House of Representatives.

Corbett, E. P. J. (1990). *Classical Rhetoric for the Modern Student.* New York: Oxford University Press.

Cornejo, M., R. C. Rojas, and F. Mendoza (2009). "From Testimony to Life Story: The Experience of Professionals in the Chilean National Commission on Political Imprisonment and Torture." *Peace and Conflict: Journal of Peace Psychology* 15(2): 111–133.

Cornelius, Q. (1997, October 31). Testimony provided to the Amnesty Committee of the Truth and Reconciliation Commission, Cape Town.

Cox, L. (2009, June 15). "Obama Must Prosecute Bush-Era Torture Enablers." *Yahoo News.* Retrieved June 15, 2009, from news.yahoo.com/s/csm/20091615/cm_csm/ycox/. Currently at http://blog.amnestyusa.org/us/obama-must-prosecute-bush-era-torture-enablers/.

Crocker, D. A. (2000). "Truth Commissions, Transitional Justice, and Civil Society." In *Truth v. Justice: The Morality of Truth Commissions,* edited by R. I. Rotberg and D. Thompson, 99–121. Princeton, NJ: Princeton University Press.

———. (2003). "Reckoning with Past Wrongs: A Narrative Framework." In *Dilemmas of Reconciliation: Cases and Concepts,* edited by C. A. L. Prager and T. Govier, 39–63. Waterloo, ON: Wilfrid Laurier University Press.

Cronje, J. H. (1997, February 24). Testimony provided to the Amnesty Committee of the Truth and Reconciliation Commission, Pretoria.

Danner, M. (2004). *Torture and Truth: America, Abu Ghraib, and the War on Terror.* New York: New York Review of Books.

Davis, M. (2007). *Buda's Wagon: A Brief History of the Car Bomb.* New York: Verso.

de Kock, E. (1998, July 29–30). Testimony provided to the Amnesty Committee of the Truth and Reconciliation Commission, Pretoria.

de Kock, E., as told to Jeremy Gordin (1998). *A Long Night's Damage: Working for the Apartheid State.* Saxonwold, South Africa: Contra Press.

Derrida, J. (1998). *Archive Fever: A Freudian Impression.* Translated by Eric Prenowitz. Chicago: University of Chicago Press.

Dube, J. (1999, February 16–17). Testimony provided to the Amnesty Committee of the Truth and Reconciliation Commission, Johannesburg.

Duckitt, J. (1992). *The Social Psychology of Prejudice.* New York: Praeger.

Eatough, V., and J. A. Smith (2008). "Interpretive Phenomenological Analysis." In *The Sage Handbook of Qualitative Research in Psychology,* edited by C. Willig and W. Stainton-Rogers, 179–194. Thousand Oaks, CA: Sage.

Ekman, P., and M. O'Sullivan (1991). "Who Can Catch a Liar?" *American Psychologist* 46(9): 913–920.

Ekman, P., M. O'Sullivan, and M. G. Frank, (1999). "A Few Can Catch a Liar." *Psychological Science* 10(3): 263–265.

Erasmus, P. (2000, November 27). Testimony provided to the Amnesty Committee of the Truth and Reconciliation Commission, Johannesburg.

Eyal, G. (2004). "Identity and Trauma: Two Forms of the Will to Memory." *History & Memory* 16(1): 5–36.

Fagan, E. (1998). "The Constitutional Entrenchment of Memory." In *Negotiating the Past,* edited by S. Nuttall and C. Coetzee, 249–262. Cape Town: Oxford University Press Southern Africa.

Fine, G. A., G. S. Heddell, P. A. Lewis, G. Ellard, and R. A. Mazer (2009, July 10). *Unclassified Report on the President's Surveillance Program.* Report No. 2009-0013-AS. Washington, DC: U.S. Government Printing Office.

Forbes, A. (1988, September 21). As cited in the "Supreme Court Reporter." *Cape Times,* 1.

——— (1997, July 14). Testimony provided to the Amnesty Committee of the Truth and Reconciliation Commission, Cape Town.

Foster, D. (2000). "The Truth and Reconciliation Commission and Understanding Perpetrators." *South African Journal of Psychology* 30(1), 2–9.

Foster, D., P. Haupt, and M. de Beer (2005). *The Theatre of Violence: Narratives of Protagonists in the South African Conflict.* Cape Town: HSRC Press.

Fourie, J. (1997, October 31). Testimony provided to the Amnesty Committee of the Truth and Reconciliation Commission, Cape Town.

Gibson, J. L. (2004). "Does Truth Lead to Reconciliation? Testing the Causal Assumptions of the South African Truth and Reconciliation Process." *American Journal of Political Science* 48(2): 201–217.

Gibson, J. T., and M. Haritos-Fatouros (1986). "The Education of a Torturer." *Psychology Today,* November, 50–58.

Giorgi, A. (1975). "An Application of Phenomenological Method in Psychology." In *Duquesne Studies in Phenomenological Psychology,* edited by A. Giorgi, C. Fischer, and E. Murray, 82–103. Pittsburgh: Duquesne University Press.

——— (1985). *Phenomenology and Psychological Research.* Pittsburgh: Duquesne University Press.

——— (2009). *The Descriptive Phenomenological Method in Psychology: A Modified Husserlian Approach.* Pittsburgh: Duquesne University Press.

Giorgi, A., and B. Giorgi (2003). "Phenomenology." In *Qualitative Psychology: A Practical Guide to Research Methods,* edited by J. A. Smith, 25–50. Thousand Oaks, CA: Sage.

Gobodo-Madikizela, P. (2003). *A Human Being Died That Night.* New York: Houghton Mifflin.

Gqomfa, L. (1997, October 27–28). Testimony provided to the Amnesty Committee of the Truth and Reconciliation Commission, Cape Town.

Greenberg, K. J., and J. L. Dratel, eds. (2005). *The Torture Papers: The Road to Abu Ghraib.* New York: Cambridge University Press.

Grossman, D. (1995). *On Killing: The Psychological Cost of Learning to Kill in War and Society.* Boston: Little, Brown.

Hallock, D. (1998). *Hell, Healing, and Resistance.* Farmington, PA: Plough.

Hamber, B. (2007). "Forgiveness and Reconciliation: Paradise Lost or Pragmatism?" *Peace and Conflict: Journal of Peace Psychology* 13(1): 115–125.

——— (2009). *Transforming Societies after Political Violence: Truth, Reconciliation, and Mental Health.* New York: Springer.

Haney, C., C. Banks, and P. Zimbardo (1973). "Interpersonal Dynamics in a Simulated Prison." *International Journal of Criminology and Penology* 1: 69–97.

Haritos-Fatouros, M. (2003). *The Psychological Origins of Institutionalized Torture.* New York: Routledge.

Harris, V. (2007). *Archives and Justice: A South African Perspective.* Chicago: Society of American Archivists.

Hart-Davis, R. (1978). Letter to George Lyttelton, April 8, 1956. In *The Lyttelton Hart-Davis Letters: Correspondence of George Lyttelton and Rupert Hart-Davis.* Vol. 1, *1955–1956.* Chicago: Academy Chicago Publishers.

Haslam, S. A., and S. Reicher (2007). "Beyond the Banality of Evil: Three Dynamics of an Interactionist Social Psychology of Tyranny." *Personality and Social Psychology Bulletin* 33(5): 615–622.

Hatzfeld, J. (2005). *Machete Season: The Killers in Rwanda Speak.* Translated by L. Coverdale. New York: Farrar, Straus and Giroux.

Hayner, P. B. (1994). "Fifteen Truth Commissions—1974 to 1994: A Comparative Study." *Human Rights Quarterly* 16(4): 597–655.

——— (2002). *Unspeakable Truths: Facing the Challenge of Truth Commissions.* New York: Routledge.

——— (2011). *Unspeakable Truths: Transitional Justice and the Challenge of Truth Commissions.* 2nd ed. New York: Routledge.

Heaney, S. (1991). *The Cure at Troy: A Version of Sophocles' Philoctetes.* New York: Farrar, Straus and Giroux.

Hechter, J. (1997, February 24). Testimony provided to the Amnesty Committee of the Truth and Reconciliation Commission, Pretoria.

Hersh, S. M. (2005). *Chain of Command: The Road from 9/11 to Abu Ghraib.* New York: HarperCollins.

Hlengwa, V. (1997, August 7). Testimony provided to the Amnesty Committee of the Truth and Reconciliation Commission, Durban.

Hodge, J., and L. Cooper (2004). *Disturbing the Peace: The Story of Father Roy Bourgeois and the Movement to Close the School of the Americas*. Maryknoll, NY: Orbis Books.

Huggins, M. K., M. Haritos-Fatouros, and P. G. Zimbardo (2002). *Violence Workers: Police Torturers and Murderers Reconstruct Brazilian Atrocities*. Berkeley: University of California Press.

Ibrahim, G. (1987). "We Are Now Facing Pretoria Military." *Azania Combat* 5. Dar es Salaam, Tanzania: Azanian People's Liberation Army.

Iglesias, D. (2008). *In Justice: Inside the Scandal That Rocked the Bush Administration*. Hoboken, NJ: Wiley.

Ignatieff, M. (1996). "Articles of Faith." *Index on Censorship* 25(5): 110–122.

Ismail, A. (1998, May 6). Testimony provided to the Amnesty Committee of the Truth and Reconciliation Commission, Johannesburg.

James, W., and L. van de Vijver, eds. (2000). *After the TRC: Reflections on Truth and Reconciliation in South Africa*. Claremont, South Africa: David Philip Publishers.

January, M. (1997, October 31). Testimony provided to the Amnesty Committee of the Truth and Reconciliation Commission, Cape Town.

Jeffrey, A. (1999). *The Truth about the Truth Commission*. Johannesburg: South African Institute of Race Relations.

Johnstone, G. (2002). *Restorative Justice: Ideas, Values, Debates*. Portland, OR: Willan Publishing.

———, ed. (2003). *A Restorative Justice Reader: Texts, Sources, Context*. Portland, OR: Willan Publishing.

Kajee, J. (1996, October 16). Testimony provided to the Amnesty Committee of the Truth and Reconciliation Commission, Pietermaritzburg.

Kassin, S., A. V. Tubb, H. M. Hosch, and A. Memon (2001). "On the 'General Acceptance' of Eyewitness Testimony Research: A New Survey of the Experts." *American Psychologist* 56(5): 405–416.

Khampepe, S. (1996, November 6). Commentary provided to the Amnesty Committee of the Truth and Reconciliation Commission, Durban.

Kingsbury, A. (2009, March 4). "Why Sen. Patrick Leahy Wants a 'Truth Commission.'" *U.S. News & World Report*. Retrieved March 5, 2009, from www.usnews. com/aricles/news/politics/2009/03/04/. Currently at www.usnews.com/news/ articles/2009/03/04/why-sen-patrick-leahy-wants-a-truth-commission/.

Kintsch, W. (1985). "Text Processing: A Psychological Model." In *Handbook of Discourse Analysis*, edited by T. A. van Dijk, 2:231–243. London: Academic Press.

Kintsch, W., and T. A. van Dijk (1978). "Toward a Model of Text Comprehension and Production." *Psychological Review* 85(5): 363–394.

Kotzé, S. M. (1997, October 21). Testimony provided to the Amnesty Committee of the Truth and Reconciliation Commission, Cape Town.

Kraft, R. N. (2000, November). "Revealing Mistakes in Personal Memory." Paper presented at the forty-first annual meeting of the Psychonomic Society, New Orleans.

———— (2002). *Memory Perceived: Recalling the Holocaust.* Westport, CT: Praeger.

———— (2004). "Emotional Memory in Survivors of the Holocaust: A Qualitative Study of Oral Testimony." In *Memory and Emotion,* edited by D. Reisberg and P. Hertel, 347–389. New York: Oxford University Press.

———— (2007, August). "Negotiating Truth in the Aftermath of Extended Conflict: An Epistemological Analysis." Paper presented at the annual meeting of the American Psychological Association, San Francisco.

———— (2009). "The Magnitude Gap: Revealing Differences in Recall between Victims and Perpetrators." In *Applied Memory,* edited by M. Kelley, 147–166. Hauppauge, NY: Nova Science.

———— (2011). "Narratives of Perpetrators: Ghastly Tales and Multiple Truths." In *Narrative Acts: Rhetoric, Race and Identity, Knowledge,* edited by D. Journet, B. A. Boehm, and C. E. Britt, 145–161. New York: Hampton Press.

Kressel, N. J. (1996). *Mass Hate: The Global Rise of Genocide and Terror.* New York: Plenum Press.

Kriesberg, L. (2000). "Coexistence and the Reconciliation of Communal Conflicts." In *The Handbook of Interethnic Coexistence,* edited by E. Weiner, 182–198. New York: Continuum.

Kristof, N. D. (2008, July 6). "The Truth Commission." *New York Times.* Retrieved July 6, 2008, from www.nytimes.com/pages/opinion/index.html/.

———— (2009a, April 25). "On the Ground: The Truth Commission." *New York Times.* Retrieved April 26, 2009, from www.nytimes.com/pages/opinion/index.html/.

———— (2009b, April 26). "Time to Come Clean." *New York Times.* Retrieved April 26, 2009, from www.nytimes.com/pages/opinion/index.html/.

Landsman, S. (1996). "Alternative Responses to Serious Human Rights Abuses: Of Prosecution and Truth Commissions." *Law and Contemporary Problems* 59(4): 81–92.

Langford, A. (1997, October 31). Testimony provided to the Amnesty Committee of the Truth and Reconciliation Commission, Cape Town.

Leahy, P. (2009, February 12). "A Truth Commission to Investigate Bush-Cheney Administration Abuses." *Huffington Post.* Retrieved February 20, 2009, from www.huffingtonpost.com/sen-patrick-leahy/a-truth-commission-to-inv_b_166461.html/.

Lecordier, M. (1999, October 11). Testimony provided to the Amnesty Committee of the Truth and Reconciliation Commission, Durban.

Levi, P. (1988). *The Drowned and the Saved.* New York: Vintage Books.

Levin, C. (2005). "Levin Amendment to Establish a National Commission on Policies and Practices on the Treatment of Detainees since September 11, 2001." Senate Amendment 2430, 109th Congress.

Lifton, R. J. (1986). *The Nazi Doctors: Medical Killing and the Psychology of Genocide.* New York: Basic Books.

Lindsay, D. S. (2007). "Autobiographical Memory, Eyewitness Reports, and Public Policy." *Canadian Psychology* 48(2): 57–66.

Lobb, P. (2010). "The Art of Caring: Women and Restorative Justice." PhD diss., Antioch University.

Lourens, J. (1997, July 8). Commentary provided to the Amnesty Committee of the Truth and Reconciliation Commission, Cape Town.

Mabela, L. (1997, February 24). Testimony provided to the Amnesty Committee of the Truth and Reconciliation Commission, Pretoria.

MacNair, R. M. (2002). *Perpetration-Induced Traumatic Stress: The Psychological Consequences of Killing.* Westport, CT: Praeger.

Madasi, V. (1997, October 28). Testimony provided to the Amnesty Committee of the Truth and Reconciliation Commission, Cape Town.

Makhubu, C. (1999, February 17–18, 1999). Testimony provided to the Amnesty Committee of the Truth and Reconciliation Commission, Johannesburg.

Makoma, G. C. (1997, July 10). Testimony provided to the Amnesty Committee of the Truth and Reconciliation Commission, Cape Town.

Malan, W. (1999). Minority Report to the *Truth and Reconciliation Commission of South Africa.* Vol. 5. Cape Town: Truth and Reconciliation Commission.

Malinowski, T. (2008). "Restoring Moral Authority: Ending Torture, Secret Detention, and the Prison at Guantánamo Bay." *Annals of the American Academy of Political and Social Science* 618(1): 148–159.

Mall, H. (1996, November 6; July 8 and 14, 1997). Commentary provided to the Amnesty Committee of the Truth and Reconciliation Commission, Durban and Cape Town.

Mamdani, M. (2000). "A Diminished Truth." In *After the TRC: Reflections on Truth and Reconciliation in South Africa,* edited by W. James and L. van de Vijver, 58–61. Claremont, South Africa.

Mandela, N. (1961, December 16). "Umkhonto We Sizwe Manifesto." Leaflet issued by Umkhonto We Sizwe. Available at www.guardian.co.uk/world/2007/apr/23/nelsonmandela1/.

——— (1985, February 13). Reported in *Solidarity News Service,* Gaborone, Botswana, 85(3): 1–2.

——— (1986). *Umkhonto we Sizwe: Born of the People.* Pamphlet published by the ANC, Lusaka, Zambia.

——— (1995). *Long Walk to Freedom: The Autobiography of Nelson Mandela.* Boston: Back Bay Books.

Mandler, J. M., and N. S. Johnson (1977). "Remembrance of Things Parsed: Story Structure and Recall." *Cognitive Psychology* 9(1): 111–151.

Manqina, M. (1997, July 8). Testimony provided to the Amnesty Committee of the Truth and Reconciliation Commission, Cape Town.

Margulies, J. (2007). *Guantánamo and the Abuse of Presidential Power.* New York: Simon and Schuster.

Martinez, J. (2009, March 2). "Room for Debate: A Truth Commission for Bush Era?" *New York Times.* Retrieved March 2, 2009, from www.nytimes.com/pages/opinion/index.html/.

Masondo, A. (1999). *Truth and Reconciliation Commission of South Africa Report.* Vol. 5. Cape Town: Truth and Reconciliation Commission.

Maxam, P. (1997, July 7). Testimony provided to the Amnesty Committee of the Truth and Reconciliation Commission, Cape Town.

Mayer, J. (2009). "The Secret History: Can Leon Panetta Move the C.I.A. Forward without Confronting the Past?" *New Yorker*, June 22, 2009, 50–59.

Mbelo, T. J. (1997, November 18). Testimony provided to the Amnesty Committee of the Truth and Reconciliation Commission, Cape Town.

Mbuyazi, B. (1997, August 1). Testimony provided to the Amnesty Committee of the Truth and Reconciliation Commission, Pietermaritzburg.

McBride, R. (1999, October 5–7, 12). Testimony provided to the Amnesty Committee of the Truth and Reconciliation Commission, Durban.

McKoon, G. (1977). "Organization of Information in Text Memory." *Journal of Verbal Learning and Verbal Behavior* 16(2): 247–260.

Mellor, D., D. Bretherton, and L. Firth (2007). "Aboriginal and Non-Aboriginal Australia: The Dilemma of Apologies, Forgiveness, and Reconciliation." *Peace and Conflict: A Journal of Peace Psychology* 13(1): 11–36.

Mentz, W. W. (1997, February 24–25). Testimony provided to the Amnesty Committee of the Truth and Reconciliation Commission, Pretoria.

Milgram, S. (1963). "Behavioral Study of Obedience." *Journal of Abnormal and Social Psychology* 67(4): 371–378.

———(1965). "Some Conditions of Obedience and Disobedience to Authority." *Human Relations* 18: 57–76.

———(1974). *Obedience to Authority: An Experimental View*. New York: Harper and Row.

Minow, M. (1998). *Between Vengeance and Forgiveness: Facing History after Genocide and Mass Violence*. Boston: Beacon Press.

Mitchell, B. (1996, October 16). Testimony provided to the Amnesty Committee of the Truth and Reconciliation Commission, Pietermaritzburg.

Mkhumbuzi, B. (1997, July 9). Testimony provided to the Amnesty Committee of the Truth and Reconciliation Commission, Cape Town.

Mlambisa, T. (1997, July 9). Testimony provided to the Amnesty Committee of the Truth and Reconciliation Commission, Cape Town.

Moghaddam, F. M. (2005). "The Staircase to Terrorism: A Psychological Exploration." *American Psychologist* 60(2): 161–169.

Morudu, S. (1997, February 26). Testimony provided to the Amnesty Committee of the Truth and Reconciliation Commission, Pretoria.

Mpshe, M. (1997, February 24). Questioning provided to the Amnesty Committee of the Truth and Reconciliation Commission, Pretoria.

Mthembu, V. (1998, July 6, 13). Testimony provided to the Amnesty Committee of the Truth and Reconciliation Commission, Sebokeng.

Mullet, E., F. Neto, and M. da C. Pinto (2008). "What Can Reasonably Be Expected from a Truth Commission: A Preliminary Examination of East Timorese Views." *Peace and Conflict: Journal of Peace Psychology* 14(4): 369–393.

Narkedien, Z. (1999, October 7). Testimony provided to the Amnesty Committee of the Truth and Reconciliation Commission, Durban.

Ndinisa, C. (1997, July 7). Testimony provided to the Amnesty Committee of the Truth and Reconciliation Commission, Cape Town.

Neisser, U. (1988). "Five Kinds of Self-Knowledge." *Philosophical Psychology* 1(1): 35–59.

Ngoepe, B. (1997, July 14 and October 21). Comments made to the Amnesty Committee of the Truth and Reconciliation Commission, Cape Town.

Nofemela, E. (1997, July 8). Testimony provided to the Amnesty Committee of the Truth and Reconciliation Commission, Cape Town.

Ntamo, S. (1997, July 9). Testimony provided to the Amnesty Committee of the Truth and Reconciliation Commission, Cape Town.

Ntsebeza, D. B. (2000). "The Uses of Truth Commissions: Lessons for the World." In *Truth v. Justice: The Morality of Truth Commissions,* edited by R. I. Rotberg and D. Thompson, 158–169. Princeton: Princeton University Press.

Nuttall, S., and C. Coetzee, eds. (1998). *Negotiating the Past.* Cape Town: Oxford University Press Southern Africa.

Ozick, C. (2010). *Foreign Bodies.* New York: Houghton Mifflin Harcourt.

Pauw, J. (1998). "Inside the Mind of Torture: The Story of Apartheid's Electrician." *Covert Action Quarterly* 63: 17–25.

Payne, L. A. (2004, March). "In Search of Remorse: Confessions by Perpetrators of Past State Violence." Paper presented at the conference on Justice across Cultures, Brandeis University, Waltham, MA.

——— (2008). *Unsettling Accounts: Neither Truth nor Reconciliation in Confessions of State Violence.* Durham, NC: Duke University Press.

Pedro, N. (1997, October 20–21). Testimony provided to the Amnesty Committee of the Truth and Reconciliation Commission, Cape Town.

Peni, N. (1997, July 8). Testimony provided to the Amnesty Committee of the Truth and Reconciliation Commission, Cape Town.

Pepper, S. C. (1942). *World Hypotheses: Prolegomena to Systematic Philosophy and a Complete Survey of Metaphysics.* Berkeley: University of California Press.

Perry, J. G., ed. (2002). *Repairing Communities through Restorative Justice.* Lanham, MD: American Correctional Association.

Phama, S. (1987). "Stepping Up Attacks." *Azania Combat* 1(5). Dar es Salaam, Tanzania: Azanian People's Liberation Army.

Pigou, P. (2002a). "False Promises and Wasted Opportunities? Inside South Africa's Truth and Reconciliation Commission." In *Commissioning the Past: Understanding South Africa's Truth and Reconciliation Commission,* edited by D. Posel and G. Simpson, 37–65. Johannesburg: Witwatersrand University Press.

——— (2002b). "The Murder of Sicelo Dlomo." In *Commissioning the Past: Understanding South Africa's Truth and Reconciliation Commission,* edited by D. Posel and G. Simpson, 97–116. Johannesburg: Witwatersrand University Press.

Pillay, R. (1999, October 13). Comments During Testimony to the Amnesty Committee of the Truth and Reconciliation Commission, Durban.

Pillemer, D. B. (1998). *Momentous Events, Vivid Memories*. Cambridge: Harvard University Press.

Portillo, N. (2012). "The Life of Ignacio Martín-Baró: A Narrative Account of a Personal Biographical Journey." *Peace and Conflict: Journal of Peace Psychology* 18(1): 77–87.

Posel, D. (2002). "The TRC Report: What Kind of History? What Kind of Truth?" In *Commissioning the Past: Understanding South Africa's Truth and Reconciliation Commission*, edited by D. Posel and G. Simpson, 147–172. Johannesburg: Witwatersrand University Press.

Posel, D., and G. Simpson, eds. (2002a). *Commissioning the Past: Understanding South Africa's Truth and Reconciliation Commission*. Johannesburg: Witwatersrand University Press.

———(2002b). "The Power of Truth: South Africa's Truth and Reconciliation Commission in Context." In *Commissioning the Past: Understanding South Africa's Truth and Reconciliation Commission*, edited by D. Posel and G. Simpson, 1–13. Johannesburg: Witwatersrand University Press.

Ramsey, M. (2006). "Servant-Leadership and Unconditional Forgiveness: The Lives of Six South African Perpetrators." *International Journal of Servant-Leadership* 2(1): 113–139.

Reid, F., and D. Hoffmann (2000). *Long Night's Journey into Day: South Africa's Search for Truth and Reconciliation*. Directed by Frances Reid and Deborah Hoffmann, IRIS Films. Distributed by California Newsreel, San Francisco, CA.

Reyna, V. F. (1998). "Fuzzy-Trace Theory and False Memory." In *Memory Distortions and Their Prevention*, edited by M. Intons-Peterson and D. Best, 15–27. New York: Wiley.

Rosenbaum, T. (2004). *The Myth of Moral Justice*. New York: HarperCollins.

Ross, L. (1977). "The Intuitive Psychologist and His Shortcomings: Distortions in the Attribution Process." In *Advances in Experimental Social Psychology*, edited by L. Berkowitz, 10:173–220. New York: Academic Press.

Rostron, B. (1991). *Till Babylon Falls*. London: Coronet Books.

Rowe, J. O., S. Halling, E. Davies, M. Leifer, S. Powers, and J. van Bronkhorst (1989). "The Psychology of Forgiving Another: A Dialogal Research Approach." In *Existential-Phenomenological Perspectives in Psychology: Exploring the Breadth of Human Experience*, edited by R. S. Valle and S. Halling, 233–244. New York: Plenum Press.

Rudof, J. W. (2000). "From the Archivist's Desk." *Newsletter for the Fortunoff Video Archive for Holocaust Testimonies*, Spring, 9.

Rutten, T. (2009, April 18). "A Truth Commission on Torture Is Needed." *Los Angeles Times*. Retrieved June 15, 2009, from http://articles.latimes.com/2009/apr/18/opinion/oe-rutten18/.

Sachs, A. (2000). "His Name Was Henry." In *After the TRC: Reflections on Truth and Reconciliation in South Africa*, edited by W. James and L. van de Vijver, 94–100. Claremont, South Africa: David Philip Publishers.

Salmon, J. L. (2009, June 12). "Religious Group Still Pushing 'Truth Commission.'" *Washington Post*.

Sarkin, J. (2004). *Carrots and Sticks: The TRC and the South African Amnesty Process.* Antwerp: Intersentia.

Schacter, D. L. (1999). "The Seven Sins of Memory: Insights from Psychology and Cognitive Neuroscience." *American Psychologist* 54(3): 182–203.

Schütz, A., and R. F. Baumeister (1999). "The Language of Defense: Linguistic Patterns in Narratives of Transgressions." *Journal of Language and Social Psychology* 18(3): 269–286.

Scoboria, A., G. Mazzoni, I. Kirsch, and M. Relyea (2004). "Plausibility and Belief in Autobiographical Memory." *Applied Cognitive Psychology* 18(7): 791–807.

Shaik, M. I. (1998, May 6–7). Testimony provided to the Amnesty Committee of the Truth and Reconciliation Commission, Johannesburg.

Sherman, L. W., and H. Strang. (2007). *Restorative Justice: The Evidence.* London: Smith Institute.

Simpson, G. (2002). "'Tell No Lies, Claim No Easy Victories': A Brief Evaluation of South Africa's Truth and Reconciliation Commission." In *Commissioning the Past: Understanding South Africa's Truth and Reconciliation,* edited by D. Posel and G. Simpson, 220–251. Johannesburg: Witwatersrand University Press.

Slovo, G. (2002, December 5). "Making History: South Africa's Truth and Reconciliation Commission." www.openDemocracy.net/.

Smith, J. A. (1996). "Beyond the Divide between Cognition and Discourse: Using Interpretive Phenomenological Analysis in Health Psychology." *Psychology and Health* 11(2): 261–271.

———, ed. (2003). *Qualitative Psychology: A Practical Guide to Research Methods.* Thousand Oaks, CA: Sage.

Smith, J. A., and M. Osborn (2003). "Interpretive Phenomenological Analysis." In *Qualitative Psychology: A Practical Guide to Research Methods,* edited by J. A. Smith, 51–80. Thousand Oaks, CA: Sage.

Sontag, S. (2004). *Regarding the Pain of Others.* New York: Farrar, Straus and Giroux.

Staub, E. (1989). *The Roots of Evil: The Origins of Genocide and Other Group Violence.* New York: Cambridge University Press.

Strang, H., and J. Braithwaite, eds. (2002). *Restorative Justice and Family Violence.* Cambridge: Cambridge University Press.

Swart, J. (1997, July 7). Cross-examination provided to the Amnesty Committee of the Truth and Reconciliation Commission, Cape Town.

Tambo, O. (1983, April). "In This Year of Unity." In *In Combat.* Pamphlet published by the ANC, Lusaka, Zambia. MSS AAM 945 AAM MSS 2503. Bodleian Library of Commonwealth and African Studies at Rhodes House, Oxford University.

Testimony of Martin S. (1986, January). Videotape recording no. T-641. Fortunoff Video Archive for Holocaust Testimonies. New Haven, CT: Yale University.

Thloloe, J. (1998). "Showing Faces, Hearing Voices, Tugging at Emotions: Televising the Truth and Reconciliation Commission." *Nieman Reports* 52(4). Available at www.nieman.harvard.edu/reports/article/102298/Showing-Faces-Hearing-Voices-Tugging-at-Emotions.aspx/.

Thompson, L. (2000). *A History of South Africa.* New Haven: Yale University Press.

Tilly, C. (2006). *Why?* Princeton: Princeton University Press.

Tisana, M. (1997, July 7). Testimony provided to the Amnesty Committee of the Truth and Reconciliation Commission, Cape Town.

Tolman, D. L., and M. Brydon-Miller, eds. (2001). *From Subjects to Subjectivities: A Handbook of Interpretive and Participatory Methods.* New York: NYU Press.

Truth and Reconciliation Commission of Canada. www.trc.ca/.

Truth and Reconciliation Commission of South Africa (1999a). *Truth and Reconciliation Commission of South Africa Report.* Vol. 1. Cape Town: Truth and Reconciliation Commission. Distributed in London: Macmillan.

——— (1999b). *Truth and Reconciliation Commission of South Africa Report.* Vol. 3. Cape Town: Truth and Reconciliation Commission. Distributed in London: Macmillan.

——— (1999c). *Truth and Reconciliation Commission of South Africa Report.* Vol. 5. Cape Town: Truth and Reconciliation Commission. Distributed in London: Macmillan.

——— (2003a). *Truth and Reconciliation Commission of South Africa Report.* Vol. 6. Cape Town: Truth and Reconciliation Commission.

——— (2003b). *Truth and Reconciliation Commission of South Africa Report.* Vol. 7. Cape Town: Truth and Reconciliation Commission.

Tshabalala, S. (1999, February 18). Testimony provided to the Amnesty Committee of the Truth and Reconciliation Commission, Johannesburg.

Tshikalanga, D. (1996, November 6). Testimony provided to the Amnesty Committee of the Truth and Reconciliation Commission, Durban.

Tutu, D. M. (1999a). Foreword to *Truth and Reconciliation Commission of South Africa Report,* 1:1–23. Cape Town: Truth and Reconciliation Commission. Distributed in London: Macmillan.

——— (1999b). *No Future without Forgiveness.* New York: Doubleday.

U.S. Institute of Peace (2009). *Truth Commissions Digital Collection.* Retrieved June 26, 2009, from www.usip.org/library/truth.html/.

Valdez, P. (2000). "The Right to Truth." In *After the TRC: Reflections on Truth and Reconciliation in South Africa,* edited by W. James and L. van de Vijver, 51–57. Claremont, South Africa: David Philip Publishers.

Vallacher, R. R., and D. M. Wegner (1987). "What Do People Think They're Doing? Action Identification and Human Behavior." *Psychological Review* 94(1): 3–15.

van der Linde, C. (1999, October 13). Testimony provided to the Amnesty Committee of the Truth and Reconciliation Commission, Durban.

van der Merwe, J. (1998, July 22). Testimony provided to the Amnesty Committee of the Truth and Reconciliation Commission, Pretoria.

van de Vijver, L. (2000). "The Amnesty Process." In *After the TRC: Reflections on Truth and Reconciliation in South Africa,* edited by W. James and L. van de Vijver, 128–139. Claremont, South Africa: David Philip Publishers.

van Ness, D. W., and K. H. Strong (2010). *Restoring Justice: An Introduction to Restorative Justice.* New Providence, NJ: Matthew Bender.

van Vuuren, P. (1997, February 25). Testimony provided to the Amnesty Committee of the Truth and Reconciliation Commission, Pretoria.

Verdoolaege, A. (2008). *Reconciliation Discourse: The Case of the Truth and Reconciliation Commission*. Philadelphia: John Benjamins.

Verwoerd, W. (2003). "Toward a Response to Criticisms of the South African Truth and Reconciliation Commission." In *Dilemmas of Reconciliation: Cases and Concepts*, edited by C. A. L. Prager and T. Govier, 245–278. Waterloo, ON: Wilfrid Laurier University Press.

Villa-Vicencio, C. (2000). "On the Limitations of Academic History: The Quest for Truth Demands Both More and Less." In *After the TRC: Reflections on Truth and Reconciliation in South Africa,* edited by W. James and L. van de Vijver, 21–31. Claremont, South Africa: David Philip Publishers.

Villa-Vicencio, C., and F. du Toit eds. (2006). *Truth and Reconciliation in South Africa: 10 Years On*. Claremont, South Africa: David Philip Publishers.

Vlok, A. (1998, July 21). Testimony provided to the Amnesty Committee of the Truth and Reconciliation Commission, Pretoria.

Waller, J. (2002). *Becoming Evil: How Ordinary People Commit Genocide and Mass Killing*. New York: Oxford University Press.

Wegner, D. M., and R. R. Vallacher (1986). "Action Identification." In *Handbook of Motivation and Cognition: Foundations of Social Behavior,* edited by R. M. Sorrentino and E. T. Higgins, 550–582. New York: Guilford.

Welgemoed, S. (1999, October 12–13). Testimony provided to the Amnesty Committee of the Truth and Reconciliation Commission, Durban.

Wells, G. L., and E. A. Olson (2003). "Eyewitness Testimony." *Annual Review of Psychology* 54: 277–295.

Wells, G. L., and D. S. Quinlivan, D. S. (2009). "Suggestive Eyewitness Identification Procedures and the Supreme Court's Reliability Test in Light of Eyewitness Science: 30 Years Later." *Law and Human Behavior* 33(1): 1–24.

Wertz, F. J. (2011). "A Phenomenological Psychological Approach to Trauma and Resilience." In *Five Ways of Doing Qualitative Analysis: Phenomenological Psychology, Grounded Theory, Discourse Analysis, Narrative Research, and Intuitive Inquiry,* edited by F. J. Wertz, K. Charmaz, L. M. McMullen, R. Josselson, R. Anderson, and E. McSpadden, 124–164. New York: Guilford.

Wertz, F. J., K. Charmaz, L. M. McMullen, R. Josselson, R. Anderson, and E. McSpadden, eds. (2011). *Five Ways of Doing Qualitative Analysis: Phenomenological Psychology, Grounded Theory, Discourse Analysis, Narrative Research, and Intuitive Inquiry.* New York: Guilford.

Willig, C., and W. Stainton-Rogers, eds. (2008). *The Sage Handbook of Qualitative Research in Psychology.* Thousand Oaks, CA: Sage.

Wilson, A. (1989). From the Judgment in the Trust Feed Trial. AAM MSS 2503. Bodleian Library of Commonwealth and African Studies at Rhodes House, Oxford University.

——— (1997, February 25 and July 8). Examination conducted with the Amnesty Committee of the Truth and Reconciliation Commission, Pretoria and Cape Town.

Worthington, A. (2007). *The Guantánamo Files: The Stories of the 744 Detainees in America's Illegal Prison.* Ann Arbor, MI: Pluto Press.

Wright, B. (2004). *Slavoj Žižek: The Reality of the Virtual.* Directed by Ben Wright. Ben Wright Film Productions. Distributed by Olive Films, Saint Charles, IL.

Yehoshua, A. B. (2003). *The Liberated Bride.* Translated by Hillel Halkin. New York: Harcourt.

Yengeni, T. (1997, July 14). Testimony provided to the Amnesty Committee of the Truth and Reconciliation Commission, Cape Town.

Zechmeister, J. S., and C. Romero (2002). "Victim and Offender Accounts of Interpersonal Conflict: Autobiographical Narratives of Forgiveness and Unforgiveness." *Journal of Personality and Social Psychology* 82(4): 675–686.

Zernova, M. (2007). *Restorative Justice: Ideals and Realities.* Burlington, VT: Ashgate.

Zimbardo, P. G. (1973). "On the Ethics of Intervention in Human Psychological Research: With Special Reference to the Stanford Prison Experiment." *Cognition* 2(2): 243–256.

—— (2004). "A Situationist Perspective on the Psychology of Evil: Understanding How Good People Are Transformed into Perpetrators." In *The Social Psychology of Good and Evil,* edited by A. G. Miller, 21–50. New York: Guilford.

—— (2007). *The Lucifer Effect: Understanding How Good People Turn Evil.* New York: Random House.

Zimbardo, P. G., C. Maslach, and C. Haney (1999). "Reflections on the Stanford Prison Experiment: Genesis, Transformation, Consequences." In *Obedience to Authority: Current Perspectives on the Milgram Paradigm,* edited by T. Blass, 193–237. Mahwah, NJ: Erlbaum.

Žižek, S. (2006). *The Parallax View.* Cambridge: MIT Press.

Zuma, J. (2003, October 3). "Address to the Community of Trust Feed." New Hanover, KwaZulu-Natal, South Africa. www.polity.org.za/article/j-zuma-trust-feed-sodturning-ceremony-03102003-2003-10-03/.

Zungu, P. W. (1999, February 18). Testimony provided to the Amnesty Committee of the Truth and Reconciliation Commission, Johannesburg.

INDEX

Abrahamsen, Therese, 41, 167n11
Abu Ghraib, 145–146
Ackerman, David, 113, 116, 158. *See also* St. James Church massacre
Action identification theory, 85–86, 124–125; focus of attention in perpetrators, 86–87
Adam, Heribert, 3, 28
African National Congress (ANC), 18, 32, 33, 56–57, 59–60, 74, 129–130, 141; clashes with other organizations, 56–60, 129–131. *See also* Umkhonto we Sizwe
Afrikaner, 29, 30, 63–64
Agency and interactionism, 81–83; situationism, 81
Alba, Joseph, 46
Ambinder, Marc, 145
Améry, Jean, 100
Amnesty Committee of the TRC, 6–7, 15, 18, 35, 36–39, 40, 43–44, 53, 133–139; biases, 107–108, 141; composition, 37–38; establishment of, 37–38; goals and procedures, 36–38, 134–139, 166n9; maintaining diversity, 141
Amnesty hearings of the TRC, 15–16, 39–49, 133–139, 147, 153–154; accountability, 135–136; amnesty applicants, 15, 34, 36, 40, 43; characteristics of perpetrator

testimony, 15–16, 95–96, 119; confrontations between perpetrators and victims, 16–17, 98–99; 100–102, 112, 115–118, 122, 123, 125–126, 127–128, 129–131, 132, 150; constraints on testimony, 167n12; cross-examination, 138, 165n6, 166–167n10, 167n12; disputing testimony, 103, 106; full and sincere disclosure, 15, 34, 38, 40; 43–44, 111, 167n11; integrating psychology, 142; lack of emotion, 44–45; neutral terminology, 169n9; oath, 39, 170n2; openness, 95–96, 137–138; procedures, 39–40, 166n9; public testimony, 40–42; reconciliation, 136–137; requirements for amnesty, 34–36; rule of law, 138–139; self-incrimination, 138–139; statistics, 37; testimony as humanizing and punishing, 140–141, 172n4; uncovering truth, 134–135; unsatisfying explanations and memory limitations, 45–49; veracity of testimony, 43–44, 167n14
Amnesty International, 3, 34, 145, 153, 168n15
Andrews, Molly, 21, 115
Apartheid, 3, 7–8, 29–34, 42–43, 49–52, 164n1, 164n2; defined by extremes, 42–43; definition, 29; Group Areas Act, 30–31; history, 29–34;

ABOUT THE AUTHOR

Robert N. Kraft is Professor of Cognitive Psychology at Otterbein University, where he teaches courses on memory, personality, cognition, research methods, and the self. His book *Memory Perceived* documents patterns of deeply traumatic memory in Holocaust survivors. For the past ten years, Kraft has been studying the testimony of violent perpetrators and the confrontations between victims and perpetrators.